DRAMA AND DIGITAL
ARTS CULTURES

D1336041

Methuen Drama Engage offers original reflections about key practitioners, movements, and genres in the fields of modern theatre and performance. Each volume in the series seeks to challenge mainstream critical thought through original and interdisciplinary perspectives on the body of work under examination. By questioning existing critical paradigms, it is hoped that each volume will open up fresh approaches and suggest avenues for further exploration.

Series Editors

Mark Taylor-Batty
Senior Lecturer in Theatre Studies, Workshop Theatre,
University of Leeds, UK

Enoch Brater
Kenneth T. Rowe Collegiate Professor of Dramatic Literature &
Professor of English and Theater, University of Michigan, USA

Titles

Adaptation in Contemporary Theatre
by Frances Babbage
ISBN 978-1-4725-3142-1

Authenticity in Contemporary Theatre and Performance
by Daniel Schulze
ISBN 978-1-3500-0096-4

Beat Drama: Playwrights and Performances of the 'Howl' Generation
edited by Deborah R. Geis
ISBN 978-1-472-56787-1

The Contemporary American Monologue: Performance and Politics
by Eddie Paterson
ISBN 978-1-472-58501-1

Social and Political Theatre in 21st-Century Britain: Staging Crisis
by Vicky Angelaki
ISBN 978-1-474-21316-5

Theatre in the Dark: Shadow, Gloom and Blackout in Contemporary Theatre
edited by Adam Alston and Martin Welton
ISBN 978-1-4742-5118-1

Watching War on the Twenty-First Century Stage: Spectacles of Conflict
by Clare Finburgh
ISBN 978-1-472-59866-0

DRAMA AND DIGITAL ARTS CULTURES

David Cameron, Michael Anderson,
and Rebecca Wotzko

Series Editors
Enoch Brater and Mark Taylor-Batty

methuen | drama
LONDON • NEW YORK • OXFORD • NEW DELHI • SYDNEY

METHUEN DRAMA
Bloomsbury Publishing Plc
50 Bedford Square, London, WC1B 3DP, UK
1385 Broadway, New York, NY 10018, USA

BLOOMSBURY, METHUEN DRAMA and the Methuen Drama
logo are trademarks of Bloomsbury Publishing Plc

First published in Great Britain 2017
Paperback edition published 2018

Series design by Louise Dugdale
Cover image: *The Power of Theatrical Madness*,
Jan Fabre, 2012. (© Wonge Bergmann)

A catalogue record for this book is available from the British Library.

ISBN: HB: 978-1-4725-9219-4
PB: 978-1-4725-9220-0
ePDF: 978-1-4725-9222-4
eBook: 978-1-4725-9221-7

A catalog record for this book is available from the Library of Congress.

Series: Methuen Drama Engage

Typeset by Integra Software Services Pvt. Ltd.

To find out more about our authors and books visit
www.bloomsbury.com and sign up for our newsletters.

CONTENTS

LIST OF FIGURES

ACKNOWLEDGEMENTS

The authors thank Dr Celina McEwen for her contributions to Chapter 5 in her role as a researcher on the Beowulf Sydney Project.

1

A Drama Framework for Exploring Digital Arts Cultures

Digital arts cultures

This book is about exciting and creative things made possible by sometimes boring and everyday technologies. It is a tour of some of the socially interesting forms of playful exploration, collaboration, and improvised performance to be found in contemporary digital arts practices drawn from games, education, online media, technology-enabled performance, and the creative industries. Some of these tools and spaces for art might still seem cutting edge, while others will be quite established and almost mundane even to those who might consider themselves late adopters of technology. Some of the specific tools and technologies referred to in this book may even have already come and gone in popularity or been replaced by a new 'killer' application, for that is the nature of working and researching in a field now heavily influenced by the exponential innovation and development paths of digital media. A companion website to this book can be found at www.drama-technology.com.

This book uses the concept of digital arts cultures as an umbrella term for a broad range of practices and aesthetic forms. It includes cases where technologies are used as a tool in the production of new hybrid forms of digital/analogue performance, and also examples where the art or practice could only exist in the procedural medium of the digital. We see characteristics of both the digital (code) and the analogue (human) working together to generate the new realities and worlds that emerge from the convergence of digital media forms with performative arts practices. This aligns with Kattenbelt's description of 'intermediality', which

> assumes a co-relation in the actual sense of the word, that is to say a mutual affect. Taken together, the redefinition of media co-relationships and a refreshed perception resulting from the co-relationship of media means that previously existing medium specific conventions are changed, which allows for new dimensions of perception and experience to be explored. (2008, p. 25)

Intermediality helps to explain how the presence of digital technology in arts cultures provides access to what Christiane Paul calls 'the infinite possibilities of recycling and reproduction', made possible by digital media that are 'interactive, dynamic, customisable and participatory, to name just a few key characteristics' (2005, p. 40). By extension, the hybrid nature of intermediality means there are also practically infinite combinations of digital and analogue performance made possible in these new dimensions.

Whose cultures?

Participation in these hybrid digital arts cultures is predicated on access to the hardware, software, and networks that are discussed as part of the 'everyday' world throughout this book. It is acknowledged that this is a view of the everyday that may only be possible to those – like the authors – with a measure of economic, social, educational, and class privilege. It is a distinctly Western perspective, although the globalizing effects of digital technology are such that many of the digital arts cultures considered in this book are increasingly 'open' – both in terms of more equitable access and in their ability to be reproduced and remixed to suit the different needs and purposes of individuals and communities. Consider the following observation in the *New York Times* from 1996, reporting differing access to technology and the internet between two Californian schools located in the heart of America's early digital revolution. One is a prestigious private school, and the other a public school serving one of the region's poorest communities, and 'the digital divide between these two schools in the heart of Silicon Valley provides perhaps the most striking example anywhere in the nation of a widening gap – between children who are being prepared for lives and careers in the information age, and those who may find themselves held back' (Poole, 1996).

The notion of a 'digital divide' contributing to real-world inequalities is possibly even stronger today than it was more than two decades ago, though sometimes it is subtler than simply having, or not having, access to a digital technology. Now a very significant divide could be around, for example, the brand of mobile device one can afford to buy, whether access to the internet is censored or monitored by a government, or whether popular software is available in a certain language or accommodates accessibility needs. As we discuss here a new wave of concern about young people not being adequately 'prepared' for modern life if they do not know how to code software and design hardware – often pitched as a case of 'programme or be programmed.' Some of this preparation is not about equity of opportunity and access to wealth but rather about serving the voracious needs of twenty-first-century capitalism for programmers, data miners, engineers, and technicians as the new labour force. This book seeks to highlight the creative and artistic affordances and opportunities that are also to be found, helping to shift young people towards making and creating as well as consuming new forms of media, entertainment, education, and performance. Digital arts cultures are a sign that people are not yet completely powerless to address the economic, social, educational, and class issues that digital technology creates or feeds.

Drama is front and centre in our approach to digital technologies for this very reason. Nicola Shaughnessy has identified how applied performance is being used to address the digital divide by focusing not so much on availability of technology, but on how to make use of it to engage in meaningful social practices. Shaughnessy's volume contains detailed examinations of the work of practitioners such as the UK theatre company C&T, who are finding it possible to tap into available technologies such as mobile phones and the internet in places like Malawi and Kenya in Africa, making it feasible to bring a blend of drama/technology to their applied theatre work in even relatively poor rural and urban areas. This allows a more authentically situated engagement by participants with the issues facing young people in a globalized world. Drama helps people to harness available technologies to develop social capital, and Shaughnessy argues that technology must be embodied to do this type of transformational creative and educational work because:

> As performance practitioners and theorists fully understand, even in activities which are not orientated towards social inclusion, the importance of a physical element via the human interface is fundamental to generating meaningful interaction. Pedagogically... technology can operate only at a basic and superficial level if it is divorced from the social and interpersonal contexts which frame and shape our everyday realities. (Shaughnessy, 2012, p. 160)

Towards invisible tools for digital drama

In Figure 1.1 is an example of a simple and free online editing tool that can be used creatively to inspect the underlying code and media elements on any web page, facilitating the editing, remixing, and publishing of the altered content.

The X-Ray Goggles tool is made available by Mozilla, the organization behind the popular Firefox web browser software, as part of a programme to help people everywhere make, learn, and play using the open building blocks of the web. In this example the serious news image and headline on the *New York Times* web page has been replaced with kitten-related news. The editing takes place on the local computer and not the actual *New York Times* website, but the ability to then publish and share the remixed version with

FIGURE 1.1 *Screenshot of Mozilla X-Ray Goggles tool 'Hack the News' activity tutorial. Used under the Creative Commons Attribution Share-Alike License.*[1]

other audiences makes this a powerful, fun, and creative tool. It can be used to teach and learn web coding, and also as a 'digital pre-text' (Carroll, 2004) that employs everyday technology for a drama-based activity to interrogate and reframe the media and news coverage. This positions X-Ray Goggles as a simple technological approach to Augusto Boal's concept of 'Newspaper Theatre'[2], an applied drama technique that helps people to make their own theatre to 'demystify the pretended objectivity of most journalism' (Boal, 1998, p. 192). In a similar vein the theatre company C&T, mentioned earlier in this chapter, is developing a web browser-based service named Prospero that allows users to add layers of interactive content over any published web page to produce applied drama, games, and learning activities.

Digital tools can be intriguing and beguiling in their own right, especially when they are new and seemingly full of promise for innovation or efficiency. However, we are also mindful that, as Clay Shirky observes, it is what people *do* with the tools once they become more mainstream and almost invisible that can be of greater significance, as

> communications tools don't get socially interesting until they get technologically boring. The invention of a tool doesn't create change; it has to have been around long enough that most of society is using it. It's when a technology becomes normal, then ubiquitous, and finally so pervasive as to be invisible, that the really profound changes happen, and for young people today, our new social tools have passed normal and are heading to ubiquitous, and invisible is coming. (Shirky, 2008, p. 105)

In a slightly different sense it is not just our social tools that have 'passed normal', but also our social forms and structures. We see technology as opening up postnormal hybrid spaces for drama, education, and artistic endeavour that combine physical and mediated tools and experiences in increasingly seamless and effortless ways. One small example of this is the case study of a youth theatre workshop described in Chapter 5. The project combined live improvised performance, large-scale puppetry, video game design, and digital media production in an examination of the eleventh-century Old English poem *Beowulf*. A week of drama and media production activities led to a performance in an old hall that was simultaneously live-streamed on social media from a roving iPad. Family and friends of the young performers formed both an audience and a media scrum, recording the show using their mobile devices and creating their own personal and sharable digital archives of performance. We believe it is necessary to examine these technologies and their role in intermedial creative expression precisely because they are, in Shirky's terms, rapidly being rendered invisible through their ubiquity. Many of the new social tools Shirky referred to in his book *Here Comes Everybody* (2008) have by now moved towards becoming invisible; recent surveys of Facebook users in Africa and Asia have found that millions of users are not even aware they are connecting to the internet when using that particular service (Mirani, 2015). This is the world of the 'interfaceless interface' between content or performer and audience (McGonigal, 2003, p. 119), for example, as applied to creating hybrid real and fictional worlds for so-called augmented reality games where the technological means of delivery seems to erase itself. This state of invisibility is central to much theatre, in which the mechanical context of a production (the stage, the lighting, the scenery) is generally so accepted as part of the experience that it does not demand focused attention to the technology itself during performance. This extends into our engagement with digital art forms where our willingness to accept what is 'real' in terms of time, space, and even physical presence can be more flexible than might at first be assumed. We explore what Bolter and Grusin label as the dual logics of 'transparent immediacy' and 'hypermediacy' (1999) – the design of interfaces so obvious and intuitive that they disappear from focus – and their connection to concepts of digital liveness further in this chapter, and then more deeply in Chapter 4. We have decided to use a drama framework that keeps the activities of people and a sense of embodied creativity central to the stories we will share throughout this book.

A drama framework

There remains an underlying historical dissonance when drama and digital technology are positioned together in the discourses of arts practice and education. This is despite millennia of technology integrated with the history of dramatic performance, most obviously in the use of stage machinery dating at least back to the ancient Greek theatre. The human body itself has often been imagined and described in terms of mechanical and computational language, and there have been many attempts to combine performance and technology in forms ranging from clockwork automata to supercomputer artificial intelligences. Performance is equally integral to the history of technology, for example, in the 'gestural knowledge' of scientific discovery in which experiments must be *performed* and *re-enacted* as part of an embodied process of interpretation and replication (Kirshenblatt-Gimblett, 2004).

Drama, performance, and the theatre have long been areas of interest for those studying the interactions between humans and computers. In the late twentieth century exploration of the nature of digital interactivity considered the 'computer as theatre' (Laurel, 1991), such that 'computers are providing us with a new stage for the creation of participatory theatre' (Murray, 1997, p. 12). In the development of the video game industry there has long been interest in concepts around engaging players both physically and emotionally in what is sometimes even described as a more theatrical experience, with efforts to produce systems capable of improvised 'interactive drama' using virtual actors. This has proved difficult both technically and aesthetically, though it continues to drive technological developments such as game 'engine' software with increasingly sophisticated artificial intelligence capabilities, virtual reality devices to produce more immersive augmented reality experiences, and more generally the creation of large-scale online game worlds with open-ended narratives and possibilities for improvised play. Still, many examinations of digital culture became locked into comparisons to the screen-based media forms they often seem most similar to aesthetically, such as cinema. As a result, 'the video game industry became closer to Hollywood and not to Broadway' (Frasca, 2001, p. 17), not just in terms of its business models but also in the way it was critiqued and researched.

As Chris Salter observes, there is now an accelerated shift to consider digital media in terms of their physical, off-screen experiences in a middle ground between traditional arts and digital arts cultures. This is based on a rediscovery of the embodied, affective, improvised, and real-time characteristics of performative practices, so that although 'obsessed in the 1990s by the ocular and the inscribed, the screen and data, now even the new media arts are discovering (or recovering) felt experience, situated context and polysensory affect that cannot simply be reduced to text, code, or photons aimlessly floating on the screen' (Salter, 2010, p. xxi). This is also a definite shift away from the 'static objecthood' of visual art forms that necessarily privilege physical artefacts. The concept of a middle ground between real and physical resonates with the concept of 'intermediality' in performance, which we shall take up further throughout this book, in which multimodal forms of expression and production might combine in creative and interdisciplinary ways that are mutually enhancing.

Drama is in many ways an ancient aesthetic means for representing, understanding, reinforcing, and transforming our perceptions of the world (Hartnoll and Brater, 2012). Like most art forms drama is more complex than simply being a pathway for artistic expression, cultural capital, or entertainment. It has many forms and applications that are educational, political, or transformative in nature. Drama also has a connection to many of the practices now emerging in what can loosely be described as the digital or media literacies of young people. We will explore why this is may be so in greater detail throughout the book but it is rooted in what Umberto Eco (1989) would call the 'openness' of both drama and digital media, or what drama practitioners such as Heathcote have called the shape-shifting qualities (2006, p. xiii) – their ability to shape and be shaped by the cultures they inhabit.

A narrative plasticity has been identified as common to improvised drama forms and digital games (Carroll and Cameron, 2005), in which the 'story' is often told reflectively or in hindsight to the lived moments of drama or game. The drama facilitator or game designer can provide elements to create the pre-text for the drama or play, but the narrative is then produced through configurative exploration, rather than fully interpretive engagement with a complete text.

Aarseth describes in *Cybertext* (1997) how computational or procedural media now allows a form of ergodic literature requiring nontrivial effort to construct and traverse the texts. Aarseth uses the Greek words *ergon* (work) and *hodos* (path) to define these as ergodic texts (1997, p. 1), and he describes a phenomenon whereby the player of a computer game, or in this sense the user, of electronic text is a closely integrated figure in the construction of a semiotic sequence.

A common element in digital arts cultures is a sense that the participants, who may to some extent include input and interaction from the computational tools and platforms themselves, must somehow 'work' together to produce the creative experience. Drama is fundamentally about action, about doing something to bring about the affective experience or the narrative whether scripted or improvised. In this sense many of the skills and conventions of drama fall into what might be termed an ergodic literacy, one that is well placed for helping us to both read *and* write the ergodic texts afforded by digital arts platforms. Participation in many of the creative practices and activities of digital arts cultures is fundamentally what could be termed a 'framed' performance activity. This concept is likely to be familiar to educational drama practitioners and teachers, and increasingly also to those working in fields of interactive media and digital games. Erving Goffman's (1956, 1974) work continues to influence many disciplines' approaches to understanding the performative nature of social and cultural interactions in our everyday lives, and these are only enhanced and extended through the use of networked digital technologies. The 'performative turn' also now has well-established roots in the social sciences and humanities as a method for understanding human behaviours and social interactions. More recently it is argued that performative research has emerged as a third paradigm to quantitative and qualitative methods, to accommodate the twenty-first-century wave of 'symbolic data' expressed in forms beyond discursive text – particularly those linked to digital arts cultures such as still and moving images, music and sound, live action, and digital code (Haseman, 2006).

The drama framework for exploring digital arts cultures shown in Figure 1.2 attempts to reconcile in a useful and applied way a hybrid generated from different physical and virtual forms of identity, performance, and experience. Taking a theatrical metaphor it is visualized as a Fresnel lens, drawing on elements of both digital media literacy and drama and refocusing them on four drama-based domains that interact, interweave, and overlap in emergent and

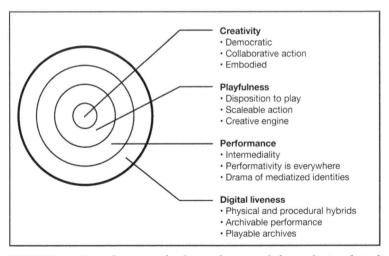

Creativity
- Democratic
- Collaborative action
- Embodied

Playfulness
- Disposition to play
- Scaleable action
- Creative engine

Performance
- Intermediality
- Performativity is everywhere
- Drama of mediatized identities

Digital liveness
- Physical and procedural hybrids
- Archivable performance
- Playable archives

FIGURE 1.2 *Four domains of a drama framework for exploring digital arts cultures.*

often fleeting ways, highly adaptive to the precarious and dynamic processes of a postnormal world.

We believe these four domains establish common ground to provide a meaningful and innovative engagement with a range of innovative, creative, and complex cultural activities emerging from within networked and mediated everyday cultures:

1   Creativity – which is a disciplined and structured process that produces valuable process and artefacts (Craft, 2003). Creativity is central to the making of theatre, gaming, and other forms of cultural production (P. McIntyre, 2012) in education, the creative industries, and beyond.

2   Playfulness – which captures in many ways the intrinsic and very human motivations behind learning, making, and doing represented by the digital arts cultures we seek to engage with. Playfulness is one engine that drives creativity. It can be emergent and contextual, based on loose collaborations or intensely focused.

3   Performance – which encompasses the role and identity play common in digital cultures, the ergodic literacies apparent in the collaborative engagement with interactive art forms, and the transmedia nature of production and content.

4   Digital liveness – based on intermediality and hypermedia, which addresses questions about participation and audience and the future possibilities of digital arts and creativity.

We will now describe and explore these four domains in more detail.

Creativity, learning, and the arts

Creative learning in arts occurs in the process and the product, in the art form and aesthetic, in the making and the performing. It occurs whether the arts are being used as a process of learning in other fields such as geography or the arts are being explored in their own right such as performing one of the great playwrights like Harold Pinter. As Jonothan Neelands argues, 'Arts education has the potential to be a discipline in its own right and a concrete and creative process for learning in other disciplinary or curricular settings' (2011, p. 168).

As such, creative learning occurs in and through the engagement with the art form and supports creative learning in other curriculum areas. It is possible to do both without diminishing either. In terms of the contribution the arts and creativity can make to networked cultures there are claims for democratic engagement, collaborative action, and embodiment.

Democratic creativity

One of the dominant mythologies that surrounds creativity is that it is only available to the elite genius few (M. Anderson, 2012). You often hear in industries such as theatre, film, and advertising the term 'creatives' used. This nomenclature is designed to delineate the 'creatives' from the 'non-creatives' or the more widely used euphemism, the technicians. This dichotomy entrenches the old idea that some are born to creativity and some are born to technicality as if these two cannot interact. Of course the technicians often practice a great deal of creativity. In the making of theatre if those who are called 'creatives' have no understanding of the technical aspects of their work, their creativity is likely to founder. Aesthetic control and understanding is always predicated on a sound base of technical understanding. Creativity is part of our daily lives and exercised by us all. Craft (2002) calls this 'lifewide creativity' as it is present and demonstrated every day and seen not just in education. This is the starting point for arts learning. Arts learning is at its core an educative process that begins with the students' immersion in artistic making and appreciating processes and then seeks to build aesthetic understanding and aesthetic control in the art form. For instance, when drama students first begin to understand and develop characters, they have begun a creative process. While this may be seen by some as elementary in the development of students' understanding of arts, it is original for the individual student. The *All Our Futures: Creativity, Culture and Education Report* (Robinson, 2001) nominates originality as a feature of creativity. Crucially this report defines originality as original for the individual involved in the activity. This is a fundamentally democratic approach to creativity that frees educators to focus their pedagogy on all students rather than just those that might one day have the potential genius required for a more restricted definition of creativity. This approach does not deny that there are different qualities of creativity; it simply argues that anyone provided with the necessary resources can be creative. Jonothan Neelands calls this ensemble approach to learning 'pro-social'. He claims, 'working together in the social and egalitarian conditions of the ensemble, young people have the opportunity to struggle with the demands of becoming' (2011, p. 176).

Creativity as collaborative action

Another myth about creativity is that it is an individual striving disconnected from others – think of stereotypes of a loner artist starving in an attic. This is perhaps the most debilitating and anti-intuitive myth that relates to creativity for arts educators: that it is an individualistic cognitive skill that has no relationship to others. As Fischer argues, 'much human creativity arises from activities that take place in a social context in which interactions with other people and the artefacts that embody group knowledge are important contributors to the process. Creativity does not happen inside a person's head, but in the interaction between a person's thoughts and a socio-cultural context' (2004, p. 485). This complexity may be difficult to measure with tests but it is a truism of creativity in arts learning that it is not an isolated cognitive skill, but rather a complex interaction of the individual learner, their learning context, their fellow learners, and the aesthetic. This complex interaction is perhaps most frequent and intensive in arts classrooms.

A cursory understanding of the collaborative processes involved in arts argues against this stereotype of creativity. For performing arts this is very much the exception that the individual is capable of creating theatre. Creativity in these areas routinely relies on the interplay of several creative approaches at once for anything to be created at all. While research has focussed more heavily on auteurship and the sources of individual and personal creativity (Jeffrey and Craft, 2001), it is evident that creativity can and is achieved in group contexts. Holbrook Mahn and Vera John-Steiner (2002, p. 51) argue that in collaboration participants create mutual zones of proximal development (Vygotsky, 1980) for each other where their intellect and emotions are brought together in a unified whole. They explain how they think collaborative creativity actually works, where 'in producing texts partners share each other's early drafts; they strive to give shape to their communicative intent by combining precision – or word meaning – with the fluidity of the sense of the words. They live, temporarily, in each other's heads. They also draw on their mutuality as well as their differences in knowledge, working styles and temperament' (Mahn and John-Steiner, 2002, p. 51).

The same processes are taking place in arts learning. For instance, if students are involved in a playbuilding process, they may develop an idea from a stimulus that is then developed further through improvisation and then worked into a performance perhaps through a theatrical style or form they have learnt about. Perhaps in this case a Brechtian performance style they learnt through studying *Mother Courage*. So you might expect in this improvisation the use of the distancing effect (Erikkson, 2011) and the use of direct address to an audience, and harsh stage lighting. The learning taking place here relies on the student to work with the group in cooperating with the understanding they have of the aesthetic demands of the form.

As teachers and practitioners who have worked in the arts well know the products of these collaborations are not always high quality. They are often banal and plodding but the potential for creativity is enhanced when the teachers are able to develop a learning environment that makes aesthetic control and aesthetic understanding prominent. Learning to be creative is an evolutionary growth that begins with the student making original discoveries (for themselves) and then building on those discoveries (iterating) in a broader social context using all their cognitive resources including the body.

Arts and embodied creativity

In many classrooms the body and the mind seem to be separated in learning. One of the unique claims that the arts has, and especially dance and drama, is the use of embodiment in the process of creation. Students engaged in arts work routinely employ embodied processes to create characters and performance. Recent experiments have demonstrated that enactment of texts enhances memory of those texts for children (Cutica, Iani, and Bucciarelli, 2014) and adults (Noice and Noice, 2001), but arts pedagogies aim to promote deeper learning beyond simple recall, to comprehension, aesthetic understanding, and control and in so doing foster creative practices (Anderson, 2012). Making and consuming digital media content is often seen as the opposite of more physical and material forms of artistic work. Gauntlett (2011) argues that making things to share online is still often very much a craft process of creative expression that leaves the makers' metaphorical fingerprints all over the digital materials. Gauntlett's argument is that working with digital and online media still implies a 'hands-on' approach to doing and making, and that the sense of embodied presence remains strong in the completed works even in heavily mediatized forms. This sense of digital liveness is very much part of the drama framework used in this book.

A key allied domain of skills and practice that can evoke democracy, collaborative action, and embodiment in creativity is playfulness.

Playfulness

Young people have a universal right to play. The United Nations Convention on the Rights of the Child (UNCRC) states in Article 31 that every child has the right 'to relax and play, and to join in a wide range of cultural, artistic and other recreational activities'. The UN's 2013 General Comment No. 17 provides a more detailed legal interpretation of Article 31, and notes that while play is often considered non-essential, it is a fundamental and vital dimension to the pleasure of childhood. The UN argues that recreation and play contribute to 'the development of creativity, imagination, self confidence, self-efficacy, as well as physical, social, cognitive and emotional strength and skills'.

We use the term "playfulness" to capture that sense of being disposed towards using play in an active and embodied way to engage in creative, artistic, and exploratory learning pursuits. It is an ambiguous and imprecise term, just as Brian Sutton-Smith emphasizes in *The Ambiguity of Play* (1997) that play is itself a difficult concept to define from any one disciplinary perspective. Play has long been recognized as a fundamental skill in human learning and several authors now consider playing as essential to the navigation of education in the twenty-first century (Jenkins, Purushotma, Weigel, Clinton, and Robison, 2009), yet we are now only beginning to understand the nuances of play as a form of social development, problem-solving, experimentation, and collaborative creativity. Recognizing playfulness as a learning skill or literacy is made harder by a tendency to view it as the opposite of work or meaningful effort. Educators and arts practitioners will understand this polarizing effect when considering comparisons made between the Arts and Science, Technology, Engineering, and

Mathematics (STEM) in education. They will also understand that like drama, play is more complex, rewarding, and potentially innovative than simply being a diversion from serious pursuits. Play is a way of prototyping and evaluating future possibilities and outcomes, and as such it is an engine to drive creativity and experimentation in many different settings. Throughout the book we acknowledge and celebrate the complex and emergent forms of creativity, embodied learning, transformation, and exploration that playfulness nurtures in both formal and informal cultural settings.

As stated in the UN Conventions, play is often viewed as a vital development activity for children. Play is also seen as something that diminishes with adulthood, and is generally not considered a component of lifelong learning. However, playfulness as an attitude or approach to exploring and learning is not limited to children. Playfulness is therefore one useful lens through which we can take an interdisciplinary path through the diverse digital arts cultures considered in this book. Although play – like drama – can be difficult to define in a universal and scholarly sense, Sutton-Smith proposes an interdisciplinary approach based on seven rhetorical perspectives on play, many directly relevant to the themes of this book (Sutton-Smith, 1997):

1   Play as progress: as noted above, this is often applied to animal or child's play, and it positions play as developmental rather than a lifelong learning skill.

2   Play as fate: applied to play as an aspect of human life that is controlled by destiny, typically represented in games of chance and gambling.

3   Play as power: sports and contests, often applied as a metaphor for warfare and patriarchy.

4   Play as identity: constructing, confirming, or advancing the power and social identities of a community of players, for example, as seen in some festivals and community celebrations.

5   Play as imaginary: idealizes playful improvisation, creativity, and innovation powered by imagination.

6   Play as the self: often applied to solitary and playful escapes from everyday life, such as hobbies, but can include high-risk activities like bungee jumping.

7   Play as frivolous: applied to the activities of the foolish and the idle, but historically linked to figures of fools or jesters; can be seen as purposeful and subversive protests against everyday order.

Taking an interdisciplinary view these rhetorics combine in different ways in an infinite range of contexts, and collectively they are a guide to the elements of playfulness that create a frame through which to view a range of individual and social engagements in digital arts cultures. Applied theatre and drama-in-education techniques can be framed as forms of playful exploration and learning. Parallel work emerging from the critical games field is exploring how game design can be used to generate critical and transformative play to address real-world issues (Flanagan, 2009; McGonigal, 2011). Ian Bogost argues that it is possible to find playful joy in even the most mundane of life's pursuits by accepting the rules and constraints that they present as part of the experience to be embraced rather than resisted:

The lesson that games can teach us is simple. Games aren't appealing because they are fun, but because they are limited. Because they erect boundaries. Because we must accept their structures in order to play them ... That's what it means to play. To take something – anything – on its own terms, to treat it as if its existence were reasonable. The power of games lies not in their capacity to deliver rewards or enjoyment, but in the structured constraint of their design, which opens abundant possible spaces for play. (2016, p. x)

The use of technology to support play as a transformative and creative platform is of interest to many disciplines, for example, the world of archives and museums is increasingly embracing creative digital arts cultures as we consider in Chapter 8. Increasingly there is interest in the scalability of play, not just in terms of massively multiplayer online games with hundreds of thousands of players, but also in ways of utilizing media technologies to generate urban experiences in public spaces as part of what has become known as the 'playable city' movement. Issues relating to this playful and often highly performative reconfiguring of urban and public spaces are considered further in Chapter 9. In the applied drama framework used in this book, playfulness offers a way to move between the 'what if' of imagination and experimentation and the 'what is' of real-world issues and problems that concern learners.

Performance

Performance remains a thread through digital cultures, despite a tendency to think of them as shedding embodiment in favour of fully virtual or mediated interactions. In our drama framework, performance is a vital means of maintaining a humanizing perspective on the digital technology that increasingly pervades the daily lives of young people. In developing the drama framework for this book we have observed the domain of performance in that basic human ability to adopt alternative identities for the purpose of improvisation and creative discovery in both real and virtual spaces.

Young people's concepts of performance, role, and individual identity are now in a state of flux in an increasingly mediated and connected world. The rationale for manipulating or editing identities is assimilated into their digital world-view, having been exposed to an array of websites, apps, games, and other media properties that encourage or even demand the creation of characters, costumes or skins, usernames, aliases, and avatars. The nature of our regular engagements with mobile phones and websites illustrates Richard Schechner's claim that 'performativity is everywhere' (2002, p. 110), particularly in an increasingly networked and mediatized world of multiple conscious and subconscious representations of self. Participants no longer seemingly choose between primarily real or virtual experiences, as new experiences emerge from the co-relationships between the 'as is' of the real world and the augmentative or representational 'as if' possibilities and affordances of digital media technologies. Status updates, tweets, texts, 'selfies', comments, 'likes', 'shares' have become a dynamic means of identity creation and maintenance within what danah boyd calls the 'networked publics' of social media 'defined as (1) the space constructed through networked technologies and (2) the imagined community that emerges as a result of the intersection of people, technology, and practice' (2007). Alice Marwick and danah boyd (2014, p. 8) have considered the performative skirmishes that occur between teens in these spaces as a form of drama, similar to the mundane interpersonal conflicts that form part of the discourse around celebrity, and which is evident in soap operas and reality TV shows. This is explored further in Chapter 3.

Intermediality

Drama and digital media are agile and adaptive cultural and technical shapeshifters, enabling opportunities to explore identities and to forge reconfigurable alliances and cooperatives in real and virtual spaces to produce creative works. Theatrical and digital practices now operate within 'hypermedia' spaces that accommodate a mutual affect created as media and performance forms interact to generate a new 'mashup' experience, to use digital culture parlance. Intermediality argues that all performances now take place in spaces (real, virtual, or even blended) that are perceived to challenge the conventional boundaries of any one particular media or aesthetic form. No longer do all participants in these creative endeavours, including performers and their audiences, need to assume synchronous co-presence in time and space. In fact, there is now less certainty that all of the participants will even be human. Experiences can scale from the intimate to the massive through personal mobile technology, now ubiquitously equipped with the affordances of cameras and microphones connected to global publishing platforms built upon social networks.

At the level of using these digital media tools, media theorist Lev Manovich describes the theatrical and performative nature of our interactions with everyday devices such as our increasingly ubiquitous smartphones and computers. He describes a form of designed theatricality in the hardware and software interfaces of these devices, with playful animations and other visual and audio responses intentionally combined to produce an experience for the user; 'as in a traditional theatrical play, these sequences unfold in time; various sensorial effects play on each other, and it is their contrast as well as the differences between the senses being addressed – touch, vision, hearing – which together add up to a complex dramatic experience' (Manovich, 2013, p. 315).

Digital liveness

The ontological nature of the performer in our mediatized world was often summarized as a distinction between live performance and technological reproduction. At a fundamental level this is about the time and place of a performance, and the relative positions of performer and audience in those dimensions. Some argue that the real-time co-presence of performer and audience in an unmediated context remains the only circumstance that can definitively be considered a live performance, and that forms involving recording or technological reproduction or transmission can never be considered 'live'. Thus some performance scholars such as Peggy Phelan argue for presence and reproduction, where 'only life is in the present. Performance cannot be saved, recorded, documented or otherwise participate in the circulation of representations of representations: once it does so, it becomes something other than performance' (1993, p. 146).

Conversely, the very notion of a live performance is not a prior condition but arises only from the technical possibility of mediatization. Conceptually, live performance emerges largely from the audience effects of broadcast mass media in the twentieth century, initially radio and then television. Before the rise of mass communication forms such as radio, an audience clearly understood the contextual differences between listening to a gramophone recording of an orchestra and experiencing the concert in person. Philip Auslander (1999) argues that this understanding was altered when the technology of radio literally created a medium between source and audience that effectively hid the nature of the performance. These broadcast media drove a parallel industry in recording and playback technologies that soon made their way from professional to consumer markets. Audiences understood that media technology could obfuscate the immediacy and presence of the original source performance, and that audience members no longer had to be in the same place as the performance to experience it as 'live'.

In the digital era young people now 'interact simultaneously with both the physical world and with digital information' (Facer et al., 2004) as they go about their daily lives. They engage in a mix of real-time and asynchronous interactions, adopting a sense of polysynchronous presence operating with both real and digital representations of themselves across a range of spaces and places including home, social groups, online games, work, and formal education. The latter presents a special challenge for arts-based teachers and practitioners seeking to use these devices and applications in institutional settings with expectations of supervision or control, or at the very least the use of technology for 'productivity' rather than experimental play or artistic creation. There has for some time been a growing divide between those that allow these tools as a teaching or creative resource and those that seek to restrict or even ban them, and 'there is a grave danger a group of young people, who are heavy users of such technology, will become even more disengaged with education, seeing it as irrelevant to the world they inhabit' (Heppell and Chapman, 2011, p. 2).

Digital liveness (Auslander, 2012) is concerned with the way digital technology transforms the boundaries and conditions of 'performance' experienced by both performers and audience. Kirschenblatt-Gimblett observes that this transformation demonstrates a dynamism in which 'performance as an organizing idea has been responsive not only to new modes of live action, but also new technologies.... If boundaries are to be blurred, why not also the line between live and mediated performance?' (2004, p. 48). The nature of intermediality in digital arts cultures is such that hybrids of physical and procedural performance are no longer seen as experimental or 'just over the horizon' technology. Auslander now uses the term 'digital liveness' to describe how we accept the procedural nature of experiences transformed by digital technology, and submit to 'the creation of the effect of liveness in our interactions with computers and virtual entities' (2012, p. 7) as a matter of course. Interaction with so-called bots, chatterbots, Non-Player Characters (NPCs), and other types of artificial agents in video games and other interactive media experiences is perhaps the ultimate mediatization of performance possible with contemporary technology. For example, it is now not uncommon to see these agents interacting within game worlds, both with the players and with each other, in increasingly realistic ways.

As performance becomes more mediatized, the concept of a digital archive of performance becomes more viable. Even highly embodied art forms like dance and theatre now have examples of both formal and informal digital documentation and archives. We are generating our own personal digital archives of live experiences through our use of mobile phones to record, store, and share moments from our daily lives. Institutional archives are increasingly providing access to digital representations of their collections in ways that are suggestive of performative interactions, built on our growing acceptance of these experiences as an enhancement or alternative to physical visits. This aspect of both creating and playing with archives is considered further in Chapter 7.

The drama framework for this book shifts away from traditional theatrical perceptions that liveness requires synchronicity of time and space, with performers and the audience both physically and temporally co-present with one another. Instead we can explore how digital arts cultures are not bound by these conditions, yet they can retain some attributes of liveness that can enhance and deepen the learner or participant experience within interactive and networked environments. Liveness, digital or otherwise, is not an objective or natural condition in the world but a subjective experience that exists primarily in the mind of the audience. Our sense that something is occurring live is therefore a premise, and 'in this sense liveness is first and foremost a frame, in Erving Goffman's sense of that term. An understanding of what is going on that allows me to define my relationship to it and participate appropriately with it' (Auslander, 2014). Digital liveness is therefore central to the dramatic and performative nature of much of the digital arts cultures we are examining in this book, and Chapter 4 is devoted to considering the intersections of intermediality and performance with everyday technology.

Digital liveness and dramatic tension

Adults and children alike can engage in dramatic and playful explorations in which they can 'intellectually and emotionally exist simultaneously and effectually in two worlds: one real but suspended as far as necessary, and one that is fictional but is the "operational" world of the drama' (O'Toole, 2009, p. 72). Digital liveness is connected to long-standing dramatic conventions such as the voluntary suspension of disbelief (Coleridge, 1817) that was attributed to literary and theatrical audiences, and then to film and television audiences, to understand how people could seemingly lose themselves in the moment of a performance. In radio, a long-held aphorism refers to the 'theatre of the mind' to illustrate how and why radio remains a powerful and effective storytelling medium despite predictions of its demise with the advent of television, the world wide web and other visual digital media forms. The concept of creating, sharing, and moving between real and imagined worlds as necessary or desired is also caught up in other concepts such as dual affect (Vygotsky, 1933/1976), the magic circle of play (Huizinga, 1938/1955), frames (Goffman, 1974), and 'metaxis' (Boal, 1979). These illustrate a range of critical perspectives on our ability to accommodate different emotional states when engaged in imaginative play or creative work. Most of these terms predate the rapid emergence, adoption, and impact of digital media, and in some cases even the full effects of broadcast mass media were not yet apparent as they entered the discourses of psychology, sociology, performance studies, education, and applied theatre.

These concepts have also retained some currency in more recent work relating to interactive media and video games. Vygotsky, Huizinga, Goffman, and Boal are familiar to many working and researching in fields such as digital media, human computer interactions, and game studies. Brenda Laurel's description of engagement evokes audience willingness to suspend disbelief, for example, though she describes it as what 'happens when we are able to give ourselves over to a representational action, comfortably and unambiguously. It involves a kind of complicity' (1991, p. 115). Mihalyi Csikszentmihalyi describes a similar phenomenon he calls 'flow' in which players of video games or other forms of interactive media seem to absorb themselves in the virtual or on-screen activity, oblivious to the passage of real-world time (1990).

John O'Toole (1992) has noted that emotional tension exists in the gap between an individual and the fulfilment of their internal purposes, and the deliberate positioning of constraints can therefore create a powerful affective dimension to a drama or learning experience. One of the drama conventions available to be used in this way is the ability of a participant to be both a performer and a spectator of their own performance:

> The dual affect of Vygotsky, where the child 'weeps as a patient, yet revels as a player', incorporates a tension caused by the gap between the real and the fiction, and a recognition of that gap. This is the tension of metaxis. (O'Toole, 1992, p. 166)

Digital liveness does not imply a total immersion in the virtual space, as that would mean giving up one reality for another. Rather, as with other dramatic conventions such as metaxis, it relies on participants to hold within them the drama emerging from the interplay and frictions between what exists in the real world and what exists in the fictional or procedurally generated virtual world. Educators and practitioners have long understood the power of drama to unlock affective experience in this way, drawing on the work of Vygotsky, Goffman, and others (Bolton, 1986; Davis, Ferholt, Grainger Clemson, Jansson, and Marjanovic-Shane, 2015; Heathcote, 1984). It is the possibility that drama participants, as themselves, can enjoy and analyse the different emotions they experience that makes drama a critical pedagogy (O'Connor, 2013, p. 132). It is still surprising that those working more from the digital games and simulation fields have not fully tapped into the knowledge and experiences well described in drama and education. For example, David Williamson Shaffer's work to develop digital simulations and virtual internships using the concept of 'epistemic frames' (2004) could easily connect with parallels in educational drama and applied theatre forms (Cameron, Carroll, and Wotzko, 2011).

Auslander himself positions digital liveness within the performative aspects of everyday life, also drawing upon Goffman (1974) to describe how we are capable of organizing our interactions with the world in many different ways, including a reframing of a clearly mediated or perhaps totally virtual experience as if it is live to participate appropriately. He argues that our understanding that digital media necessarily separates participants physically and temporally from each other is actually what drives this sense of dramatic performance, just as a theatre audience knows that they are distanced – even if within touching distance – from a live performer on the stage:

> The idea that we can appreciate a performance as live without being in the place where it is occurring is fundamental … the power of liveness is in fact a function not of proximity but of distance. Or more precisely: the power of the live resides in the tension between having the sense of being connected experientially to something while it is happening, while also remaining at a distance from it. (Auslander, 2014)

This recruitment of temporal and physical distancing is a key to dramatic tension, with time and space two elements that are commonly manipulated and reshaped creatively to produce performative explorations of real and imagined events. Physical co-presence of the participants in digital art forms is often not necessary, and in fact networked technology such as the internet and mobile telephones makes it possible to scale social co-presence in ways that are not possible in real life.

Conclusion

If there is one common theme that runs throughout this book, it is that the performing arts have become increasingly mediatized at the same time that digital art forms have rediscovered the performative nature of creativity. As Salter describes it:

> Performance as practice, method, and worldview is becoming one of the major paradigms of the twenty-first century, not only in

the arts but also the sciences. As euphoria for the simulated and the virtual that marked the end of the twentieth century subsides, suddenly everyone from new media artists to architects, physicists, ethnographers, archaeologists, and interaction designers are speaking of embodiment, situatedness, presence, and materiality. In short, everything has become performative. (Salter, 2010, p. xx)

We have taken a practice-led approach to researching the performative and dramatic aspects of arts practice and education in both formal and informal settings for this book, at times embracing idiosyncratic and individual cases of practice as a means for considering emergent forms of creativity in new digital arts cultures. Taking a cue from Brad Haseman (2006, p. 3) we have been led 'by what is best described as "an enthusiasm of practice": something which is exciting, something which may be unruly, or indeed something which may be just becoming possible as new technology or networks allow (but of which they cannot be certain)'. Throughout the book we have therefore attempted to provide a number of diverse experiential hooks upon which to anchor further practice, criticism, and research.

This book is a critical guide to the profound changes to the creative practices of people made possible by digital media, in a world in which 'normality', such as historical practices and experiences, can no longer be taken as signposts to the immediate future. This is the liquid world of postnormality (Sardar, 2010) marked by rapid, global changes and challenges fuelled in part by technology. This book positions drama, with its very human and fundamentally embodied calls to *act* together within and upon the world, as a powerful way to engage with technology and help all people, and particularly young people, contend with a future infused with precariousness. Drama and technology can be seen not as binary opposites but rather as two elements that can mashup to produce new and complex hybrid forms that are part of learning and living as we move forward together. This postnormal world, and the potential for drama in arts and education contexts to confront its emerging contradictions, chaos, and complexities, is explored further in Chapter 2.

2

This Liquid World: Intermediality, Postnormality, and New Opportunities for Arts and Education

Imagining the unimaginable

For some reason it is very difficult for humans to imagine a future in ways other than it is at the moment. For instance, our not too distant ancestors thought human mechanized flight unlikely or unwise despite a series of rapid developments involving kites, balloons, and gliders. In a more banal way, we find it difficult to imagine it raining if we are in the middle of brilliant sunshine, even if now highly scientific meteorological forecasts predict a sudden summer storm. We think the same might be true of the kinds of ways technology, learning, creativity, and performance might interact in the very near future. It is difficult to imagine a future for schooling that is dominated by creativity, the arts and integration to support the academic and non-academic outcomes of students (including personal, economic, artistic, cultural, and vocational benefits) yet the research discussed in this chapter points to this as a way to future proof and enrich schooling (Jefferson and Anderson, 2017; Martin et al., 2013).

This phenomenon is also reflected in the work of science fiction. Carroll and Cameron's (2014) analysis of the prominent writer William Gibson gives us some insights into how the sometimes disconnected technologies that are 'over the horizon' will become commonplace in a 'mashed up' near present as digital arts cultures become living sites of liquid modernity (past, present, future mashed up in different ways, e.g. in games, music, and videos). Carroll and Cameron (2014) argue:

> As a successful author he [William Gibson] makes a living using science fiction as the tool to snap together the scattered pieces of a contemporary reality that many of us find difficult to observe or imagine as we go about our lives. As much as we might wish it to be so, daydreaming and soothsaying are probably not actually specified in most of our job descriptions. (p. 168)

This book contains an effort at some focused daydreaming in Chapter 11, and like the rain analogy the forecasts are in and they predict a future that is both exciting and unlike our current circumstances. We have entered in Zygmunt Bauman's terms a phase of liquid modernity:

> in which all social forms melt faster than new ones can be cast. They are not given enough time to solidify, and cannot serve as the frame of reference for human actions and long-term life-strategies

because their allegedly short life-expectation undermines efforts to develop a strategy that would require the consistent fulfilment of a 'life-project.' (2000, p. 303)

These new fluid social structures in some ways impede our ability to imagine what the future might look like and they indeed make reimagining the future far more difficult than it ever has been before. Theatre and performance provide an example of this imagination gap. The history of theatre has been littered with critics claiming that its demise is certain. One of the more contemporary claims was delivered by the father of Performance Studies, Richard Schechner, when he said 'the fact is that theatre as we have known and practiced it – the staging of written dramas – will be the string quartet of the 21st century: a beloved but extremely limited genre, a subdivision of performance' (1992, p. 8).

In some ways this is an easy out – it does not require any imagination about what theatre might be, it just imagines that it won't be. This book attempts to overcome this difficulty by imagining the possibilities of convergence and integration of technology and live performance and education that we identified in Chapter 1 as 'intermediality' and 'digital liveness'.

In a similar way, technologies such as books, radio, and film have had their obituaries written and read prematurely over the last few decades. In essence digital and theatre forms are similarly evolutionary and adaptive to a 'liquid' environment. Our intent in this chapter is to describe the challenges and opportunities of this liquid state by referring to discussions around society and modernity that set the scene for the possibilities explored in the remainder of this book.

From convergence to intermediality

Our conceptualization of an intermediality of hybrid art forms moves beyond convergence culture and beyond the media and technology-focussed applications. It considers the role of live engagement with technologies and the implications these kinds of convergence will have for our cultural and educational institutions. Henry Jenkins defines the term in this way:

> By convergence, I mean the flow of content across multiple media platforms, the cooperation between multiple media industries, and the migratory behaviour of media audiences who would go almost anywhere in search of the kinds of entertainment experiences they wanted. Convergence is a word that manages to describe technological, industrial, cultural, and social changes, depending on who's speaking and what they think they are talking about. (Jenkins, 2006b, p. 2)

There is an interdisciplinary intent and action in this kind of convergence. As we have already suggested, with the notions of intermediality and digital liveness, the barriers between fields of understanding live and not live performance in different kinds of media have dissolved even further since Jenkins wrote *Convergence Culture* in 2006. Mediatization has turned many aspects of our daily lives into performative actions, occurring in hypermedia spaces that mix physical and digital modes of expression and communication. This has implications for the world of work and education and the way we position and understand the role of cultural institutions in our society. The changing skill sets required to understand, create, and manage these new convergences are critical questions for those considering the future of our schools, workforces, and communities.

These requirements are compelling drivers for a major change in the way that we 'do' 'education' and 'culture' currently. The old systems and approaches that have been built for the twentieth-century world or earlier do not need refining; they require wholesale change. Taking education and the formal setting of schooling as one key site where young people experience many of these challenges and opportunities first hand, this chapter considers some of the change that is possible when the old models are redesigned to encourage creative mashup rather than the maintenance of knowledge silos. This chapter will argue for interdisciplinarity as a starting point rather than an afterthought in education and will discuss the spaces for creativity and innovation that make use of the rich yet currently largely disconnected cultural resources locked in our cultural and social institutions. The intermediality we imagine integrates many of the assets that currently sit in the 'culture', 'education', or 'play' containers in our conceptions of the world. It democratizes these resources and makes them available for creative play and invention. This is not only critical for learning but also central to providing skills for the changing patterns of work that are becoming apparent, and the emergent class systems that go with them.

The precariat and the proficians

In the face of these changes, sociologists and historians have been reimagining the implications of the new normal on our society and our communities, in a world where newly pervasive technology has impacted to make working lives more fluid and transferrable. The rise of Uber with its technology-driven labour distribution is a potent example. Employees in the pre-Uber era could expect to work as a licensed taxi driver or as a waged driver. The advent of Uber means that work and employment is more fluid and based on the availability of the individual driver's time and the local market's demand at any specific times for drivers. This makes the labour market inherently more fluid, less secure, and allows those involved to switch from one job role to another (computer programmer to musician to driver) when and where the needs exist. This change has implications for the way schools consider their approach to curriculum and suggests that traditional models of subjects may be at least a decade or two out of date. One of the most persuasive analyses comes from Guy Standing's theories, where he identifies emerging class categories including *the precariat* and *the proficians*. The precariat are those who do relatively low-skilled work (such as the example of the Uber driver discussed earlier) and the proficians are those, such as paediatricians, who have high levels of training and sustained demand for their services. Standing argues:

> The globalization era has resulted in a fragmentation of national class structures. As inequalities grew, and as the world moved towards a flexible open labour market, class did not disappear. Rather, a more fragmented global class structure emerged... [the] 'precariat', [is] flanked by an army of unemployed and a detached group of socially ill misfits living off the dregs of society. (2011, p. 12)

He argues that the proficians are an emerging class that does not seek the old certainties of a stable or even a salaried job; instead they use their fluid interdisciplinary skills to make a living:

[Proficians] combines the traditional ideas of 'professional' and 'technician' but covers those with bundles of skills that they can market, earning high incomes on contract, as consultants or independent own-account workers. The proficians are the equivalent of the yeomen, knights and squires of the Middle Ages. They live with the expectation and desire to move around, without an impulse for long-term, full-time employment in a single enterprise. The 'standard employment relationship' is not for them. (2011, p. 13)

The class that is least able to deal with these emergent uncertainties are the precariat who cannot take advantage of this fluency of 'opportunity' and instead find themselves at the whim of the local and global marketplace. The precariat cannot rely on the certainties of job, housing, or food security of the past. Standing defines the precariat as being 'characterized by living with unstable labour and chronic economic insecurity. Millions of people are being forced to live through unstable jobs, with fluctuating incomes and periodic unemployment. The precariat faces chronic uncertainty' (p. 13).

There are some prescient implications for digital arts cultures in these emerging classes. One of Standing's concerns is that the connection and omnipresence of technology in our lives can lead to a dangerous lack of reflection and risks for those with fewer resources. Standing argues (2011, p. 16) that this situation threatens our capacity for reflective thinking. Of course, there are potential benefits in work flexibility such as the ability to decide where and when labour can be provided based on the needs of the supplier rather than the demands of the market (which due to poverty may be no choice at all). But we need to deal with the risks. The precariat is most endangered, because those in it have least control over their time.

The new realities of work are just one feature of a fundamentally changed world from that of our parents and grandparents. It's possible to consider the realities of this shifting, liquid world through Ziauddin Sardar's concept of postnormality, articulated as three forces that have to some extent created the liquidity of contemporary society: chaos, contradiction, and complexity (Sardar, 2010).

Postnormality or the new normal

The continuing geopolitical uncertainty in the Middle East – while a long-standing narrative of conflict and refugee movement – illustrates the state of postnormality that we find ourselves contending with. In the modern world these entrenched uncertainties are further fuelled by the rapid movement of capitals of all kinds through technological advancement. We are also witnessing the seemingly unstoppable rise in the power of technology multiplying what might be possible in terms of economic growth while simultaneously putting at risk up to 47 per cent (Frey and Osborne, 2013) of the jobs that will be rapidly computerized in the next decade. Reports by the CEDA (2015) and OECD (2016) found similar trends. Yet we as a community often lack the vision to contend with the near future. We need to push beyond our limitations and imagine what a new and more liquid education system might be that prepares young people for the challenges of postnormality, and equips them to create and innovate across disciplines rather than repeat outmoded education approaches in pursuit of jobs that may no longer exist or offer any kind of security. In short we need to imagine the near future so the prevailing international context and the rapid rise of technology can be navigated to provide hope and peace for future generations rather than endless disruption and oppression.

The Western world is moving uneasily from one uncertainty to the next. The ravages of the Global Financial Crisis (GFC) at the end of the first decade of this century have once again brought into sharp focus the disparities between the rich and the poor. The overwhelming greed of bankers and corporations has led to continued 'austerity', which for citizens of Greece, Ireland, Spain, and many other countries has really meant poverty. At the same time many of those responsible for the worst outcomes of the GFC have remained not only largely untouched by law or untarnished by reputation, but in many cases they have also been monetarily rewarded. While there is nothing novel about corporate greed, contemporary capitalism and hyperactive market economies have created globalized and networked economic misery. This crisis of confidence and trust has developed in the midst of other global crises such as climate change, food security, and mass refugee movements as a result of asymmetrical wars. The rapid exchange of information that technology now allows has contributed to a maelstrom of crises that are complex, contradictory, and confusing. As Marshall and Picou ask, 'the critical question is not how do we reduce uncertainty, but rather how do we make better decisions in a world of irreducible uncertainties?' (2008, p. 230). US President Barack Obama said in his 2009 inauguration speech:

That we are in the midst of crisis is now well understood. Our nation is at war, against a far-reaching network of violence and hatred. Our economy is badly weakened, a consequence of greed and irresponsibility on the part of some, but also our collective failure to make hard choices and prepare the nation for a new age. Homes have been lost; jobs shed; businesses shuttered. Our healthcare is too costly; our schools fail too many; and each day brings further evidence that the ways we use energy strengthen our adversaries and threaten our planet. (Obama, 2009)

These coinciding conditions have moved international relationships to the situation already described in this chapter as postnormality (Sardar, 2010). The term first emerged as science philosophers Silvio Funcowitz and Jerome Ravetz sought to understand 'unpredictability, incomplete control and a plurality of legitimate perspectives' (1993). They argued that beyond the certainties of scientific method a new understanding was required that 'facts are uncertain, values in dispute, stakes high and decisions urgent' (Funtowicz and Ravetz, 1991). The 'post-truth' demonstrated in the UK's Brexit referendum and the 2016 US presidential elections have confirmed the prescience of Funcowitz and Ravetz's work. As Fish (2016) argues:

Recent developments in international politics have highlighted the uneasy attitude that politicians are beginning to develop towards information, truth, evidence and expert opinion. In the United Kingdom, where the 'Brexit' referendum has now concluded, we found members of the 'Leave' campaign claiming that the British people 'have had enough of experts'.

Beyond the paradigm of long periods of normality in the sciences espoused by Kuhn (2012), Funcowitz and Ravetz developed a way of thinking about science and more recently the humanities that pushes the bounds of certainty and engages with the ambiguity of the modern liquid condition of the world. While Funcowitz and Ravetz do not argue that the postnormal paradigm completely replaces the scientific method, they do argue that 'we would be misled if we retained the image of a process where true scientific facts simply determine the correct policy conclusions' (1993). Policy in science and other spheres is still somewhat driven by a principle of normality supported by perceived facts.

The normality paradigm is however an inadequate and to a large extent discredited starting point for education and schools, and yet schools are almost universally predicated on assumptions that arise from normality: cause and effect, economic growth, and industrial prosperity (Darling-Hammond, 2004). The testing and reporting regimes imposed on schools by governments in Western economies such as Australia and the UK have created a market-driven schooling system that is much more about training than it is about coping with imagined futures. As Thomson, Lingard, and Wrigley suggest (2012, p. 1):

> Governments around the world are committed to changing education. These changes are framed by national economic imperatives and driven by the need to be globally competitive in today's globalised economy. This is not change driven by an imaginary of a better and more socially just future for all, but of a more competitive economy, powered by improved human capital and better skills.

An example is the current focus on computer coding in school curricula, examined in Chapter 8, which is often framed as meeting the needs of industry rather than accommodating these skills into creative pursuits for social outcomes. A condition of postnormality presents challenges to participants in education to reconsider the old 'normalities' and reimagine what schooling could be in a 'post-fact' world (Manjoo, 2011) where students require the skills and understandings to confront the contradictions, chaos, and complexities of the future. As discussed earlier, one of the rising issues in modern life is the precariousness of work. This precariat class is different to the working or middle classes of the twentieth century as it transcends these labels. The emergence of this class has an impact on the ways work and education will change in the fluidity of the twenty-first century.

A postnormal tomorrow?

The emergence of the precariat has occurred at a time when many of the old normalities are rapidly disappearing. In some ways the technological convergences and new interdisciplinary art forms discussed in this book are both the cause and the outcome of some of the issues that are emerging for the education sector and communities generally. For instance, the prevalence of video creation from mobile devices and distribution via social media create an implicit community demand for learning about online film and video. The challenge for educators is not to reproduce the seas of mediocrity that can be found online but to harness the technologies through intermediality across English, drama, mathematics, and so on, to make learning connected, credible, beneficial, and relevant.

But before we consider the challenges and the opportunities that intermediality presents we would like to consider the circumstances and features of the postnormal world that is bringing with it this societal change. According to Sardar (2010), the postnormal age is

> characterised by uncertainty, rapid change, realignment of power, upheaval and chaotic behaviour. We live in an in-between period where old orthodoxies are dying, new ones have yet to be born, and very few things seem to make sense. Ours is a transitional age, a time without the confidence that we can return to any past we have known and with no confidence in any path to a desirable, attainable or sustainable future.

Sardar argues that the combination of complexity, confusion, and contradiction has fuelled a shift from normalcy to postnormality, sweeping away the institutions and understandings society has clung to for thousands of years and replacing them with uncertainty. Sardar argues that this condition is different to other shifts in history as the combination of networked systems facilitates rapid and chaotic shifts. This is demonstrable in two distinct and interacting ways in science and global conflict. In economic terms the pressures bearing down on the global economy from networked greed and environmental change created new and unprecedented challenges to the 'normalcy' of market economics. Ringland (2010) argues that economic models have been in decline long before the GFC struck and 'concerns about energy, environmental and security issues, food price increases, growing economic and financial imbalances and asset price inflation should have suggested that all was not well with this model'.

While financial crises are not new, the rebalancing of labour and resource economics from the West to the East means that the 'debt and deficit' business-as-usual model has become vulnerable. Ringland argues:

Recovery from the crisis is likely to be slower than that of the new competitor nations. Competition will be intense, and on new terms. Global systems issues – such as environmental change, but also international law and finance, access to raw materials and the management of intellectual property – all require the rich nations to sacrifice some of their power. This combination of power rebalancing and an institutional vacuum implies that the next decade will be a turbulent one.

We are now well into that next decade, and the ongoing fallout from the GFC has seen a demand for change that has led to strong and prosperous countries such as the UK retreating into a form of isolationism given voice in the 2016 Brexit referendum. While isolationism might be politically attractive to some, 'global systems issues' remain. An inability to respond to them adequately has led in some measure to the growing international tensions around refugee movements.

While science and technology can drive economic growth in many economies, there has been a less welcome rise in the side effects of these technologies. As Marshall and Picou argue:

These same advances tend to manufacture environmental problems that are increasingly complex, large-scale, and destructive. This is the paradox of the twenty-first century. We are increasingly reliant on science and technology to solve 'normal' environmental problems, but some of these solutions in turn create 'postnormal' environmental problems. (2008, p. 243)

There is a paradoxical bind here, one which is often present when we consider technology. Society has become reliant on the network and market economies but the combined fruits of both of these can be poisonous. The certainties of 'facts' and 'normality' have been supplanted by societal conditions that Sardar nominates in a postnormal world: complexity, chaos, and contradiction.

Complexity

One of the most compelling demonstrations of postnormal complexity is the ongoing 'war(s) on terrorism'. These involve both state sponsored and independent actor organizations. These conflicts are often in response to an abhorrent act such as a terror attack in a major urban area or the use of chemical weapons on civilian populations during civil unrest. There are however complex forces at work as the networked global community assesses the cost of action and/or non-action. Morality in these cases is shaped and driven at least in part by energy security and the economic pressures higher oil prices could bring to bear on local economies. The networking and linking of these geopolitical and economic factors integrated with the rapid delivery of live or almost live coverage brings new complexities to bear on decision-makers and creates complicated tensions for political leaders. In one of the main theatres of the war on terror, Afghanistan, the United Nations Mission to Afghanistan records the civilian death toll there as more than 22,000 (by mid-2016) in addition to the 2,996 people killed in the 9/11 attacks on the United States in 2001. These wars on terror with their theatres and incidents in locations such as Syria, New York, Washington, London, Paris, Brussels, Bali, Afghanistan, Africa, and Iraq have taken an enormous toll in human life and human hope. These are complex conflicts that are to a certain extent about big issues such as international esteem, Western confidence, oil, and the place of the United States in international power plays. The problem with coming up with a coherent response to the war on terror is the complexity this global war produces. The attacks of 9/11 remain abhorrent but do they justify the torture and civilian deaths that have been the legacy of the West's response? This 'war' seems in some ways more complex than many others from our past, as Condoleezza Rice said (2002): 'we're in a new world. We're in a world in which the possibility of terrorism, married up with technology, could make us very, very sorry that we didn't act'.

This complexity is demonstrated as the affordances of social media are being used for both radicalization and deradicalization. In the Paris attacks as Robyn Torok explains (2015):

> social media has become a means of institutionalized socialization, drawing in new recruits by dispersing potent narratives around the globe. While YouTube is the key delivery mechanism for ISIS's imagery and 'theater', it is social media platforms such as Facebook that allow for interactions and socialization, including the delivery of extremist narratives. By better understanding these mechanisms of radicalization, authorities around the globe can develop more effective strategies for countering ISIS's highly successful recruitment campaign.

And perhaps this complexity is a contributing factor to Sardar's next C, Chaos.

Chaos

Chaos has become more prevalent in our once civil societies. In 2005 Australia saw a race riot being coordinated on mobile phones (Goggin, 2006). Racist anarchy briefly reigned in the sleepy seaside Sydney suburb of Cronulla, exploding in the most violent and chaotic bigoted violence seen in that country for years. In 2011 in the UK, a series of riots in Hackney, Brixton, Chingford, Bristol, Manchester, Birmingham, and Liverpool also stained the landscape (Baker, 2011). In other places networked and social media have been used to organize and mobilize protest against the targeting of minorities by police in places such as Ferguson with the #BlackLivesMatter movement (Garza, 2014) in response to the death of seventeen-year-old Trayvon Martin. As Stephanie Baker points out, protests and riots are not novel but 'new social media played a key role in organising the recent riots with smartphones giving those with access to these technologies the power to network socially and to incite collective disorder' (Baker, 2011, p. 45). Protest in the postnormal world is routinely organized, coordinated, and delivered through mediated crowds for the voracious and instant twenty-four-hour news cycle.

Contradictions

Sardar's third C is Contradictions. He says we now live in 'a complex, networked world, with countless competing interests and ideologies, designs and desires, behaving chaotically, can do little more than throw up contradictions… It is the natural product of numerous antagonistic social and cultural networks jostling for dominance' (2010, p. 439).

Teacher education internationally is one such site of this contradiction. We know of the importance of sustained supported teacher preparation (Darling-Hammond, 2004) that attends to theory and practice. Yet we see governments in the UK, Australia, and the United States delivering programmes where six weeks of training makes you 'ready to teach' in school. Even though the weight of evidence indicates these alternative pathways such as methodical and reflection-based pre-service training that mix practicum and reflection provide a more effective model (Ludlow, 2013), governments continue to roll these schemes out.

Another example of the contradiction of our times in education. An overwhelming weight of research shows that large and frequent testing does not sustainably enhance student learning. Yet testing regimes persist in schools, which effectively make testing the goal of learning. As Thomson et al. argue, 'in stark contrast to this imaginary of a socially just world, and often driven by PISA[1] envy, educational policymakers mobilise various forms of audit and intervention designed to produce measurable increases in "performance" at system, school and student levels' (Thomson et al., 2012, p. 2).

Fundamentally contradictory pieces of evidence become policy and practice. These contradictions have become so entrenched that often the practices go on largely unchallenged. Contradictory policy is allowed to stand because in postnormal times society seems to have lost its ability to discern or trust 'normal' sources of evidence.

In the face of this, researchers need to consider the multiple audiences for their research and the ways they conceptualize and present evidence. We must consider in the face of postnormality how researchers provide 'evidence' to shape policies where many have lost faith in evidence and expertise. Critically, for education we need to connect with their audiences through digital channels to promote their research rather than solely through traditional scholarly channels of publication (for more discussion on research see Chapter 10).

Dimensions of intermedial learning

In the face of these emergent features postnormality in a liquid world we would like to provide some dimensions of intermedial learning that guide our reflections in the remainder for the book. These fit within the broader drama framework outlined in the previous chapter, and connect with the concepts of creativity, playfulness, performance, and digital liveness. Although our broad interest is the impact within digital arts cultures, these features are agnostic to the relative 'value' of a live or mediated experience, for we believe the divisions between live and mediated learning will continue to dissolve as the immersive affordances of technologies make more 'as if live' experiences possible. In any case the choice of learning we imagine possible through intermediality should be motivated by each learner's context and opportunities so that we always suit the learning experience to the needs of the learning and not whether we have a preference for live or mediated forms.

Intermedial learning is creative learning

Sardar suggests that one of the ways to exist in a postnormal state is to concentrate on creativity as the driving force for change. The interdisciplinarity of creativity (Sawyer, 2015) provides a strong foundation for intermediality being a productive rather than destructive phenomenon. The discussions for creativity in education have shifted substantially in the last five years. Several key international initiatives have brought the profile for creativity in primary, secondary, and tertiary education to the fore (Anderson and Jefferson, 2016). While there has been a significant shift in the discussion of creativity internationally over the last two decades, with the inclusion of creativity as priorities in some national curricula, notably Australia and South Korea (Anderson and Jefferson, 2016), this has not effectively filtered into the classrooms, curriculum, or schooling systems as a mainstream priority. As Robinson argued more than fifteen years ago (2001), schools often extol the virtues of creativity but are organized against any possibility of it actually emerging, so that 'if the government were to design an education system to inhibit creativity, it could hardly do better ... Governments throughout the world emphasise the importance of creativity, but often what they do in education suppresses it' (2001, p. 41).

The boom in discussions and research around creativity is continuing unabated even in the face of indifference from some governments and the cancellation of schemes such as Creative Partnerships in the UK. It may be that this drive is emerging from the corporate sector spurred on by the Creative Industries and Creative Class discussions (Florida, 2014) demanding creativity or perhaps to use another common term 'innovation' in its workforce. For educators marketization and commodification of 'what industry demands' can be problematic (Harris, 2014) as it makes the endpoint of education a job, usually at the expense of a broad liberal and developmental education. There is however an opportunity for educators to make a case for creativity being the 'must have' attribute of the current century for future citizens as well as future workers. The book *The Future of Employment: How Susceptible Are Jobs to Computerisation?* predicted a major shift in workforce towards creativity and interpersonal skills that is supported by several other national and international studies. The authors of that book concluded the 'findings thus imply that as technology races ahead, low-skill workers will reallocate to tasks that are non-susceptible to computerisation – that is, tasks requiring creative and social intelligence. For workers to win the race, however, they will have to acquire creative and social skills' (Frey and Osborne, 2013, p. 44).

Additionally, research published in the *Journal of Educational Psychology* from research at the University of Sydney (Martin et al., 2013) provides strong evidence that young people who engage in subjects where creativity is taught explicitly in schools have enhanced outcomes in academic and non-academic spheres. The Australian Research Council study examined academic and personal well-being outcomes over two years. The research found that students who engaged with the arts in schools as active participants – in creative processes – were more likely to do better in academic and social spheres than those who passively consumed the arts.

Creativity learning provides new ways of thinking and communicating that provoke ingenuity, imagination, and possibility.

Creative learning enables young people access to the tools of creation (M. Anderson, 2012). These tools are central to creativity learning – but are also vital in a rapidly changing world that will require citizens not just to be consumers of 'their' world but also to be able to actively change the world in the face of complex and pressing problems, such as global warming and overpopulation.

Stevenson's concept of cultural citizenship is concerned with issues of exclusion and inclusion in civil society and addresses the struggle between civil cohesion and cultural diversity in current and future societies. Going beyond notions of behaviour and relationship to authority, cultural citizenship embraces issues of inter-connectedness, representation, rights, and widespread participation. Cultural citizenship

> has been more concerned with issues related to respect. Cultural understandings of citizenship are not only concerned with 'formal' processes, such as who is entitled to vote and the maintenance of an active civil society, but crucially with whose cultural practices are disrespected, marginalised, stereotyped and rendered invisible … cultural citizenship is about the ability in a shared cosmopolitan context to participate in the polity while being respected and not reduced to an 'Other'. (Stevenson, 2010, p. 276)

In this way the tools of creativity can be taught with the critical reflection that cultural citizenship empowers to construct public space, identity, and difference, all paradigms that education can and must recruit, often simultaneously. Within this, the construction of various perspectives is an inter-subjective process and constituted by the ability simultaneously understand and hold one's own and another's viewpoint (Stevenson, 2010). This process is central to the understanding of what the present is and what the future could be. To make these changes happen in schools will require active, transformational creative leaders and leadership teams. The next critical dimension of mashup culture is interdisciplinarity.

Intermedial learning is de-siloed

None of the real-world problems that society and the education system struggle with respect the disciplinary boundaries that the world currently places around them. The organization of schools mostly partitions knowledge in discrete timetabled blocks. Yet the issues that face the world and which young people must prepare themselves for as citizens do not respect silos. While knowledge has always had an interdisciplinary quality, the fluidity of the modern world has meant that learners require agile intelligence to notice and understand the connections between ideas and knowledge in discrete fields like mathematics, music, economics, environmental studies, and so on. Intermedial learning, which takes its raw materials from live performance, media, and other forms to suit the emergent problem or challenge and is ideally suited to these kinds of interdisciplinary understandings. As Robinson argues, 'creativity depends on interactions between feeling and thinking, and across different disciplinary boundaries and fields of ideas' (2001 p. 268). We are not arguing here that disciplinary knowledge is irrelevant or redundant. Quite the contrary, disciplinary understandings and knowledge is critical in the development of deep learning that enables interdisciplinary understanding and creative making. The gap currently seems to emerge, however, not in the disciplines but *between* the disciplines. Although almost all teachers understand that disciplines do not exist in a vacuum, the structure of secondary and tertiary education militates against the crucial linkages between knowledge domains being cultivated, strengthened, and understood. Through the creativity and learning processes intermedial learning encourages a blurring and re-configuring of these elements as a foundational component of learning. An example of the ways intermediality can work effectively is discussed in Chapter 5 in the Beowulf Sydney Project. The next and perhaps most critical dimension of intermedial learning is the building and sustaining of partnerships.

Intermedial learning is about partnerships

One of the persistent unrealized potentials in many communities is the partnership between educators, arts practitioners, and others. There is significant possibility in engagement between storehouses of culture, such as the GLAM sector of galleries, museum, archives, and libraries (considered in Chapter 7), and the education sector. Of course partnerships such as these are not new (Hunter, 2015) but the affordances of rapidly evolving technologies in Western societies mean that the opportunities have exponentially multiplied. Internationally with non-Western school-based partners, the UK-based theatre in education company C&T created a collaboration with young people in the slums of Korogocho, Kenya, to support and enhance cultural citizenship through online and drama-based pedagogical tools. Paul Sutton (2016, p. 154) argues that this approach can be a tool for social justice:

> Young people know these technologies are powerful instruments for social engagement and organization. Enabling the schools

they learn through to recognize this potential too is the next step .... Our shared common goal is to develop a permanent hub of C&T-derived activities in Korogocho that can be independently maintained in the medium to long term: a practice that is both economically and creatively self sustaining, bringing benefits to all sides of this glocalized efficacious practice.

Today these global partnerships can enable a student studying space exploration in the regional city of Hamilton in New Zealand to connect to NASA or the European Space Agency directly through the web. It is commonplace now for the Royal Shakespeare Company or the National Theatre in the UK to produce high-quality broadcast performances[2] that reach vastly larger and different audiences than traditional live performances (NESTA, 2010). Yet these cultural assets do not currently connect effectively with education because they are designed to be viewed, rather than being integrated resources for creative learning. The opportunities in young people transforming from passive receptors of culture (e.g. recorded theatre) and information (e.g. NASA and ESA) to *makers* where they can engage with these partnership opportunities as active contributors is the necessary next step to meet the potential of the arts sector and GLAM organizations. While there is considerable further potential for the integration of curriculum and cultural resources, this is occurring sporadically. The emergence of new technologies and greater levels of understanding in resource design and delivery and pedagogy will support this change. The continued digitization of the archives will further accelerate the access and malleability of these cultural resources. When this occurs the images, recordings, facsimile objects, and other archival data and objects will be available for all to reimagine and remake in deep partnerships between schools and cultural institutions. Mary Ann Hunter articulates the qualities of these partnerships as they are now, and as they might be:

> schools must scaffold opportunities for this interplay of certainty and uncertainty as well as model what a curious and discerning approach to life's many available communities of reference might look like. At this historical moment, however, it takes more than the schools and dispositions of teachers alone to do this. Caught in the difficult dilemma of contemporary schooling, teachers must themselves connect with other communities of reference to collaborate on offering quality education. Professional artists make natural partners in this effort... Curiosity and inquiry are the professional tools of trade. (2015, p. 369)

Hunter nominates here the benefits of strong partnerships (in this case with artists in schools) being the ability to awaken curiosity and inquiry in a liquid world. Partnerships that position a collaborative making process at the centre of the educative process have the potential to radically alter the relationship between education, cultural institutions, and society generally. All of these places become not only sites of reception, but potentially also for invention, co-creation, and innovation.

Precarious platforms

While artistic work has historically been framed as a 'precarious' way to make a living, and just as likely to be driven by passion and creativity as financial benefit, the impact of technology has led to a blurring of amateur and professional practice, for example, in journalism. This is fuelled by neoliberal views within technological industries that see free competition and disruption to established markets as a democratic capitalist imperative. Technology platforms pitched at artists and craft makers, such as Etsy, emphasize a handmade aesthetic while promoting the affordances of e-commerce and networking. Less obvious are concerns of intellectual property theft, including claims of large clothing brands 'stealing' designs from Etsy producers. Underlying this is an attitude that small-scale producers with a minimal digital presence are part of a sharing, open arts culture that can be plundered for ideas and innovation. In this sense even those artists choosing to take a proficians approach to trading their skills and talent on the free market might find themselves easily transplanted into the precariat by those same market forces, aided by technology.

As an online marketplace for craft and vintage goods, Etsy has courted controversy among users with changes to the company's interpretation of what constituted 'handmade'. The company had built a strong brand by positioning itself as an online platform that would be sympathetic to the ideals and needs of 'cottage' craft producers. However, with Etsy's success came a realization that some individual producers now struggled to meet demand for their goods. *Wired* described the pressure on one home-based embroiderer, Terri Johnson, as she worked long hours in her basement to fulfil growing orders. Despite her growing business, 'she feared that if she hired help, invested in new equipment, or rented a commercial workspace, she might run afoul of Etsy policies and get kicked off the site' (Walker, 2012). Etsy began to reconsider its position on the nature of being an artisan or cottage 'maker', and although sellers of new goods are expected to be personally involved in the design and manufacturing process, policies allow for certain types of outsourcing to third parties. Etsy's policy rhetoric still doggedly frames this as a sympathetic form of collectivist production, though it is a clear shift towards allowing at least some industrialization. Similar stories now play out with regularity in the online world where 'free' services used for creative production can change functionality, commercialize, or disappear altogether with little or no warning to the thousands, perhaps, millions, of users.

Coupled with the precarious nature of these online platforms, there is a growing expectation for artists, designers, and writers to do work for free, for the benefit of exposure rather than earning a living. This begins at the exit from education, where young people find themselves in a job market where seemingly endless, unpaid internships – particularly in the arts and media – are the norm in exchange for 'experience'. A Sainsbury's supermarket in North London provoked a furore in May 2016 after posting an ad seeking a volunteer artist to refurbish the design of their staff canteen with no offer other than to 'get your work recognised'. The multi-million-pound supermarket has since apologized for their 'error in judgement', but this incident exemplifies a culture where creative work is undervalued or expected for free in return for supposed recognition or exposure. One begins to wonder when that exposure will turn into offers of professional work, once a willingness to work for free is clearly established.

Digital media do provide channels of distribution, but blur the lines between amateurs and professionals. Jenkins, Ford, and Green (2013) suggest that the concept of E.P. Thompson's (1971) 'moral economy' is destroyed by the duality of expectations of free content provided by unauthorized peer-to-peer distribution of media, and the demand for free labour from media and creative industries. Crowdsourcing, a term coined by Jeff Howe in *Wired* in 2006, 'documents the way media producers solicit insights and contributions from a large base of amateur or pro-amateur creators' (Jenkins et al., 2013, p. 247) for free or on some platforms for a very small fee. Artists and researchers are turning to crowdfunding websites such as Kickstarter, Pozible, and Indiegogo – demand-driven funding models out of Silicon Valley – to fund work. This is part of the new working world that educational systems must consider so concepts of values and ethics can be understood as coexistent with forms of creative and cultural production.

Conclusion

The liquid world we now inhabit with its postnormal features is often justifiably characterized in negative terms. The change in the accessibility and rapidity of knowledge generation and acquisition is often considered problematic but for those who see education as a creative process it also constitutes a massive opportunity to change the way education positions, enacts, and activates knowledge. Knowledge as an intermedial concept encourages a playful experimentation with cultural assets that starts with a deep understanding of disciplines and fields and then seeks to make creative and interdisciplinary connections between them. This is a shift to an unimaginable present.

In many ways an intermedial reality is being played out in our lives through the mashing up of multiple media for our entertainment and leisure. The unimaginable present in education is using these affordances to power education to make it more relevant and engaging for twenty-first-century learners. This will be possible when schools manage to reach the potential of an integrated curriculum that has strong connections with the shared cultural archive held in theatres, museums, libraries, and galleries throughout the world. We are not there yet. There are several stars on the horizon that indicate where learning in a creative, integrated, and intermedial world might take us. The chapters in this book will provide rough coordinates to have some of those stars, starting in the following pages with consideration of the role and nature of identity formation in these collaborative and creative digital arts cultures.

3

Drama and Identity in Digital Arts Cultures

Digital arts cultures provide hypermedia stages for us to present multiple and sometimes contradictory aspects of our selves to a variety of audiences that may be distributed in time and space. Just as we choose to present different kinds of our real-life selves in different everyday contexts (Goffman, 1956), we often voluntarily shape our online identities to suit different audiences on a site-by-site basis. As Charles Cheung observed in his analysis of early personal homepages on the web, 'a family making a site for grandparents may choose to present their happy family life, but conceal the fact that both parents recently got the sack' (2000). Ironically, homepages now seem somewhat anachronistic carefully planned productions compared to the more spontaneous and liquid self-representation that is typical of today's social media applications, accompanied by the messaging and 'selfie' cultures associated with mobile phones. New technology brings with it not only new ways of presenting and representing identities but also new demands on our abilities to juggle these multiple identities to avoid accidental or deliberate misrepresentations. Even when considerable time and effort is spent self-curating different online personas, individuals must now be even more 'prepared to see that the impression of reality fostered by a performance is a delicate, fragile thing that can be shattered by very minor mishaps' (Goffman, 1956, p. 63).

The risks associated with managing online identities are heightened by the networked nature of these mediated spaces. Social researcher danah boyd identifies four key properties of interest that feature in this chapter's consideration of how identities are performed in digital spaces (2007).

1 *Persistence*

   Our digital representations are now recorded for posterity. The notion of comments or actions passing with the moment can longer be taken for granted when they can be archived and saved in large databases and personal storage devices.

2 *Searchability*

   Finding our 'digital body online' can now be as simple as a few keystrokes in a search engine. Not only do we leave text traces behind but also social media tools like Facebook lead in technology for facial recognition and other potentially searchable markers of our real-world identity.

3 *Replicability*

   The original can be impossible to distinguish from the copy. While in face-to-face representations hearsay can be directly deflected as misinterpretation, this is increasingly difficult when comments and content can be distributed far and wide from the original publication or source without context or control.

4   *Invisible audiences*

> While we can generally detect our audiences in unmediated spaces, digital cultures contain many possible networked audiences that can be far removed from our immediate awareness, and detached from the time and space of the original source due to the nature of the first three properties.

Digital identity is therefore a complex and sometimes perplexing aspect of our daily lives, now enacted in highly mediatized spaces through performative acts of self-presentation to a range of known and unknown publics. When considering the dramatic role performance of online identity, the link between drama conventions and digital cultures is strengthened (Carroll, 2002). New forms of entertainment and performance of role have emerged as young people participate within digital cultures. There has been some interesting ethnographic and social research in the last few years looking at young people and their engagement with digital media that drama and arts practitioners may not be so familiar with or might find useful. This chapter presents some key themes from that work as part of the discussion of the latest forms of digital drama as a way of performing identity.

Online identity and performance

In their white paper on new media literacies, Jenkins et al. suggest that 'role play, in particular, should be seen as a fundamental skill used across multiple academic domains' (2009, p. 52). Of course, this is what drama educators and practitioners have advocated for years. Digital media offers young people many ways to play with identity and social roles, from the development of avatars in online role-playing games to representations of self through curated images, status updates, and shared and liked links to content using social media. Though the affordances and popularity of digital spaces change with time and new technologies, collectively they are now sites where young people undertake 'identity tourism' (Nakamura, 1995) and other playful and performative aspects of understanding their place(s) in a connected world. Within digital cultures young people assume fictive identities that help them 'develop a richer understanding of themselves and their social roles' (Jenkins et al., 2009, p. 47). Paul Sutton of UK drama and technology company C&T argues that 'the construction of new identities on the internet is an accepted convention and that this could be regarded as another form of being "in-role"' (Shaughnessy, 2005, p. 206). Drama teachers are often uniquely positioned to understand and explore the emerging performance conventions in new media forms (Carroll, 2002). Identity has always been at the heart of cyberculture studies because it is something that technology can obscure, enhance and alter. You can play with reality and become gender, race, and species fluid. Identity tourism or play is both a powerful means and an end for a range of entertainment, artistic, and social practices enacted within networked digital media cultures. Not all of this is innocent or well-intentioned performance, as we are reminded in warnings about online sexual predators, scammers, and bullying 'trolls' hiding behind false identities. A 2015 YouGov survey of over 4,700 13–18-year-olds from across the world found that one in five young people reported being bullied online.

There has been a long interest with identity play in digital worlds and how people represent different selves through an online frame (see, for example, Turkle, 1995). A liminal threshold of game play, especially Massive Multiplayer Online Role-Playing Games (MMORPGs) such as *World of Warcraft,* is the creation of the avatar: what creature are you, what gender are you, what do you look like, what are you wearing, and what weapons do you have? This common aspect of many digital role-playing games extends to collecting objects such as clothes or weapons and additional special powers or skills that may further embellish your character. The performative style of avatar development and the more general ability to explore combinations of 'as if' possibilities in relatively open world game spaces is why drama performance conventions and studies have been a useful tool in interrogating these conventions (Carroll and Cameron, 2005; Dunn and O'Toole, 2009; Flintoff, 2009; Nicholls and Philip, 2012). While games studies scholars have established connections between online digital cultures and some performativity-oriented theoreticians like Goffman, there has historically been a tendency for drama scholars to see online digital games cultures as something other than drama and theatre. In the past ten years or so, this has shifted, and there has been more engagement as social media and mobile media have penetrated all disciplines and aspects of our lives. For example, digital storytelling has emerged as a method of applied theatre praxis that combines live performance with digitally mediated representations through still images, text, animation, video, and audio (Alrutz, 2015; McGeoch and Hughes, 2009; Wales, 2012). Young people have developed their own forms of playful and theatrical storytelling to inject themselves into their favourite fictional media narratives, for example, the popularity of costumed role-play (cosplay) seen at comic conventions and movie screenings. While not a new phenomenon, the media sharing and critiquing afforded by social media extends cosplay from physical performance to a highly mediatized form of vernacular digital storytelling for a much larger audience. This type of identity play is explored later in this chapter.

Representations of the authentic self

As the classic and oft-cited *New Yorker* cartoon by Peter Steiner says: 'on the Internet, nobody knows you're a dog'.[1] Each new platform or media channel that emerges presents a growing tension between the representation and performance of a fictive and authentic self. At the time of the cartoon's publication in 1993 the internet was very much a space where users could choose to represent themselves in any number of ways through text and images, with markers such as gender, age, and race often being hidden or distorted as part of the experience of communicating in cyberspace. As Lisa Nakamura noted when considering these forms of identity tourism, the ability to hide behind textual descriptions and visual avatars presented opportunities to avoid real-world social prejudices and power structures:

> The cartoon seems to celebrate access to the Internet as a social leveller which permits even dogs to express freely themselves in discourse to their masters, who are deceived into thinking that they are their peers, rather than their property. The element

of difference, in this cartoon the difference between species, is comically subverted in this image; in the medium of cyberspace, distinctions and imbalances in power between beings who perform themselves solely through writing seem to have deferred, if not effaced. (Nakamura, 1995)

As social media has become increasingly part of our everyday lives, social networking platforms encourage creating an online profile that represents your 'real' self as opposed to online pseudonyms that were widely accepted in the past. The adoption of social networking tools in the workplace from services such as LinkedIn, Facebook Workplace, and Google's G Suite make it harder for users to keep their real and playful identities separated. The terms and conditions for signing up for social networking site Facebook demand the 'real' you: your real name and birth date. Facebook was originally created as a relatively restricted 'book of faces' for Harvard University students to identify each other. There are policies in place to remove users who are overtly identified as having fake accounts. In 2015, the monthly user population of Facebook reportedly exceeded the population of China for the first time at 1.39 billion users (Chan, 2015). It hasn't taken long for the power structures in capitalist financial/technology hubs like Silicon Valley to realize that the personal data that users pour into these platforms are worth monetizing. Facebook was valued at over $350 billion in April 2016 (La Monica, 2016). What at first seems like a playful, innocent, and helpful interface to create an online profile (e.g. list your favourite books or films) is a mode of eliciting information out of users to add value to the company's user data sets.

As is the way of things, young people will of course sign up for these platforms by using fake names and birth dates. They can hide themselves (especially from parental surveillance) as long as they have communicated to their real-life friends who their online persona is so that connections can be made from behind false identities. While some of these identities may be playful or even subversive in their choice of names and images, this is not necessarily a conscious act of performance compared to other types of identity tourism. As danah boyd, who has conducted significant research into young people and their use of networked cultures, suggests, 'most teens aren't enacting an imagined identity in a virtual world. Instead, they're simply refusing to play by the rules of self-presentation as defined by these sites' (2014, p. 46). As savvy as this may seem, young people are still creating a digital footprint which is not necessarily protected by their alternative use of role. Companies like Facebook are increasingly adept at algorithmically piecing together scraps of text, images, geo-location data, website visits, online searches, email addresses, and other data crumbs to predict or verify the 'real' identity of users. Such tracking can extend beyond the immediate and obvious use of Facebook, through the use of software code to track and report a user's activity across the web. Increasingly, young people – or at least their parents and guardians – are becoming aware of the persistent, searchable, and replicable properties of mediated spaces with invisible potential audiences, and are attempting to clean up some of these data trails to prevent them being seen by future employers. There has been a rise of companies that promise to erase online history (e.g. https://www.abine.com/deleteme/), correct mishaps of self-presentation, and enable a fresh start using social media and other internet services.

Scholar danah boyd (2014) emphasizes that online representations of identity need to be considered in the context of their intended audience. Different platforms can offer different contexts of communication. Again, we can draw on Erving Goffman's (1956) work and the conclusion that the presentation of self is based on both context and audience. The work of Belgian digital media artist Dries Depoorter provides a relevant example to highlight these different contexts. In 2015, Depoorter compiled a series of images comparing the representation of self in profile pictures between contrasting social media platforms: LinkedIn, a business and career-oriented site, and Tinder, a location-based dating app. The resulting gallery, 'Tinder In' (http://driesdepoorter.be/tinderin/) juxtaposed portrait photographs in business attire from LinkedIn with informal images from Tinder showing more than a head and shoulders – invariably dressed informally and often exposing bare flesh. Depoorter sourced the publically accessible images as a Tinder user himself, and then searched for LinkedIn profiles after viewing users' connected Instagram accounts (Roet, 2015). The work was criticized for initially showing only women, which Depoorter explained was the gender he was searching for as a Tinder user. The gallery was later expanded to include men, including Depoorter himself. There was also criticism about the potential violation of privacy, although Depoorter explains that the work, like many of his projects, mocks and challenges privacy issues (Depoorter, 2015). The work highlights the different selves presented in social media, and perhaps the naivety of users who think they can separate these identities.

Instagram, a mobile photo-/video-sharing application and social network, is a particularly popular channel for identity creation and maintenance. Young people upload imagery to embody the poses they see celebrities presenting – all seemingly impromptu, for example, poses snapped in front of bathroom mirrors. The underlying message is that with the right look, and the right number of followers, you too could be a Kardashian.[2] As the Pew Research Centre's report into *Teens, Technology, and Friendships* (Lenhart et al., 2015) found, young people in the United States feel pressure to present and curate a popular and 'well-liked' stream of media content. In 2015, an Australian Instagram user, Essena O'Neill, who had amassed more than half a million followers and attracted several sponsorship deals made international news by 'quitting' social media. In an outburst that proclaimed that 'social media is not real life', O'Neill edited the captions of previously posted images to reveal their constructed nature by detailing how much she was paid for wearing a particular brand of clothing, or how many shots were taken to achieve an image she perceived worthy of publishing on her Instagram account. As her account developed into an income stream for O'Neill, the pressure to curate and perform within that online identity was increased. The more popular a social media channel becomes, the more likely they are to be commodified, as the users behind them are targeted by public relations and marketing companies as 'influencers'. Some companies are also not above creating fake social media accounts, known as 'sock puppets', to artificially inflate follower numbers or contribute to fake grassroots support and commentary in a process known as 'astroturfing'. As Jenkins et al. (2013) note, contemporary audience participation does not exist in a vacuum of democratic co-creativity, free of economic constraints. Non-disclosure of sponsorship raises ethical questions about the exploitation of audiences around the ideal of authenticity in contemporary online identity performance. Following on from O'Neill's quitting of Instagram, she created a website called Let's Be Game Changers with video blogs posted to encourage young people to reconsider the artifice of social media channels like Instagram. Ironically, her rebranding faced a backlash from peers as just another form of self-promotion and the new website was subsequently taken down, with the address redirected to a temporary holding page.

A counterpoint to Essena O'Neill's Instagram that garnered substantial interest in 2015 was @socalitybarbie, an account that showed a Barbie doll in a range of carefully constructed photographs that satirized the so-called 'hipster' subculture and an aesthetic of 'authentic living': portraits of adventures in wild landscapes, or close-ups of cups of organic coffee. A popular hashtag on Instagram is #nofilter to prove that an image has not been manipulated and that the image is showing an unfiltered, although still mediated, reality. The then anonymous photographer behind the @socalitybarbie account said in an interview with *Wired*, 'People were all taking the same pictures in the same places and using the same captions... I couldn't tell any of their pictures apart so I thought, "What better way to make my point than with a mass-produced doll?"' (Glascock, 2015). The aesthetic promotes a perception of individuality and authenticity, however it is highly constructed. Coincidentally, the creator behind the @socalitybarbie account, Darby Cisneros revealed herself not long after Essena O'Neill's well-publicized 'quitting', to thank her followers and conclude the project. Although we know that @socalitybarbie is a playful and performative construct, the revealing of the producer behind the online persona strips away the dramatic frame.

New forms of celebrity

Participatory media has given rise to new forms of emergent and home-grown celebrity. Gauntlett (2011) argues that digital tools like YouTube are platforms that, like theatrical stages, can be considered spaces for a hands-on approach to production, and which are 'agnostic about content' (albeit with some legal boundaries) and tending to be open to a wide variety of uses and contributions (p. 91). There is a broadening of the concept of audience in these spaces to include incentives for all participants to make and share content, actively support each other, share knowledge and skills, and to engage in debates. Of course, all of these activities can be considered both positive and negative, for example, engaging in 'debate' in some of these online spaces can be more like a public riot than a thoughtful exchange of views. Broadly these spaces contribute to a 'participatory culture' (Jenkins, 2006b), which finds its roots in fan-based media production linked to a variety of media texts. Celebrities from more traditional media spaces such as popular music, television, and cinema have made use of them as a way to speak directly to their fan base. The pervasiveness of digital technology and networked media has made these participatory cultures more widely distributed and easier for newcomers to enter, compared to the often closed shops of traditional and largely industrialized media. In a post-lonelygirl15[3] world where fake identities and staged videos are portrayed as genuine in the hope of 'going viral', social media has opened up channels of distribution and entertainment that are used by celebrities and non-celebrities alike. In the media performance genre of vlogging,[4] where ordinary people are producing their own videos often with little more than a webcam, some popular presenters have amassed millions of subscribers and fans. Vlogging is an 'emblematic form of YouTube participation' (Burgess and Green, 2009, p. 53). Popular YouTube celebrities include names like Jenna Marbles, Zoella, HolaSoyGerman, ThatcherJoe, and communitychannel, each with millions of subscribers. Their video blogs cover fashion, beauty, relationship advice, and general musings or rants about everyday life. The self-shooting production method behind vlogging gives it a sense of raw authenticity as opposed to the production values provided by a professional film production crew. Vlogging has a sense of 'liveness, immediacy and conversation … [that] inherently invites feedback' (Burgess and Green, 2009, pp. 53–54), an example of the presence generated within the condition of digital liveness explored further in the following chapter. Viewers can respond by clicking on a thumbs up/thumbs down icon, by typing a comment below a video, or by filming a video reply using their own webcam or a mobile phone. Young people consume YouTube in the same way that their parents watch television, except now they can hold the remote and control what's on the screen. In this sense digital arts cultures around channels like YouTube are highly performative identity spaces, often framed around the creation and sharing of screen-based identities reflected both audio-visually and through text in exchanges between producers and viewers.

There is a feedback loop between online forms of entertainment such as YouTube and popular forms of television programming. Internationally successful reality television talent search programmes like *The Voice, The X Factor, So You Think You Can Dance,* or the *Got Talent* franchise proliferate the Cinderella story, where seemingly ordinary citizens are transformed into celebrities at the press of a button or swivel of a chair. YouTube contains many videos of vloggers and song covers, perhaps vying for their big break. Indeed, Justin Bieber, one of the top selling pop artists of recent times, started his journey of fame as a teenager on YouTube with a cover of a Chris Brown song. This first video remains the most popular on his YouTube channel (kidrauhl) with over 50 million views. Other sub-genres of reality television such as fly on the wall docudramas like *Keeping Up with the Kardashians* use seemingly unscripted collections of 'raw' or handheld footage to maintain a sense of authenticity through unprotected role performance. As with other forms of reality programming, from *Big Brother* through to more recent 'real-life' docudramas like the *Kardashians*, the screen identities of these performers is crafted and manipulated, with a production crew behind them, plotting narrative arcs. There is even a fan community dedicated to revealing the constructed nature of the programme: *Keeping Up with the Kontinuity Errors* (http://kuwtke.tumblr.com). The 'theatre of surveillance' (Carroll, 2002) found in these genres has not lost its popularity, but rather has come to dominate the television schedules in many countries.

Performing drama

Given the popularity of vlogging and these reality television forms, young peoples' identity work in digital cultures involves playing out their own real-life dramas using social media as the broadcast channel (Lenhart et al. 2011; Marwick and boyd, 2014). The disembodied, often text-based interaction makes the performance of drama happen, though the development of live video streaming services from mobile phones incorporated into services like Facebook is increasingly making these interactions seem televisual. Marwick and boyd (2014) suggest that the use of the word 'drama' by teens to describe negative events online gives them a sense of agency and acknowledges both participants and audience. The demand for the 'real you' represented online in dominant platforms like Facebook and Instagram[5] means that young people do not have what in applied drama terms would be known as role distance to protect them in the play and performance of identity. We know from drama in education that when you take away role distance, you make it more difficult for people to perform without being self-conscious (Carroll, 1986; Carroll and Cameron, 2005). In online spaces where 'users/operators are free to perform via avatar icons or text-based identities with any identification they choose; gender, race and class, become performative differentiation, not fixed, hierarchical assignments within a social order' (Causey, 2006, p. 59). When you take away the possibility to be dynamic with the performance of an online identity, and as more real social constraints and structures impinge on the virtual world, the greater the likelihood of being caught up in 'real-life' conflicts. This is particularly relevant for young people as they are in a time of identity experimentation, termed by psychologist Erik Erikson as a 'psychosocial moratorium' (1968). Of course, there are still channels where identity play and detachment occur, but as David Buckingham (2008) notes, it can require digital literacies beyond basic practical skills to assist young people in critically selecting and participating in these forms of media.

When working in media production with young people, we need to consider that they can have a blurred perception of amateur and professional media production due to the proliferation of both popular YouTube content, and fly on the wall styles of reality television programming. When teaching a documentary making subject to undergraduate media and communication students, we have found that students are often drawn to 'mockumentaries' as a genre for their major projects, as it offers them a form of role protection and distance from more serious forms of performance. In a media culture where parody, quick jibes, and one-liners are a popular form of discourse, this makes sense. Mockumentary is an accepted form of entertainment and documentary production; however, we have encouraged students to produce a different mode of documentary first to demonstrate an understanding of the genre they are going to satirize. This is another refutation of Prensky's (2001) concept of 'digital natives' as it highlights that although young people are often engaged in performative forms of expressions through digital media, this confidence or comfort does not always transfer to other media performances or contexts.

Alternate role play

Participatory fan culture is another place to turn when examining notions of identity and identity play that are distanced from a real self. Social media platforms can be demanding in terms of time and attention, and engagement with real issues and relationships, and so are not necessarily easy to escape. In a mediatized world the opportunity to resist reality and be empowered on an alternate channel is appealing. Turkle (1995) considered identity play in terms of early virtual worlds like MUDs (multi-user dungeons) and MOOs (MUD, object-oriented) and finds that social empowerment is a powerful motivation for participation. Fan-based activities range from the curation of images, mashups, fan fiction, blogging, and participation in discussion groups through to physical aspects of participatory culture such as cosplay. This participation is often a way of expanding engagement with texts that have high production values such as television programmes like *Game of Thrones*, *Doctor Who*, or *Sherlock*. This is in opposition to the online video forms discussed earlier. Events like Comic-Con, a US convention around comics, games, and popular culture strip away the production elements of these programmes by featuring panels with actors and production crew such as writers, directors, and producers. Fan participation is not only encouraged but also rewarded. Cosplay is a popular form of participation in events like Comic-Con that bridges the live and mediated experiences. Maker skills like 3D printing have now made it possible to print detailed replicas of character costume elements and props.

Conclusion

Digital arts cultures are highly performative, and in many early forms offered opportunities for different types of identity play. Avatars and role play were common in text-based virtual worlds, and then massive online game and graphic virtual world spaces. Increasingly, the demands of newer social media platforms to confirm identities and build profiles of real people has created situations where users can feel obliged to break the stated terms and conditions of service to continue using the application. In turn, the more users are required to 'keep it real', the more likely they are to replicate the drama of everyday life played out in popular culture forms like reality TV and online celebrity cultures. Digital arts cultures are as dynamic, chaotic, and complex as any other. We therefore echo John Carroll's (2002) suggestion that we need to consider – and keep considering – what dramatic performances young people value as clues to how they will generate their own presentations of self in the performative mediatized spaces. A critical view of the performance of identity online will inform both our classroom and applied drama practices, and perspectives of new media and entertainment forms. Research on digital identities is part of a wider need to continue to develop literacies in participatory media cultures. In the next chapter we further examine notions of blurred live and mediatized performance in and around digital arts cultures.

4

Digital Liveness: Playing with Time and Space

This chapter develops the position that digital media requires an interdisciplinary approach as a contemporary starting point for understanding, sustaining, and transforming arts practices among young people. This is not to diminish the values and traditions of individual arts disciplines founded on passionate interests, mastery of skills, and core knowledge; rather it acknowledges that digital arts cultures are a complex system of mediatized performative practices that reconfigure and recombine at multiple levels of engagement, expertise, and reliance on technology. Young people today have many opportunities to pursue individual creative and learning opportunities in a spectrum of formal and informal settings. These can be fleeting engagements or deep pursuits. These may be personalized journeys, or more likely they may be social experiences in which technology plays a central role in connecting participants and allowing them to share their views and practices around common interests on a potentially global scale. How the mutable and transformative cultural

DNA of digital media contributes to these processes is a characteristic of the liquid modernity outlined in Chapter 2.

One of the key affordances of networked digital media is the creation or enhancement of physical and online space(s) where common passionate interests can be turned into a shared endeavour. James Paul Gee (2004) defined these sites as 'affinity spaces' to emphasize that the activities within the space are formed by participants following their individual goals around a shared interest. The individuals moving in and out of an affinity space do not necessarily see themselves as belonging to a community of practice with common values and goals, as understood from the work of Jean Lave and Etienne Wenger (1991), but rather find that the space affords the voluntary pursuit of activities or projects through a dynamic mix of learning, social and cultural practices that emerge around a shared interest.

Research on web-based affinity spaces around literature and video games popular among young people has found these online sites to be rich in self-directed and multimodal production of creative content, social learning, distributed knowledge, and awareness of public audiences for their activities (Lammers, Curwood, and Magnifico, 2012, pp. 48–50). One of the immediate challenges for people working in traditional disciplinary models of mastery or formal cultural or educational settings is to consider affinity spaces 'not for how we should manage them or necessarily accommodate them within existing educational structures, but for what they tell us about the forms of learning and literacy that are already instantiated within the use of these media' (Duncan and Hayes, 2012, p. 3).

There are signs that drama educators and practitioners are becoming increasingly aware of the applied learning and artistic production emerging in the multiple, globally distributed, multimodal spaces in which young people learn about themselves and their world through play, enactment of identity, creative production, remixing, sharing, and connecting (Anderson and Cameron, 2013). This approach is consistent with the rise of references to so-called 'slash arts' or hybrid arts that Sandra Gattenhof notes within the cultural and media industries:

> as globalisation and technologies change the way in which we communicate and how we create, it may be these spaces that will be crucial in the ongoing support and development of young people as artists … The majority of young people are adept at constructing new realities for themselves. There is no taking young people back to one world. They live in many within the global compass. (2004, p. 107)

As Chiel Kattenbelt suggests, 'media' are a critical element of this global compass as both a facilitator and distribution channel for the mutable conventions, interconnections, and co-relationships between art, technology, and performance that play a central role within this new global art ecosystem, thus enabling the social construction and sharing of these new realities and many worlds (2008). Digital technology and live or dramatic performance generate mutual affect within the dynamic and ubiquitous mediatization present in postnormal arts cultures, and intermediality has quickly become a context for daily engagements with entertainment, information, and educational institutions and events. This can be seen in an example of recent work that skilfully blends media technology and live performance, creating animated characters that are beautifully rendered into a lively and engaging show. 1927's production of *Golem* is also about the seductive and potentially destructive obsessions many people have with technology.

Golem: Setting the stage for hypermedia

Move with the times, or you'll be left behind... Say yes to progress... Do you want to be a nobody, or an everybody?

Those are some of the advertising slogans that compel the lead character to buy and continually upgrade his technology in London-based theatre group 1927's production of *Golem* (Andrade, 2014). The work is an imaginative exploration of the 'Jewish Frankenstein' myth of the Golem, a creature often made from clay or stone that can be brought to life. The production by 1927 frames the Golem as a must-have piece of technology that like a magical genie will do its owner's bidding, initially at least, but then the roles of master and servant become blurred.

The same slogan could easily be applied to any number of fields touched by technology, including theatre and staged live performances like *Golem* itself, in which there is a sense that to resist the exponential changes brought about by technology is to deny 'the times'. The subject matter and themes of *Golem* capture some of the tensions now present in the world and the everyday use of technology in many societies. The staging of this production also provides a useful example of intermediality and the mutual affect made possible by 1927's skilful leverage of the co-relationships possible when combining live and pre-recorded media and performance.

In this staged version a nerdy young man named Robert Robertson works in a data centre responsible for 'backing up the back up', a dreary and robotic task. Robert is urged to buy a Golem, which is represented in the production by projected vision of an animated and wonderfully voice-performed clay figure that is projected onto the set. In the beginning of course Robert feels in control of the Golem and uses it to take on the menial tasks in his life. It's not long however before Golem begins to manipulate Robert, in a metaphor for the technologies and social media that now infuse the daily lives of millions. He is soon being told what to buy and what to think, for example, echoing Golem's statements like 'I adore Benedict Cumberbatch', a comment on the symbiotic nature of celebrity and social media. Soon Golem needs to be upgraded to the smaller and faster Golem 2.0, and the similarities between Golem and devices such as smartphones and tablets and their relentless upgrade cycle become apparent. Eventually the Golem product line moves towards version 3.0, a chip implanted in Robert's brain.

The interactions between the live performers, musicians, and the stop-motion animation of the Golem are a seamless example of the hypermedial stage. The audience is aware of the obvious artifice of projected imagery and Golem's animated character, exaggerated by a general handcrafted aesthetic that is matched by the sets, lighting, and costumes. This handcraft aesthetic is an interesting sub-element of a number of new media works, for example, as seen in the video games of Media Molecule described in Chapter 6. The audience members are also willing to ignore the interface between the real and animated, and experience the production as a new perspective generated by the co-relationships between these elements. This is the double logic of what Jay David Bolter and Richard Grusin have described as 'remediation', which they consider a defining characteristic of digital media (1999), and which produces an intense experience by combining the 'as is' and the 'as if'. In *Golem* is seen firstly the logic of 'transparent immediacy' in which the aim of the production is to blend physical and media components so seamlessly in real time so as to create an 'interfaceless interface': 'one that erases itself, so that the user is no longer aware of confronting a medium, but instead stands in an immediate relationship to the contents of that medium' (Bolter and Grusin, 1999, p. 24).

Secondly, there is seen the logic of hypermediacy, in which performers and audience remain intensely aware that the stage contains numerous raw materials such as sound, sets, lighting, vision, and movement that are creating something new and exciting. The writer and director of *Golem*, Suzanne Andrade, acknowledges that the performance does rely on media technology like high-definition projectors to combine the animated characters with the actors, but this is staged so as to make the interaction appear as close to a live performance as possible rather than screened:

> We try to use it in a way that is a bit disruptive, not to let it dictate to us how to do things. I think technology can make us passive. I mean I have heard people say they are busy creating and really

they are just rearranging their photos on a screen; they can spend hours doing that. (Adams, 2014)

Golem illustrates the stage as a hypermedium in that when images and sound are used in this way, they are, as Kattenbelt asserts, 'not only screened or played back, but also staged, and, in this capacity, not only cinematic, televisual, videographic or digital, but at the same time theatrical' (2008, p. 23). Although *Golem* relies on pre-produced animations that are recorded and projected onto a set like a film, each performance of *Golem* is a live and irreproducible experience for the audience. The musicians and performers must live out each performance, with any flaws and imperfections in their timing, delivery, or physical positioning on stage a part of that embodied moment. Although animated from a combination of clay and digital compositing, the character of Golem is an integral member of the cast with a distinctly 'as live' performance, and there is a sense in which audiences accept the perceived 'liveness' of the claymation performance as readily as they do that of the human actors and musicians in the show.

One reason that intermediality is accepted in staged productions like *Golem* is that it also operates at the everyday level, in the personal space of individuals who may not necessarily consider themselves engaged in creative or dramatic work as defined in traditional discipline-based approaches towards mastery. When the digital is combined with even a minimal sense of embodied creativity and agency, it is creating a hybrid of producer and user within the ontology of performance in ways that challenge and expand the material, temporal, and spatial understandings of traditional drama-making conventions.

Digital liveness

As we have noted in Chapter 1, Auslander (1999) initially argued that distinguishing a performance as live is a direct effect of broadcast media technology. His initial work focused heavily on television, labelling it the dominant mass media form of the twentieth century. Early experiences of radio and television in the domestic setting still framed the moment in terms of an audience gathered together around the radio or television to listen or watch together, echoing both the conventions of theatre and cinema, and for many decades radios and televisions were designed to be dominant pieces of furniture taking up a significant footprint in living room spaces. The rise of transistorized technology and other technical improvements consistently drove down the cost and size of radio and television receivers in the decades following the Second World War. Similar trends can be seen in which consumer computing experiences have shifted from being tethered to desktop-scale PCs towards more portable laptop computers and now to smartphones and tablets or even smaller, wearable devices. In some emerging economies, mobile devices are the primary means of personal computing and accessing the internet as governments bypass the costs of investing in wired communication infrastructure. The rise of digital networked technology has required a retuning of the liveness concept.

The last couple of decades have seen a shifting media landscape where content is not just a mediatized representation of a performance, but where elements of the performance itself may have been generated procedurally by computer software without any 'real' physical presence at all. Using television as an example, there has been an increasingly sophisticated use of computer-generated images to provide content, ranging from high fidelity rendered special effects through to live on-screen graphics to enhance news, sports, and entertainment broadcasts.

Digital media are often generally referred to as a 'disruptive' innovation for their impact on traditional business, social, and creative models and this is no less true in the sense that the intersections of procedural digital media and live performance have disrupted understanding of liveness by removing the need for both co-temporal and co-spatial synchronicity (e.g. Bower and Christensen, 1995). As Clair Read notes, one example can be found in the live streams of video and other real-time data to be found online, in that

> a confusion concerning the definition of liveness has evolved as events that offered co-temporal and co-spatial liveness were labelled as live, in addition to performances that could not offer both co-temporal and co-spatial liveness but offered instead one element of liveness or an overall 'sense' of liveness. (2014, p. 68)

An example of this in the digital culture of young people falls broadly in the emerging category of 'e-sports', which combines multiplayer video game competition with live, televised (e.g. via dedicated cable TV channels), and online audiences. This is discussed further in Chapter 7, however it is worth considering briefly here as an example of how 'digital liveness' can operate to produce significant audience engagement in a live event, generating the same tensions and emotional responses as any closely fought sporting competition in the physical realm, even though audience and player/performers may not be located in the same space. In South Korea for example, where professional e-sports is a significant popular entertainment segment, competitors take advantage of the spectator technologies built in to the software for some games titles, notably *Starcraft 2* (Blizzard Entertainment, 2010). This science fiction strategy game pits players in head-to-head competition that can also be played with a third party in-game observer present in the game world, who can see activity in the game but not participate, and thus can act as a cameraperson by sharing their screen view with audiences in real time. As with any mediatized sporting competition, expert commentary can be added. Matches can also be recorded and uploaded to distribution channels like Twitch TV and YouTube to document the competitions, a form of performative archiving discussed in more detail in Chapter 7.

Far from being a passive experience for the live and online audiences for these competitions, they are highly performative at several levels, for

> although the game sits in the center-stage, it does not mean that the only performers are the players. The work of the broadcasters (observer-cameramen and commentators) is another level of performance. Beyond that, the Crowd engages in little performances, trying to out commentate the official commentators with their own analysis and prediction, or stirring up the emotions of their peers, and other reactionary performances. (Cheung and Huang, 2011)

Janet Murray (1997, p. 71) observed in the relatively early stages of today's hypermedia environments that 'it is surprising how often we forget that the new digital medium is intrinsically procedural'. What can now be readily described as live or social interactions within digital spaces are still fundamentally governed by the execution of rules embedded in software code, but it has become simpler and cheaper to engage with these digital media forms as part of daily life for many. In this form, it becomes clear that what is considered live is very much driven by the willingness of audiences or participants to accept a mediatized or perhaps even procedurally generated interaction as if it is live. This is live in the very broadest sense, encompassing both that the interaction is occurring in real time and with real people.

In practice, liveness occurs without a need for deeply immersive and authentically rendered virtual worlds or software agents. Like drama, much of it happens in the heads of the participants at a range of conscious and subconscious levels. The effect of liveness routinely alters perception of the geographical and temporal distances operating in networked environments, and is key to the often superficial acceptance of new media as generating intrinsically interactive and potentially social experiences. The 'as if' possibilities that are so central to drama and human creativity are also a key to understanding why mediated or even virtual experiences are readily accepted as real or live by people, even when they are confronted with the obvious technical artifices of procedural representations generated on screens from computer code, and input interfaces such as headsets, keyboards, trackpads, and mice. The connection between drama and computer interface design is not new, and stems from works such as Laurel's foundational *Computers as Theatre* (1991). Laurel emphasizes that the human-computer 'interface', though suggestive of a surface or membrane between human and non-human, actually represents a shared space for co-creation of output.

Auslander has mused on the nature of interactions with virtual entities and makes the point that they are not recordings, but are procedural responses to direct human input often designed with the intention of trying to fool the human interlocutor as to the nature of the respondent (2002). His use of the term 'digital liveness' is also intended to capture increased interactions with software agents. To some there is no escaping that no matter how sophisticated the algorithm might be in choosing appropriate responses or questions to ask, there will always be a limitation in their ability to appear 'live'. For example, in response to Auslander's article, Herbert Blau argues that although some theatrical performances can appear so thoroughly coded and familiar as to give equal status to mediated or virtual performers, a proper sense of liveness stems from human 'liabilities' like 'stage fright, lapses of memory, a stomach ache on stage, a coughing fit, unscripted laughter – that give a local habitation, in the body, to the succinct and apposite admission of imperfection that no bot will move us by – "We are all frail" – no less the myriad inflections of a performance that, intended or unintended, really make it live' (Blau, 2002).

These discussions fall back on the nature of the interface between audience and performer, with an assumption that interaction with software agents will always make the encounter a mediated experience because it must occur through a technological interface such as keyboard and screen. However, there are now ways to introduce a human performer interface between the human audience and the software, and this throws up even more questions about the nature of live performance.

An example of this interface is found in London School of Economics research with a hybrid of human performer and software 'chatterbot' that has been termed an 'echoborg' (Corti and Gillespie, 2015). In these experiments a human performer wears a discrete microphone and earpiece while engaging in a conversation with a human interactant. The interactant's input is relayed by the microphone to another location, where it is typed into the chatterbot software application. In time, more sophisticated speech interpretation software could remove the need for typing intervention at this stage. The chatterbot's software response is then read from the screen in the remote location, relaying it to the earpiece of the live performer or 'shadower'. They deliver the chatterbot's response in as seemingly natural and appropriate way as possible. Using their acting skills, the shadower tries to cover up as naturally as possible the inevitable small delay between the question being input to the chatterbot and the response being returned to their earpiece. They might try to give the impression of thinking deeply of their own response, or they might use a smile and other facial gestures to keep up a stream of non-verbal connection with the questioner to avoid heightening the sense of delay or emphasizing the procedural tone of the response. The nature of these experiments is to hide the involvement of the software agent, and the findings suggest that the human interacting with the echoborg is more likely to attempt to clarify any subjective misunderstandings in the conversation with the shadower when they are unaware of the role played by the chatterbot.

Example sessions of the echoborg experiments can be viewed online (e.g. at https://youtu.be/NtWLCZZYM64), and they show how the use of a human interface radically alters previous impressions of interacting with a non-human performer. However, increased use of software agents, for example, Apple's Siri or Microsoft's Cortana, suggests that revealing the technology behind the human interface of an echoborg would not necessarily diminish a participant's willingness to interact under the right circumstances. If framed dramatically these interactions seem to fit with the 'as is + as if' nature of digital liveness as a potential dramatic convention operating in digital arts cultures. The LSE experimenters have indicated an interest in extending beyond just conversational interfaces, to explore embodied echoborgs by

> developing a bot that delivered to the shadower's left ear monitor words to speak while delivering basic behavioral commands (e.g. 'smile', 'stand up', extend right hand for handshake) to the shadower's right ear monitor. This would grant the bot greater agency over the echoborg's behavior. (Corti and Gillespie, 2015, p. 15)

These echoborg experiments take software agents known as chatterbots and use them to drive a human performance, exploring the nature of presence and liveness when the human body is treated as the mouthpiece for an algorithmic scriptwriter. The ability to fool the human interrogator, or at least to enable them to accept the moment as a form of human-human communication, further explores the potential for new forms of artistic expression and drama that might be considered live performance within emerging digital arts cultures.

Digital liveness, intermediality, and everyday performance

Chapter 1 described digital liveness as not requiring total immersion in a virtual space, which would be substituting one reality for another, but like the dramatic convention of metaxis, it relies on participants to hold within themselves the drama emerging from the interplay and frictions between the real world and fictional or virtual world. In this sense digital liveness contributes to a sense of dramatic tension that produces a sense of affect and therefore embodied presence in the experience. These tensions exist in daily engagements with many different types of digital devices that can be seen as inherently theatrical and performative.

Nick Couldry (2004) notes two types of liveness operating in this context that now permeate everyday lives: 'online liveness' and 'group liveness'. First, there is online liveness in social co-presence on a variety of scales from very small groups in online chatrooms to huge international audiences for breaking news on major websites, all made possible by the internet as an underlying infrastructure. Large social networking applications like Facebook are seeking to combine all aspects of online liveness into one service, further emphasizing the sense of social co-presence.

Secondly, there is 'group liveness', the mutually accepted liveness of a mobile group of friends who are in continuous contact via their mobile devices. Couldry suggested in 2004 that this was primarily through calls and texting, but today's young people are now accustomed to intermedial digital and performative identity maintenance technologies such as instant messaging, status updates and geo-location check-ins, live video chats, and selfie photos. These forms of digital liveness might be experienced directly among curated groups, or via more public-facing open networks, and most afford instant feedback and criticism via tools for liking, sharing, or rating individual posts or contributions. Auslander notes that distancing is common to all these experiences, and a sense of liveness matters in these daily interactions through technology, because it holds out the promise of compensating for not being in the physical presence of the people to whom we feel connected (2014).

Although, as noted earlier, some media theorists have argued that the goal of many designers was to create an 'interfaceless interface' (Bolter and Grusin, 1999) that is intended to render the technology invisible to the user, in practice many consumer technologies now consciously treat interactions as small, designed events which combine to create a carefully orchestrated user experience (Manovich, 2013, p. 311). The software operating systems, icons, and interfaces of these devices are now dissected, previewed and reviewed, fetishized, and debated as part of a fan culture around particular brands, and the user experience plays a key part in the commercial success of many of these products in an aesthetic as well as functional sense. Clearly the user of technology is part of the procedural or software loop that forms the interface with that technology, as she or he both initiates and reacts to events and information on the screen. A user is simultaneously the performer and the audience for the myriad of audio and visual cues enacted upon the interfaces of media devices. Bolter et al. (2013) also propose that new media theory needs to find space in its canon to acknowledge this embodied and performative aspect of the digital medium, and 'the irony is that procedurality is dominant in digital theory at precisely a moment when digital media forms are expanding in ways for which procedurality cannot account' (Bolter, MacIntyre, Nitsche, and Farley, 2013, p. 329).

Bolter et al. (2013) use the example of social media such as Facebook, which represent a form of simultaneously interpersonal and procedural communication forms. They highlight the performative and ritualistic nature of the media forms, such as the act of 'friending' on Facebook that in turn creates a new audience member for an individual's status updates, original photos, 'likes', and curated media 'shares'. These acts effectively form a contract in which each user agrees to become an audience for the other. The true success of these forms, they argue, is that they are flexible enough to keep adding new dimensions to an otherwise fairly simple and well-defined communication ritual.

The strength of these behaviours has grown over a relatively short period of time, as these web-based social media have become more readily accessible via mobile media devices such that they now extend into most facets of many living environments, not always to the comfort and safety of those involved. The implications for young people are quite significant, especially as it is becoming more apparent that the digital footprints left behind in this experimentation with mixed realities are resistant to erasure or may be detached from appropriate context, as already explored in Chapter 3. Returning to the theme of intermediality and the everyday nature of media engagements in the lives of young people requires consideration of how the gap between technology and the human is diminished in the postnormal world.

Mixed realities: Betwixt and between physical and virtual performance

Technology blends into lives in myriad ways, altering how people live, learn, work, and play in these new mixed realities. For example, game designer Jane McGonigal argues that players in task-driven video games like *World of Warcraft* (Blizzard Entertainment, 2004) can come to feel more productive in the game world than they do in their everyday lives, because

> although we think of computer games as virtual experiences, they do give us real agency: the opportunity to do something that feels concrete because it produces measurable results, and the power to act directly on the virtual world. And, of course, gamers are working with their hands, even if what they're manipulating is digital data and virtual objects. (McGonigal, 2011, p. 60)

This sense of agency and manipulation in virtual spaces has been an ongoing focus of technological development, including in the home entertainment market. Video game hardware developers sought to design more natural or embodied ways for players to control and interact with virtual characters. One example is Microsoft's Kinect, which is

> a motion sensing input device by Microsoft for the Xbox 360 video game console, which can capture, track and decipher body movements, gestures and voice. The auditory and visual information serves as commands to interact with digital contents presented in games or software programs. In other words, users are not bound by keyboards, mice or joysticks and thus have intuitive and virtual experiences with digital contents. The kinaesthetic and gesture-based interaction enabled by Kinect definitely is the dream application that computers are envisioned to support. (Hsu, 2011, p. 365)

Drama practitioners, researchers, and educators have noted the potential applications of these devices in digital performance settings, for example, experiments with a 'time of flight' camera in an interactive dance and media performance (Carroll and Xu, 2012). Fans shared software to 'hack' devices like the Kinect to use for creating their own embodied entertainment and artistic applications of these embodied digital interfaces (Tanz, 2011). Some considerations of adapting the technology for non-gaming purposes have focused on rehabilitation in medical settings; however, others like the 'Trigger Shift' project helped young people appropriate the Kinect 'as a creative tool, allowing them to help hack and re-appropriate this common consumer technology' for creative play and performance for its own sake (T. Schofield et al., 2013).

These technologies are gaining new interest as part of a resurgence of interest in the consumer applications of virtual reality (VR) devices. Manovich (2006) has identified how the wave of interest in VR throughout the 1990s was marked by iconic representations of cyberspace as the future of human–computer interaction; however, it transpired that this was rapidly superseded in the 2000s by the ubiquitous nature of screens large and small used to augment the physical world with data:

the research agendas, media attention, and practical applications have come to focus on a new agenda – the physical – that is, physical space filled with electronic and visual information. The previous icon of the computer era – a VR user traveling in virtual space – has been replaced by a new image: a person checking his or her email or making a phone call using a PDA/cell phone combo while at the airport, on the street, in a car, or any other actually existing space. (2006, p. 221)

However, the second decade of the twenty-first century has seen a wave of new development of entertainment devices promising 3D video and virtual reality experiences. By 2016 products such as Oculus Rift, Samsung Gear VR, HTC Vive, Google Cardboard and Google Daydream, Sony PlayStation VR, and Microsoft Hololens were dominating enthusiastic discussions and product reviews in technology media, particularly those focused on entertainment – primarily gaming – and educational applications. There have even been proposals for a new Mixed Reality Service protocol to more easily enable the mapping of data to real and virtual spatial coordinates that could easily spark mass adoption of virtual and mixed reality media and support other technologies such as drones and autonomous vehicles (Pesce, 2016).

At the time of writing, how this new wave of VR will impact on digital arts cultures is yet to be fully realized; however, Laurel observed following the first wave of VR in the 1990s that VR has a strong connection to drama in the sense that beyond entertainment applications it creates a space for free-form, imaginative, and even playful exploration of real life:

> Running counter to the traditional ethos of computers, VR is a context for exploring how to make us whole within a technological frame. It is a context in which we encounter technology with passion. The primary concern of VR is not constructing a better illusion of the world; it is learning to think better about the world, and about ourselves. (Laurel, 1991, p. 214)

In this sense virtual reality technologies are not ways of escaping the real world, but they are hypermedia spaces in which the spectrum of digital liveness shifts towards greater incorporation of the human sensorium as part of the experience, generating new sites for performative identity play.

Not quite live: Into the uncanny valley

In a consideration of the new forms of identity and digital role performance being explored by young people more than a decade ago, John Carroll noted that technology was already expanding the definition of what might be considered performative spaces in their everyday lives:

> So move over Arnold Schwarzenegger and the clunky cyborgs, digital performance is being created in the minds and computers of online interactors enhanced by digital imaging. It's going to produce some interesting notions of what constitutes dramatic performances in the future. (Carroll, 2002)

In Mary Wollstonecraft Shelley's classic novel *Frankenstein or, The Modern Prometheus* (1818), the titular Frankenstein feels revulsion at the creature he himself has stitched together:

> Oh! no mortal could support the horror of that countenance. A mummy again endued with animation could not be so hideous as that wretch. I had gazed on him while unfinished; he was ugly then; but when those muscles and joints were rendered capable of motion, it became a thing such as even Dante could not have conceived. (Shelley, 1818)

Shelley readily conjures up the creature's gloriously grotesque appearance in the minds of the reader. Almost two centuries later popular culture is littered with similar imagery in the form of zombies and other monsters rising or being risen from the grave, and they can be found in popular media forms such as film, television, graphic novels, video games, and young adult fiction. The modern mashup of Frankenstein's monster into the playfully performative aspects of young people's lives can be seen in the enjoyment of cosplay (costumed roleplay) such as 'zombie walks' organized as public events, of the type promoted and curated in websites such as Death By Zombie (http://deathbyzombie.com). The gruesome outward appearance of these fantasy creatures certainly shocks and thrills audiences in transmedia entertainment phenomena like *The Walking Dead* (Kirkman et al., 2010); these are the new interdisciplinary dramatic properties being created by the emerging proficians class of project-oriented and highly entrepreneurial creative workers considered in Chapter 2.

There are lessons to be learnt from these forays into the horror genre as part of the examination of the impact of technology on the arts and creative learning in postnormal settings through a drama lens. Yet more visceral than the horror derived from the visual imagery is the dramatic tension derived from an awareness of the (re)animation of these fantasy creatures, and the immediate threat to life and limb that this unnatural mobility implies to the living protagonists in these narratives. In *Frankenstein* it is indeed the 'animation' and the 'motion' of the monster that renders it so terrible for its maker, more than just its horrific countenance. It is the almost human form of this creature imbued with muscles and joints capable of movement that highlights how even the suggestion of embodiment is recruited as a powerful element of dramatic storytelling, as relevant in today's transmedia creative environment as it was in the nineteenth century. Although the divisions between live versus mediated experiences are diminishing as focus shifts to ways of ensuring choice and opportunities for creative expression and learning, this is still in a transformational stage.

As such, one of the most direct challenges to traditional understanding of dramatic production and performance occurs at the friction zones between humans and their technology that challenge notions of synchronous presence in artistic performance. Historically the injection of technology into drama has been seen as producing something else, at the very least a hybrid form, such as early experimentations with the use of film in stage productions at the turn of the twentieth century. For some the presence of media technology in a performance setting requires a different ontological position; like Frankenstein's monster it may simulate live performance but it is intrinsically something 'other'. The early uses of mass media forms in drama to some extent emphasized this difference, as it is difficult to avoid the sense that the addition of these tools to drama is in some ways an effort to make the drama seem more like those forms (Auslander, 1999). For example, the use of projected film and video onto the stage can easily be seen as twisting a dramatic performance to an experience more like watching cinema or television. Global digital media networks and powerful graphic software and hardware have made photorealistic digital art, high-definition projectors, and real-time audio and video streaming relatively inexpensive and accessible via domestic technologies even in developing economies.

The need for performers and audiences to occupy the same space at the same time for something to be called a live performance seems anachronistic to many young people who now regularly consume live or even 'as live' media and data streams as part of a daily diet of mobile and online interactions. Live television now regularly comes with a social media backchannel that incorporates viewer comments into the broadcast itself as superimposed data feeds. The willingness to accept even the simplest of mediated interactions with daily technologies as a live, performative act is fundamentally shifting the understanding of liveness. In fact, it may be that people are more willing to accept these obviously mediated performative moments as live more than those digital encounters that attempt to mirror the appearance of real-world experiences.

As with Frankenstein's monster, a willingness to engage with technology is tempered by concerns and assumptions about the nature of embodied presence in performance. In the contemporary world of digital arts cultures there is to some extent a questioning of the nature of increasing encounters with a range of robots, animations, 3D avatars, and video game characters attempting to appear, act, and react in terms that might be perceived as human. The term 'uncanny valley' comes from the work of a Japanese robotics professor, Masahiro Mori, and describes how likely responses to a humanlike form can rapidly switch from empathy to revulsion as it approaches but never quite reaches a lifelike appearance. The uncanny valley refers to a hypothesized chart of likely human emotional responses to anthropomorphized robots, registering positive and negative reactions to forms that develop progressively from obviously mechanical towards genuinely human in appearance. While people might initially start to feel increased empathy as robots adopt more human forms, there reaches a point where an artificial human begins to appear real without being accepted as real. This becomes creepy, and the chart of emotional responses records a dip into negative territory – the uncanny valley. Theoretically, as the robot forms then continue to progress towards more realistically human forms, empathy increases again. Interestingly for this discussion of performance, Mori's work found that movement intensified the positive and negative feelings towards the robot, amplifying the peaks and valleys represented in the uncanny valley graph (Mori, 1970).

Concepts such as the uncanny valley are a very practical concern for creators and performers seeking to work with the emerging possibilities of digital art forms. In early twenty-first-century cinema, for example, a number of big budget films have sought to render photorealistic digital animations based on the performances of real actors, which some audiences and reviewers have found difficult and unsatisfying to watch because of the creepy effect coming into play. A string of notable Hollywood examples from one major production company and director/producer Robert Zemeckis include *The Polar Express* (2004), *Beowulf* (2007), *A Christmas Carol* (2009), and *Mars Needs Moms* (2011). Similar concerns vex the designers and producers of video games, with many titles seeking to combine data capture of actors' movements from live action performances with the powerful graphics rendering hardware available in computer devices to produce photorealistic and immersive game experiences. The developers of the detective fiction game *L.A. Noire* (Team Bondi, 2011) went so far as to use elaborate multi-camera setups to capture finely detailed facial expressions of actors from every angle. They then created highly nuanced digital facial animations that invited the player to make judgements about whether a character was lying or telling the truth under interrogation. Given this desire of some artists to climb out of the uncanny valley by devising increasingly realistic digital characters, it is ironic that the inability of realistic humanoid robots to feel empathy with us creates the nightmarish scenarios of science fiction films such as *Blade Runner* (Ridley Scott, 1982) and *The Terminator* (James Cameron, 1984).

The uncanny valley should strike a chord with drama practitioners and educators, as it touches on current debates around the nature of performance in an increasingly mediated world. This is not an esoteric topic on the periphery of drama theory and practice, but rather points to increased challenges to what constitutes performance and drama when some of the participants might not be physically present, may be represented through graphical or textual avatars, or in the case of software 'chatterbots' perhaps might not even be human. There is a risk that the pursuit of combining live presence with digital representations will plunge the participants into hybrid spaces more notable for their creepy not-quite-live affect rather than the affordances and creative opportunities that they offer.

Conclusion

Drama now operates as part of the interdisciplinary, hypermedia landscape of digital arts cultures that is denoted by the concept of intermediality. This represents a complex and rapidly evolving and reconfiguring system of mediatized performative practices that can be difficult for both participants and observers to navigate. However, powerful and transformative new mashup experiences are now made possible. Digital liveness expands the creative and educational boundaries beyond time, space, and even the assumption of human-only social presence in daily engagements with entertainment, information, and educational institutions and events.

The next chapter continues to explore how these pervasive digital technologies have altered and expanded the conventions and affordances available to artists. Perhaps not surprisingly in the historic context of institutional adoption of technological change, these new multimodal performance approaches although now commonplace in the daily lives of young people have not permeated to a large extent schools, universities, and other places of learning. Chapter 5 considers some attempts by performance makers and educators working with young people to collapse the boundaries between forms and styles, in works that are brazenly interdisciplinary and defy easy categorization.

5

Proto-pedagogy, Intermediality, and Drama Making

At certain periods, innovations in the art forms do not necessarily translate into pedagogy or classroom practices. For instance, hip-hop is a contemporary dance and music form that predominates popular culture through music videos, but it is not a mainstream study in most music classrooms. In the same way, there is scant evidence that intermediality, by which we mean performances that hybridize live and mediated forms as discussed in Chapter 4, has reached drama classrooms. This has implications for the relevance of drama education to the art form, and, perhaps more critically, it represents a lost pedagogical opportunity to connect the affordances of performing intermediality to the learning of young people. As theatre education researcher Amy Petersen-Jensen wrote almost a decade ago:

The authors would like to acknowledge the substantial contribution that Dr Celina McEwen made to this research and its subsequent development for publication.

the world has changed, radically, dynamically, and continuously through media and technology. These changes create an opportunity for arts educators to actively engage these media in the best forms of literacy – through examining them, commenting on them, and representing them in original and thought-provoking contexts. With this accomplished, arts education moves from the margins to the center. If we support our students by listening to, learning from, and using their new vocabularies, we engage with them in significant conversations about public life – theirs and ours. We can reside together, practicing and learning in the complexity and contention of the digital world. (2008, p. 25)

Of concern is that the vast array of aesthetic opportunities made possible in part by advances in technologies are not commonplace in drama classrooms. For instance: how could the digitally driven performativities of groups such as Blast Theory, that have been discussed elsewhere in terms of drama and technology (Carroll, Anderson, and Cameron, 2006), become accessible in pedagogy for teachers and learning experiences for students?[1] This concern was the precursor for the Beowulf Sydney Project, the case study discussed in this chapter.

The project itself was *proto-pedagogical* in the sense that it took the practices of intermedial performance as the raw materials to create pedagogies for secondary drama classrooms. The prefix 'proto' is used to denote the prototyping nature of the process, which also fits with the concept of a playful experimental element to the drama framework described in this book for engaging in new works.

This chapter describes some of the processes used and analyses some of the implications for pedagogy that intermediality affords. The following discussion is a kind of mashup that combines the processes of performance, mediatization, and pedagogy to understand how these practices can create a viable classroom experience. The project collected data that are relevant in several areas but this chapter is focused on issues that arose in this case study that relate directly to intermediality and pedagogy. The chapter first tells the story of the Beowulf Sydney Project to 'paint the picture' of the project and then moves to some of the reflections of the students to analyse the potential for new pedagogical models that incorporate pedagogy, performance, and intermediality. These developments have the potential to lead to new drama-making models and pedagogical possibilities, especially when co-devising with students who are digital residents (White and Le Cornu, 2011). They also have the possibility of transforming students from consumers of art and learning into producers/users or 'produsers' (Bruns, 2008). This shift is critical not only for drama and theatre education and practice but has potential implications for other learning areas coping with liquid modernity (Bauman, 2000) discussed in Chapter 2.

About the Beowulf Sydney Project

Beowulf is an Old English poem structured as a hero quest that features monsters, heroes, and sword battles in the underworld. It is worth noting here that this project is literally Anglocentric. That said, the processes and approaches here could be used with stories from classical African, Asian, and many other cultures. Arguably many of the techniques used in this project such as choreographed movement and tableaux, oral storytelling, staged combat, large-scale scenic imagery, and puppetry derive from or mirror performance methods drawn from non-Anglo cultures. In essence the intent is to engage in a flexible multimodal manner to reinterpret cultural texts and present them anew notwithstanding their cultural origin.

Here is an excerpt of Seamus Heaney's translation to give a sense of the language and the content of the story (Allard and North, 2014, lines 2971–2091):

> Then Wonred's son, the brave Wulf,
> Could land no blow against the aged lord.
> Ongentheow divided his helmet
> So that he buckled and bowed his bloodied head
> And dropped to the ground. But his doom held off.
> Though he was cut deep, he recovered again. With his brother
> down, the undaunted Eofor,
> Hygelac's thane, hefted his sword
> And smashed murderously at the massive helmet
> Past the lifted shield. And the king collapsed,
> The shepherd of people was sheared of life.

In late 2015, a team[2] of artists, academics, and digital games makers worked together to investigate how intermedial performance could be designed and implemented with a group of young people. The Beowulf Sydney Project was the 'colonial' offshoot of the larger Playing Beowulf Digital Transformations project funded by the Arts and Humanities Research Council in the UK and led by Professor Andrew Burn of the Institute of Education, University College London. That UK-based project focused on developing a game-authoring tool to create game levels devised from the Anglo-Saxon epic poem *Beowulf* for use by literature students in schools and universities, curators, and library visitors. Excerpts from the game and gameplay were used as some of the performance materials in the Sydney project. The story of the Anglo-Saxon poem *Beowulf* was the core 'dramatic property' (Sutton, 2012) transcodified across a range of media and performance forms.

One of the goals of the project was to fuse mediated or procedural (e.g. game-based) performances with more traditional drama forms, such as large-scale puppetry, to create a hybrid dramatic experience. This aligns with the concept of intermediality (Kattenbelt, 2008) outlined in Chapter 4, in which 'previously existing medium specific conventions are changed, which allows for new dimensions of perception and experience to be explored'. In some ways, *Beowulf* may seem an unlikely candidate for the opportunities that intermediality affords performance makers. It is, after all, an ancient, rambling epic poem with seemingly few resonances with modern experience. Yet there is something appealing in the epic and the archetypal that suits the larger palette that intermediality provides to this unwieldy poem. It lends itself to creative interpretations of what remains a debated text, along with playful embodied and mediatized performances of action sequences and heroic victories.

The project team was interested in the mutual affects of complementary performance-based conventions of digital gaming and drama making, viewing both as play-based and highly performative practices operating within the realm of the imagination or suspension of disbelief, and framed by abstract roles, narratives, and shared conventions. In both cases, 'rules of one kind or another operate; and [...] players deploy resources to meet challenges or overcome obstacles to achieve some kind of goal or outcome' (Burn, 2013, p. 5). For this project, live and digital performances were not positioned in this project as opposing or as dualities. In the language of digital cultures, these elements merge in a 'mashup' – a less formal way perhaps of describing intermediality and the way in which elements form a new and more complex whole for both performers and audiences.

Making intermedial *Beowulf*: A proto-pedagogical story

A group of eighteen young people (7 girls and 11 boys), 11–15 years of age, joined a week-long school holiday workshop offered by The Australian Theatre for Young People[3] (ATYP). They were invited to explore a variety of storytelling and drama-making art forms using the Anglo-Saxon poem *Beowulf* as inspiration. With a teaching team of eight adults, the young students took part in a range of activities including:

- story interpretation and performance adaptation
- puppetry
- video game design

- video making

- voice acting

- directing and performing.

Their efforts culminated in a live twenty-minute long performance for family and friends. A range of qualitative tools was used to gather data. Parents and carers provided consent for the young people to take part in the research and participation in the interviews and online survey was on a voluntary basis.

The methodological process of this project will be described in this chapter so that the approach can be understood and then modified in other contexts. While there has been a substantial and ongoing discussion of the opportunities that intermedial performances present, there is still scant evidence of actual classroom practice. One of the possible reasons for this poor take-up is the lack of coherent pedagogical stories (case studies) from which classroom teachers can apply and adapt their practice. The detailed description and analysis of the limitations and implications for practice here are an attempt to bridge that gap.

Understanding the narrative

The devising phase began with a process that aimed to acquaint students with the narrative of Beowulf. To help students explore the epic poem, the workshop opened with Dr Daniel Anlezark, a scholar in Old and Middle English language and literature from the University of Sydney, leading a session on understanding the narrative of *Beowulf*. In this session, students were immersed in the story and the broader Anglo-Saxon culture. They looked at *Beowulf* as a tale structured around three battles and taking place at two different stages of the hero's life. During the talk, students drew or took notes about aspects of the story that appealed the most to them.

Students were also given the opportunity to discuss the dichotomies of heroes versus cowards, humans versus monsters, and territory versus community as well as unpack issues of gender representation, revenge, and dignity. After this process, the group collaboratively storyboarded (see Figure 5.2) the elements of *Beowulf* to be included in the performance. They also chose which modality of performance they felt would be most effective to tell each aspect of the story. They could choose between:

FIGURE 5.1 *A student's drawings of young and old Beowulf. Used with permission.*

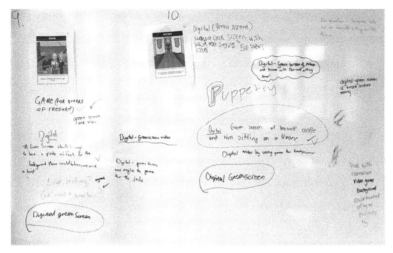

FIGURE 5.2 *Collaborative storyboarding to develop the* Beowulf *narrative into an intermedial performance.*

- live performance,

- puppetry, and/or

- digital (which was anything that was based on the video game, video, sound recording, or a mashup of any of these).

Devising and rehearsing intermedial performance

Following the introduction to the *Beowulf* poem, the students attended an initial session where they were introduced to notions of sequencing, production, and stage design. This allowed students to start working on creating vignettes/tableaux and storyboarding key aspects of the poem. Students then had a choice of becoming part of:

- the directors group,

- the puppetry construction and performance group, or

- the digital creation group.

Later, a smaller group of students collaborated with the teachers[4] on making decisions about the staging as well as the logistics of creating a performance. Students discussed and negotiated which of the three elements (gaming, puppets, theatre) would help tell different parts of the stories most effectively, which spaces to use for the performance, which characters might be required on stage, and which props and digital assets to use.

This process was similar to playbuilding processes that are a standard feature of drama education (Anderson, 2015). The exception being that instead of being limited to dramatic staging techniques (blocking, use of props, actor-audience relationships), they had a larger selection of choices (gameplay sequence, video sequence, voiceover, etc.). Pedagogically, this is both a challenge and an opportunity. It provides more options for creating a story but also creates an expectation that students can make aesthetically adept choices that even some theatre professionals find difficult. In this project, that issue was somewhat overcome by the specialists guiding the making and devising process but this 'expanded devising palate' will require careful scaffolding when transferred to classroom learning environments.

The devising process was in reality a mix between student devising and teacher guidance. In terms of the age and maturity of these students, there was no real intention to allow the whole process to be student-led, and this became more of a concern later in the week as attention turned to creating a final performance for family and friends. When teaching drama with Year 7 and 8 students, a blend of approaches that moves between modalities from the so-called 'sage on the stage' to the 'meddler in the middle' (McWilliam, 2008) is not only preferable, it is more likely to produce a performance event that is genuinely co-constructed and allows experimentation, risk taking, and productive error making.

Rehearsing of scenes was introduced during the second half of the week. In the rehearsal phase, the teacher-as-director approach was used more prominently to make the loosely associated segments of the devising process gel in a clear and coherent public performance. Early rehearsals took on the form of walk-throughs of sequences using guided improvisation to help key moments in the story emerge. During these sessions students were also introduced to basic elements of physical performance, thus bringing new skills and knowledge to their acting experiences. Final rehearsals saw students practise staged action to block acting, puppets, and digital sequences in the space with props, lighting, and projection.

The performance

Prior to the performance, spectators (mainly parents and friends of the students) were invited to gather in the main workshop room to attend a short presentation outlining the processes the students had engaged in during the week and from which the performance had emerged. At the end of the presentation, the audience was led through the Old Teachers' College to the Assembly Hall. This performance setting is a Gothic Collegiate style hall large enough for performers and the audience to move about. The hall's heavy wood panelling and high windowpanes were reminiscent of the mead hall Heorot which is featured prominently in the poem, and which is also represented digitally in rooms within the game-making software used for the workshop. As such, it provided an ideal setting for the promenade performance that was created. The performance was attended by approximately forty people as well as streamed live using the Periscope app for Twitter. The physical audience stood in a semicircle around the performance and followed the performers around the room, with most filming and streaming the performance on their own devices creating a multilayered virtual presence and representation of the performance. In effect, the audience was generating a set of personal digital archives of the performance that could be re-experienced and shared with a wider circle of family and friends later.

The performance lasted approximately twenty minutes and took the audience through the background story of the monster Grendel's fury against the humans and how Beowulf's party came to be involved; the battles between the young Beowulf and Grendel and his mother; and the final battle of the old Beowulf against a dragon. Static scenes were used for gatherings and battle scenes while roving through the hall space was used to transition between the scenes. A teacher, Howard Matthew, guided performers through the live action. The characters on stage included:

- Beowulf, a proud warrior,
- Geatish and Danish warriors,
- the monster Grendel,
- Grendel's mother, and
- a dragon.

Other characters from the story, such as the Danish King and Queen, were seen in projected video sequences recorded from video game footage created specifically for that purpose, a form of the game-based moviemaking genre known as 'machinima', which is described in more detail in Chapter 7. Beowulf was embodied by several male and female performers who moved in and out of character by donning or removing symbolic costuming. All performers remained on stage throughout, swiftly changing role, in turn becoming one of the main characters, a warrior and/or a puppeteer. The performance took place on the main floor as well as on stage. Chairs and tables were still present in the corners, pointing to the room's current educational purpose. Some of these chairs and tables were also used as props to represent the ageing Beowulf's throne and his burial vessel. The performers' black clothes emphasized their equal non-gendered status as performers. The black clothes also helped with the changeover of performers in the main roles and assisted in the use of performers as elements of props, for example, when performers stood in an oval formation to represent the boat on which Beowulf and his warriors sailed.

Simple versatile props and lighting were used throughout. They included bamboo sticks to signify, in turn, weapons and oars. Some basic accessories, such as a helmet, sleeveless jacket, a sword, and a shield, helped the audience identify the main character of Beowulf. A large white sheet held by several performers was also used as both a projection screen and the sails of a boat.

Puppets were used to represent the monsters/animals in the story. A two-metre tall green puppet was used to animate Grendel, as seen in Figure 5.3. The body was harnessed to a backpack frame and operated by one performer whose feet were attached to the puppet's. Each arm was operated by a separate performer. For expediency,

FIGURE 5.3 *Rehearsing a scene between Beowulf and Grendel.*

Grendel's mother was represented by placing a wig of long drab black locks on the puppet of Grendel. The dragon was represented by a deconstructed puppet made of a giant red head with an articulated jaw, operated by one performer, and two broad detached unfolding wings with hooks on each end, made of red flowing fabric, each operated by two performers.

Student voices were recorded to narrate key sections of the story (using Seamus Heaney's translation of the original text) and other sounds (Celtic music, the sea and monsters' growl) were woven into a twenty-minute soundtrack for the production. The recording of the narrative content freed performers from having to learn their lines in the short time available and allowed them to focus on movement, puppetry, and the sequencing of the performance.

Performers' movements, as travellers, were also emphasized by the Celtic music that accompanied the journey of the hero. Finally, the puppets were brought to life through the deep threatening growls and plaintive howls projected against the performers' battle and victory cries. These sounds and voices were played through two mini Bluetooth speakers covered in hessian and carried around on rods by performers. The two rods not only served as stands for the speakers but they also functioned as flags for the audience to follow, and poles to delimit performance spaces as the action moved to locations around the hall.

The backdrop was provided by scenery projected on two large screens (one fixed on stage and another mobile). Projection was also used to show the audience Grendel's point of view (represented by video and game scenes with Grendel's arm superimposed using digital compositing techniques). Further, projection was used as a device to help transition between the scenes and mark the passing of time (e.g. an animation of the ageing Beowulf represented by a series of drawings made by one of the students, as seen in Figure 5.1). In addition to this, and as with the speakers, a mobile screen placed at the back and a projector on a mobile trolley located at the front of the performance were also used to frame and delimit the space of the performance at certain times.

The lack of material separation between front and back stage allowed for the 'strings' to be visible. Combined with the non-refined (semi-guided, semi-improvised approach) staged action, these aspects of the performance gave it a particular aesthetic that sought to highlight the devising process, the complexity of the story and project, and students' effort in putting together a performative product within such a short period of time. This intertwining of process and performance, representation and artifice, live and digital, play and work, real and proxy also served to create an atmosphere of playful learning or productive fun. Finally, it emphasized the principle that the 'how' and 'why' of creating an original piece is as central to the experience as the end result or the staging of the performance. This draws an analogy between the devising process and the journey of the hero, where the overall journey is perhaps more critical to the development of the hero than the slaying of the monsters.

Having described this workshop as a case study in intermediality, the chapter now outlines the processes used to research the performance. These include a number of decisions and approaches that are built upon more broadly in Chapter 10, where the research implications are considered for those starting to work and research in intermedial performance, especially with young people and digital arts.

Research approach

The processes for researching theatre and education have been well established over decades. The intersections between theatre, education, and technology in intermedial performances are less well established. The techniques employed in this project (ethnographic observation, surveys, interviewing) represent traditional social sciences approaches to understanding student and teacher experiences in learning. Again, there are included here in some detail and situated with the narrative of the workshop to record the approach and give a sense of the fit and limitations of these approaches so that researchers might learn from these experiences.

Ethnographic observation

Ethnographic observation of workshop activities, the devising process, and several teachers' meetings was undertaken during the week. Notes were made about actions, dialogues, and interactions and complemented by photographs. Workshop activities were also recorded with video cameras setup in the workshop spaces. The final performance was also streamed live to research partners in the UK using the Periscope application for Twitter, and these partners provided their own ethnographic observations on the performance.

The performance was ethnographically observed and analysed using Gay McAuley's (1998) performance schema. McAuley's schema is a practical socio-semiotic tool that helps analyse a performance by describing the relationship between the performance's presentational system (the material signifiers and the patterns, such as repetitions, contrasts, and redundancies they form) and its narrative structure of fictional events (the story told and its segmentations).

Student and teacher interviews

Teachers were interviewed at the end of the project via Skype sessions that lasted on average thirty minutes. The questions asked related to teachers' experiences of integrating drama and gaming in performance and on ways of improving the model of practice explored. On several occasions during the week, students were interviewed one-on-one, in pairs, or in focus groups. Interviews were brief (between 5 and

15 minutes) and focused on eliciting an initial understanding of students' interest and expectations of the workshop as well as their experience in drama making and game design, and their opinions about the relationship between live and digital performance making. The interview questions were also used to stimulate reflection in students prior to completion of an online questionnaire.

Online survey

On the last day, students were asked to fill in an online survey. This survey comprised eighteen questions and was designed to explore the student's experience of and attitudes towards:

- drama making and gaming,
- classic and ancient texts,
- devising the *Beowulf* performance, and
- the relationships between digital and live dramatic creation processes and performance.

Research findings

The following findings have been selected from a much larger group as they touch on the themes of this book: intermedial making and learning. The student's responses are available in full in the project report but for the sake of readability they have been summarized here and are interspersed through the findings to feature the student's voices.

Participatory pedagogy

As mentioned earlier in this chapter, the design of the workshop mixed student agency in the making process with more teacher-directed processes leading towards the performance event at the end of the project. This flexibility offered students the opportunity to explore themes and ideas, as well as to problem-solve and make decisions about how to best convey the story. It also gave them a certain level of control and ownership over some of the processes and the final product of the workshop (the performance).

The participatory activities and flexible approach allowed students to make sense of their experiences. The problem-solving approach helped them find connections between and thread together the different performative and digital elements of the intermedial performance, making sense of them as a new form emerging from the different elements. Conversely, this agile pedagogical approach that allowed for more possibilities to emerge and the flexible repurposing of elements, also required young students' dexterity in flipping between genres, and tested their capacity to embrace and negotiate digital technology.

Live and mediated performance

Though different elements initially attracted students to the workshop, once engaged in the process and the materiality of the performance, there were no dominant or major and minor elements (which was surprising to many of the researchers and teachers). Indeed, a majority of students had no reservations about bringing together video games and live performance. Students saw connections between live performance and game making in the way they were both used to present a story and/or characters to an audience. They also saw similarities between live and digital productions like games, especially comparing video and drama making, in their heavy reliance on resources (time, skills, equipment) and team effort as well as the fact that they are framed by rules and conventions ('There's a set of rules which you need to follow, and a script that gives you all the necessary commands') and their capacity to entertain ('entertaining story. Making the audience experience emotions e.g. sadness, joy, humour').

However, students also said that beyond those broad connections, there were specific differences between making a live performance and making a video or a game in terms of the use of time, space, emotions, physical presence, control or predictability in the making ('A live performance can be messed up more easily'), and the level of interaction with the story or responsiveness to the audience ('When you are in a performance, you can really connect with the audience. A video doesn't really connect because people just think it is something to watch and don't actually think why they are watching it'). Further, they saw these differences between real and virtual elements as allowing different performative effects. For example, some students reflected that staged performance could be used to create emotional conflict, because of its immediacy and presence ('with performance you use your emotions and passion to express to the audience'), and digital performance used to heighten dramatic tension through the use of special effects ('in a video game it is much easier to do special effects') and enrich the backdrop ('digital software can be used effectively to create more atmosphere for the audience').

Devising intermediality

Digital art is not bound by the conditions of liveness. It does not require synchronicity of time and space, with performers and the audience's physical and temporal co-presence. Yet, digital art can retain some attributes of liveness that can enhance and deepen the learner or participant's experience within interactive and networked environments. This was the case of most students in this project.

Engaging in these activities and processes helped students develop common sets of vocabulary and provided a basic framework for them to collaborate on devising the performance. The switching between processes and integration of elements was made straightforward because of the participant's prior experiences in drama making, their willingness to take part in the processes offered and to work to combine media. Though they expressed preferences in terms of what they wanted to do for the workshop, they conveyed no sense of hierarchy between the elements in the performance making.

Combining live and virtual and representational and ludic performance and drama-making elements allowed for students to define the rules – '[t]he rules determining which way a player might go, what resources are made available and when, how such resources are balanced finely against the difficulty of challenges and obstacles, and what conditions need to be met to achieve the outcome' (Burn, 2013, pp. 5–6) – rather than these be solely dictated by the teachers or the elements.

Students alternated roles on stage, sharing responsibility for representing the main characters and the narration of the story. They alternated roles in the devising process as directors, actors, puppeteers, game designers, and film-makers. They also had the opportunity to shift from a role of consumer to a role of producer when exploring game design with *Missionmaker*.[5] Using *Missionmaker* they were able to explore particular aspects of the poem within an explorable and interactive game environment as well as co-construct narratives. *Missionmaker* also contains a set of procedural rule-making tools that can be applied to objects and characters, giving the students opportunities to shape events, puzzles, and interactions within the game world of the story they are creating and sharing. Experimentation with the rules and objects was in itself a devised performance process.

By handling a range of instruments and experiencing different roles and genres, students had the capacity to explore new possibilities in terms of identity formation, as Carroll and Cameron (2005, p. 3) argue: '[t]he field of identity formation that both drama and video games encompass means they are uniquely positioned to grapple with this issue in a cultural climate of increasing openness and identity relativism'.

Students worked individually and in groups to generate material, evaluate the range of options, and decide on the most appropriate solution(s). The combination of individual and collaborative processes led to rich and varied information gathering and solution finding. Further, by working together across genres to design a blended physical and digital space in performance, they had the opportunity to look beyond the limitations of one particular genre, which led some students to a new reading of 'what is already known or imaginable' (Fryer, 2010, p. 559) and a sophisticated understanding of the value of ancient or classic texts ('It gives us an insight as to the culture and values of peoples throughout history'; 'they strengthen our culture'; 'for us to appreciate how far science and technology has come'), the workshop processes ('I learnt how to cooperate with other people'), and drama making ('I learnt how to utilise various media forms, including green-screen and game sequencing, in conjunction, thus creating a more engaging performance'; 'we were looking at how to take a bunch of different media forms, like puppetry, filming, game sequencing etc., and seeing how we cold mash it all up into one big performance, so the different media forms complemented each other').

Limitations and implications

The workshop resulted in positive outcomes for the students, the convergence of various performative elements, and the emergence of an intermedial drama-making process. The quality of facilitation skills and experiences, and the level of access to a wide range of resources, were key to this result. As well, the flexible structure of the workshop allowed teachers to respond to students and adapt their processes and directions to the group's needs. Though this flexibility created many opportunities, it also created some challenges and led to some of the workshop's shortcomings, including loose expectations and unclear workshop parameters. In a sense, this looseness is a feature of the emergent experimentation with pedagogy and form that was taking place in this project.

In future iterations of the project, intermediality could support the shaping of a more contemporary approach to performance making. For instance, live gaming and other digital assets could have been included more effectively from the beginning design phase of the project with the students. In this project, game sequences were presented as a background projection to add gaming to drama in the final performance. This was only a small sample of the game-design work that the students undertook in the week, with playable game levels another possible element that could be added to the mix. There are also more opportunities to explore the role of audience members equipped with mobile phones that can live stream the performance, or share collective archives of the performance. These opportunities were unforeseeable in some ways until the participants became immersed in the storytelling process.

Also, the project was constrained by several external and pragmatic factors. This project was one case study within a larger research project, with a primary focus on exploring how young people engage with culturally significant texts through gaming activities than on intermedial drama-making processes. In addition to this, for practical reasons, the recruitment of students was conducted by ATYP, resulting in the participation of a group of young people with a higher than average level of experience in drama making in contrast to most school-based drama cohorts.

Finally, though the workshop was not intended to have a strong performative element, there was a need to include a performance to show parents the outcome of their children's efforts. This created a shift in focus towards the end of the workshop away from exploratory process-based activities. Combined with time constraints linked to ensuring the delivery of a product, this might have detracted from the initial democratic and participatory approach used and led, in the latter stages of development, to teachers taking control of the process more than initially intended. That said, student direction as mentioned earlier is an appropriate and, in some ways, a necessary technique for teaching drama with students at this age, stage, and skill level.

Other limits to the participatory nature of the activities included the work around the script and segmentation, the techniques used to create the puppets and other practicalities, such as the use of props, lighting and projection, rotating roles, and the use voiceover narration. For example, the choice of the twelve-scene storyboard,[6] the excerpts used for the script, and the final performance segmentation was made by the teachers for reasons of expediency. In this context, students were still, however, able to exercise choice and make decisions in the devising of tableaux, linking the segments and creating the Grendel puppet. They were also regularly consulted on some of the decisions made by teachers, including the decision to contain the roving of the performance to the Assembly Hall despite original enthusiasm at using a range of nearby locations. Thus, though some of the teachers' decisions might have caused some loss of control or agency by the students, there was still enough scope and opportunities for students to feel a sense of ownership over the process and outcomes.

Conclusion

In the Beowulf Sydney Project, a group of young people and teachers experimented with possible ways of integrating different live and digital elements in performance. This led to the development of an experimental intermedial drama-making model and the reconfiguration of dramatic frames into a hybrid or hypermedia dramatic space opening up new learning opportunities for young students.

Unlike more traditional performance workshops for young people, this workshop did not focus on developing acting and performing skills. Though the immersive character of performance and video gaming could have been more fully explored, the workshop led to a problem-solving approach to mashing up live and digital elements. Further, teachers used participatory learning and action processes to help the students problem-solve and role-play a range of fictional and professional roles.

More specifically, students uncovered new ways of performing and being a game designer, and incorporating this game design in a performative manner. They developed a more sophisticated understanding of Beowulf and live and digital drama/performance making/storytelling as a creative endeavour framed by given rules and conventions. As the students negotiated some of the parameters of performance making, they were able to explore options and boundaries of the intermedial 'stage'. The combined effect of the different elements of the performance creating different aspects of 'distance' that created a liveness affect.

By taking part in interdisciplinary and intermedial activities, the students learnt that narrative can be told and experienced in different ways. They were also able to explore how to interpret ideas of combat, heroic quest, and monster figures in drama and game. By moving in and out of gaming and design and devising, as well as by operating puppets and designing game environments, they were able to engage with notions of control, agency, and manipulation and explore where and when the 'actor/player' is just another variable and when it can become a 'master'.

Through action and intent, students were not just retelling the story or choosing to perform one of several versions of the story, but given the opportunity to develop their own understanding of *Beowulf*. The workshop emphasized the design of narrative experiences (affective, active). The adaptation of *Beowulf*, a fantasy-based story that is larger than life, yet grounded in real life, to the stage with puppets and video game elements, opened up ways for students of connecting the Anglo-Saxon poem to contemporary popular cultural contexts. It also allowed students to have a certain level of authorship over the story.

The workshop provided a case study that raised several questions: How to better integrate digital media as a performative element rather than just as a mode of performance? What is the natural fit/commonalities between the elements of embodiment and experience? How can we make these types of creative learning approaches an integral part of learning in and for liquid times?

This project was 'proto-pedagogical' as the learning experiences provided the research team with rich insights into the integration of live and mediated performance with young people. Prototyping of these kinds of pedagogies is critical as we consider the challenges and the opportunities of intermedial performance. While there are still several critical questions to be answered through further research, this evolving model of intermedial drama making is one example of developing a better understanding of the pedagogical implications for learning in the twenty-first century to ensure that the contemporary art form and the classroom can reflect and learn from one another.

The workshop processes of the Beowulf Sydney Project enabled students to move between roles as audience, performer, and produser (Bruns, 2016) by exploring the creative and dramatic potential of the Beowulf story as they navigated ways of combining different media forms. In the next chapter, the concept of engaging game players as game designers and co-creators of new content is explored more deeply in the context of the commercial video game industry.

6

Games as Co-creative Dramatic Properties

The materials used in the game worlds of *LittleBigPlanet* and *Tearaway*, created by studio Media Molecule, are reminiscent of a craft afternoon at school: paper, corrugated cardboard, fabric, stickers, sponges, and pencils. The comfortable familiarity of these craft objects offers a low barrier to entry into both game play and the digital fabrication enabled by the games. The common craft aesthetic as a catalyst for play and creativity in these games suggests they are dramatic properties, a digital text 'structured to be collaborative, drawing participants into their ludic narrative, [and] inviting them to be part of an on-going process of authorship' (Sutton, 2012, p. 609). These games are interesting cultural artefacts in the resurgent DIY maker culture due to the bridging of the mediated and real-life fabrication processes. Both *LittleBigPlanet* and *Tearaway* position the player in real-world roles as a maker: in *LittleBigPlanet* as a game designer, and in *Tearaway* as a paper-craft artist. This chapter examines the collaborative creative activities within games *LittleBigPlanet* and *Tearaway* and an associated fan community. In particular, consideration will be given to the informal and formal spaces or communities in which these digital arts cultures perform their creative works in engagement with the underlying dramatic properties. As with the previous chapter, some of the research methodologies used to examine these fan communities are described in order to provide another useful case study of practice.

LittleBigPlanet

Almost invariably with everyone there's this 'aha!' moment where you realise 'holy crap, this is the art media that I've always been looking for and I didn't even know that I wanted'. Like, I'm not an artistic person and for me, this is my canvas. I had no idea that I had any sort of creative ability until I got this game. This is my ink and paper.

–LBP player and former fan community manager, interview.

Released in 2008 bundled with Sony's PlayStation 3, *LittleBigPlanet* is a platform game designed to encourage collaborative play and user-generated content, released with the tagline, 'Play, Create, Share'. Since its initial release, the *LittleBigPlanet* title has expanded to include *LittleBigPlanet 2, LittleBigPlanet Karting*, and *LittleBigPlanet 3* for the PlayStation 3; and *LittleBigPlanet PSP* and *LittleBigPlanet PS Vita* for Sony's handheld devices. The titles are available in multiple languages across different regions.

The 'Play, Create, Share' tagline from *LittleBigPlanet* prompts players to be active participants in the game world. 'Play' encourages players to complete the game story, 'Create' refers to the building of game levels which extend the game narrative, and 'Share' emboldens players to share their creations with other players online, through the portal lbp.me. The game is of course not the first to incorporate the sharing of user-generated content (UGC) as part of gameplay. Alex Evans, co-founder of Media Molecule, suggests that UGC exists on a spectrum between drawing lines in games such as *Line Rider* (InXile Entertainment, 2009) and the activity of modding (Westecott, 2011; Wired, 2008). Evans positions *LittleBigPlanet* in the middle of this spectrum (Westecott, 2011; Wired, 2008). User-generated content in levels, from sets through to villains, are constructed with digital objects collected during gameplay. Objects are assembled with digital glue, springs, and rubber bands. Creative storytelling and game-building tools in *LittleBigPlanet* are highly accessible as players do not need to know a line of code to participate in the creative process. Game design as a learning strategy and other game authoring tools are discussed further in Chapter 8.

The opening video clip for the first *LittleBigPlanet* game describes a universe, 'Craftworld', created by all the ideas and dreams floating out of human heads while we sleep. Eight creator-curators govern Craftworld, and dramatic conflict is created by one of the creator-curators – The Collector – going rogue. The Collector has started hoarding ideas and creativity from the universe, including kidnapping the other creator-curators. The Collector is the antagonist of a world where shared knowledge and creativity is valued, much like in the digital media landscape. The first game concludes with the protagonist, Sackthing, confronting The Collector who apologizes: 'I'm sorry! I'm not really a bad guy. The reason I don't share is that I have no friends!'. At that moment, the freed creator-curators appear with a message to The Collector, and a call to action for the players: 'All the Little Big Planet community can be your friends! Get out there and be part of it!'.

Play, learning, collaboration, and creativity are clearly embedded within *LittleBigPlanet*. These elements map well to the drama-based domains for exploring digital arts cultures of creativity, playfulness, performance, and digital liveness. Drama offers us an interesting framework to understand the fostering of community and participation in *LittleBigPlanet*. Despite being positioned as a platformer game, it could be argued that *LittleBigPlanet* is a role-based game where players are put in role as game designers, commissioned to develop game levels. As a digital artefact, the game contains many characteristics of a 'dramatic property'. Coined by Paul Sutton of C&T, a dramatic property is a term that describes a digital text that draws on the collaborative features of digital media and provides a life for a drama beyond a text, performance, or workshop (2012). The main performance is the gameplay contained on the disc, and the life beyond it exists in the official and unofficial game communities and the content created by the community. *LittleBigPlanet* is a dramatic property on a commercial, global scale. The first levels in the game teach players how to use the controls to move (Jump! Grab! Swing!) and to successfully collect score and prize bubbles throughout the game. Prize bubbles contain digital artefacts that reward players with objects such as costumes for their Sackthing avatars, and textures, decorations, sets, and audio that will aid in the construction of game levels. The sequel, *LittleBigPlanet 2*, expands what can be created, adding digital puppetry and mini-games. The game comes packaged with level creation tutorials that teach players how to manipulate objects to create their own levels. Completing tutorials unlock more prize bubbles, rewarding players for learning. Collaborative play is required throughout the game to unlock particular prizes: for example, a problem-solving challenge that cannot be completed without four players.

Collaborative creativity ('co-creativity')

Collaborative creativity or 'co-creativity' refers to the process where people work together towards a creative outcome. This working process is also inherent in applied drama forms. The term has gained renewed currency within digital media where technology enables groups of people to work together.

The concept of user-generated content finds its roots in fan-based media production linked to a variety of media texts, including games (Jenkins, 2006b). This practice forms part of 'participatory culture', where 'fans and other consumers are invited to actively participate in the creation and circulation of new media content' (Jenkins, 2008, p. 331). It can't be assumed everyone wants to or can participate in this culture, but arguably there are now more opportunities to do so. In considering the concept of 'participation' more widely in terms of the practices of a culture or community, and especially when framed in a learning or collaborative setting around performance and media, we must be mindful of the danger of excluding those who choose to contribute in less publicly visible ways. In critiquing the current discourse around engagement and active learning in higher education, Lesley Gourlay reminds us that

> mainstream conceptions of student engagement emphasise practices which are observable, verbal, communal and indicative of 'participation', and that private, silent, unobserved and solitary practices may be pathologised or rendered invisible – or in a sense unknowable – as a result, despite being central to student engagement. (2015, p. 402)

Despite the risk of this 'tyranny of participation' in education, fan culture has a long history of engagement in many diverse forms, and the pervasiveness of digital technology and networked media has made participatory cultures more widely distributed and easier to access. Jenkins et al. (2009) describe a participatory culture as one with

> relatively low barriers to artistic expression and civic engagement, strong support for creating and sharing creations with others, some type of informal mentorship whereby what is known by the most experienced is passed along to novices, members who believe that their contributions matter, and members who feel some degree of social connection with one another (at least, they care what other people think about what they have created). (Jenkins et al., 2009, pp. 5–6)

Within participatory culture can exist French cyber theorist Pierre Levy's idea of 'collective intelligence' (Jenkins, 2006b; Lévy, 2000) where there is too much information about a topic for one person to know so the knowledge is both shared and pooled within a community. Jenkins suggests this 'knowledge space' is realized by online fan communities where 'consumption has become a collective process' (2008, p. 4). Collective intelligence is not limited to media consumption; the power of the group can be used for collective action, creativity, and play (McGonigal, 2003; Rheingold, 2002; Shirky, 2008). As an informal learning environment, James Gee (2004) calls this culture an 'affinity space'. Gee considers affinity spaces an alternative notion to Etienne Wenger's concept of 'communities of practice' (1998) and suggests that labelling a group of people as a community of practice is problematic owing to varying levels of engagement within the group. Gee suggests that by starting with spaces, 'we can then go on and ask to what extent the people interacting within a space, or some sub-group of them, do or do not actually form a community' (Gee, 2004, p. 89). Jenkins (2008) acknowledges that not all participants are equal in a participatory culture: corporate media producers exert power from the top-down and there are varying levels of skills for engagement from individual participants within the culture.

Gee (2013) has summarized some of the common features of affinity spaces that make them a critical area for research and development. People are in such spaces by choice, and their affinity for each other is based on a shared endeavour. Participants come from diverse areas and backgrounds and are not ranked by age, gender, or class. People bring different skills and levels of expertise. Leadership and status are flexible, with different paths to mastery. Some people have an interest, others have a passion for the endeavour; the affinity space is built to support development of interest into passion. Affinity spaces link to other related spaces to incorporate outside knowledge, but each retains a distinctive culture and vision negotiated over time.

Those with passion set high standards, and are inclined to discuss and animate the pursuit of excellence in the activities undertaken. Affinity spaces focus on production and solving problems – on knowing and doing. People can specialize, but general skills are shared and collaboration is coordinated towards larger projects. Affinity spaces use a range of powerful tools and affordances to enable the work done in the space. Contributions can be big or small, but every contribution can make a difference. There is not a tight distinction between work and play, as people are already motivated by an interest or passion. These are social spaces, but the endeavour is always the primary work/ play focus of the space. Endeavours are guided by a collective sense of authenticity, with claims of truth tested and the evidence debated by the people in the space in a form of collaborative critical reflection.

Games scholars would not be surprised to find that play and simulation are considered to be part of a set of new literacies connected to taking part in participatory culture (Jenkins et al., 2009). The intersection of play, user-generated content, and affinity spaces in *LittleBigPlanet* is thus relevant to those interested in player production practices in digital games cultures, and more widely it offers a sense of how creative practices and learning opportunities emerge around many different interest-based projects when supported by the affordances of tools and spaces for sharing outputs.

LittleBigPlanet fan communities

As Jenkins and Squire noted back in 2002, 'as players engage more directly in the design process [of a game], the line between gamers and designers begins to dissolve. To participate fully, players will need to learn more about the art of game design' (p. 75). Game design, like drama, can be a way of playful exploration across curricula as demonstrated by other authoring tools such as *Minecraft* and *Missionmaker*, discussed further in Chapter 8. In-game tutorials teach *LBP* players how to create levels but how do they learn to get better at game design and make meaningful contributions to the *LBP* community? A fan community attached to a game where players are commissioned to design levels seems a useful place to start exploration of how informal channels are supporting the creation of user-generated content.

A simple Google search can reveal a variety of fan sites linked to *LittleBigPlanet*. Often these sites will list a directory of other sites, and cross-pollination of members across sites is not uncommon. To narrow down the list of potential fan communities to explore, it can be filtered to those spaces whose creative competitions (a challenge to create a certain style of level, or to create a special in-level feature) were posted in current in-game news on the PlayStation console. The inclusion of fan site content in the in-game news indicates an acknowledgement from the game developers of the importance of these sites in keeping the momentum of the game rolling. The sites in the in-game news were used as a starting point to initiate contact. Fan site administrators and moderators were targeted to participate in interviews.

A connection was made with 'Lindberg', a site administrator of *LittleBigPlanet Central* (*LBPC*), and a past *LBPC* moderator, 'The Mole' (both pseudonyms were self-selected by the participants). LBPC is the largest and most active of the *LittleBigPlanet* fan communities, and was recognized early on by Media Molecule's then community manager as 'an amazing resource' (Spaff, 2009). Interestingly, quite a few involved in *LBPC* have gone on to work for Media Molecule and Sony. The site contains a forum, wiki, blog tool, and the space extends to channels including a Twitter account (@lbpcentral) and a profile on the in-game community, lbp.me. Participation in the site has diminished over time, as *LittleBigPlanet* was first released in 2008; however it still remains a useful resource for players discovering – or rediscovering – the games.

Learning to create better levels

An analysis of the interviews with a *LBPC* site administrator and a former *LBPC* moderator identified the following level creation related themes: the positive sense of community; the role of the fan community in sharing player-created levels; the importance of feedback; and how the community learns about level creation over time. The following discussion will offer a developing insight into how *LBP* players learn how to create better levels.

With over 9 million community levels published (*LittleBigPlanet*, 2014), an issue faced by *LBP* players on contributing their first level is how their creative work will be found by other players to be played, receive feedback, and perhaps be 'hearted', a method of tagging favourite levels. As Lindberg suggests, part of the function of *LBP* community sites is the sharing of player-created levels. By posting your level on a website, 'You're trying to get other people to play your level ... you're trying to get feedback on your level because that's the "golden ring" ... you want people to play it and give you feedback'. To enable this, to occur there is a team of volunteers who play all the levels posted to a level forum thread on *LBPC*, rate them, and curate a list of the best levels which are published to a level hub profile on lbp.me, the in-game community linked to the Sony Network, as well as in the community spotlight section of *LBPC*. With potentially hundreds of levels posted each week, this is no small feat. An extension of this is The Mole's creative work with the game, which has included creating trailers for YouTube for levels other players had designed, which helped promote exemplars among members of *LBPC* and the broader *LBP* community. These trailers drew thousands of views, creating further exposure for levels specific players had created, and more opportunity for feedback, and opportunity for other players to learn.

The structure for feedback that Lindberg suggests, and models for other members of the *LBPC* site is 'you start off with something good, you hit them with something bad, then you finish with something good ... I also like to list out three good things and three bad things, and then three suggestions on how to fix them'. This method of constructive criticism is useful for encouraging improvement on level design. Learning to provide feedback as a player and as a creator is a skill that Lindberg values highly: 'This is something that I have had to just learn, this is another reason why I think this game is so amazing, it's just a good life lesson to learn these things.'

A cycle of production and documentation drives ongoing improvement to the creative process and Lindberg indicated how those in the *LBPC* space have collectively learned over time. When describing what makes a bad community level design, Lindberg explained:

It's a level where somebody has failed to incorporate feedback in some way from prior experience or pay attention to what's going on. If you say look, people don't like it when you use just plain wood materials and have no obstacles. Nobody does that anymore because everybody's figured out that that's terrible and then people will publish with that and it's like 'I'm sorry, I don't know what to tell you, if you've been paying any attention at all then you'll notice that nobody does that because it's a bad idea.' That sort of thing, I guess it's just lack of attention to one's surrounding and perhaps what the rest of the community is doing. But that's really a slippery slope because some of the best levels I've ever played have no focus at all on what they look like and are just remarkably well choreographed and use plain wood. Generally just people who aren't with it, I suppose. They want to get the benefits of the community without putting the time in and their levels usually reflect that.

Both interviewees had opinions on what makes a bad level design in the *LBPC* community. The Mole expresses this through the creation of 'bad tutorials', video tutorials created by a persona that 'is a really bad creator, but he thinks he's really good'. There is humour behind this media creation, with the bad creator persona creating a video tutorial called 'how to make a dog' that presents him making a cat. 'What not to do' or 'How not to design a level' is a recurrent – and often humorous – theme within the *LBPC* affinity space. With a touch of reverse psychology, discussions around the worst practice may help players strive for overall better practice.

Both Lindberg and The Mole described the positive and nurturing nature of the *LBPC* community behind the feedback, and the *LBP* player community at large, and how it compared to other game player communities. Lindberg explains:

> [LBPC is] very accepting of the new people and the people who come in and go 'hey, I don't understand what to do'. There's very little 'hey, can't you search for yourself, we don't feel like answering this question... it's an interesting community for allowing the newbies in and nurturing them as creators, because a lot of the time the person you brought in learns things that you didn't know, or looks at things you taught them in a different way, then teaches something back. You really need that sort of nurturing environment, which really does exist in the community; it really trends towards a nurturing environment versus a destructive one, which is what many other video games trend towards, destructive environments. Because most of the other video games are, I don't know, competition based, go and blow each other up, whereas *LittleBigPlanet*, okay, fine, you can also blow other people up but that's really not the core.

The Mole echoes this sentiment by suggesting 'other games aren't as community driven as Little Big Planet'. The passion Lindberg and The Mole both share for the *LBPC* community reflects the emphasis placed on community as part of the game design. The nurturing nature of the community helps foster creativity as players have an accepting, authentic audience for their creative works. The creative challenges/

contests posed by the *LBPC* 'Contest Crew' provide ongoing stimulus material for level creation and help players strive for bigger and better creations, inspired by the kudos of winning a community accolade.

Tearaway

Initially released on one of Sony's handheld devices, the PS Vita, *Tearaway* is another Media Molecule title. It unfolds as the story of a messenger, Atoi/Iota, travelling through a papercraft world to deliver a message to you, the player. The player is referred to as You throughout the game, breaking the fourth wall between player and screen. *Tearaway* is a single player game, and a very personal journey is created through the use of the handheld PS Vita. Like *LittleBigPlanet*, *Tearaway* has a handicraft aesthetic, except the digital world is constructed entirely from paper. Every item in the game can be recreated in real life using paper, scissors, and glue. Templates for the papercraft objects created in the game are unlocked as the player progresses through the game levels.

The game makes use of the technical features on the PS Vita – front- and rear-facing cameras, microphone, and a touch pad behind the screen to embed the player in the game, operating within 'hypermedia' (Kattenbelt, 2008) to blur and bridge the boundaries between live and mediated performance.

When the player taps the touch pad with a finger, a digitized finger can be seen on screen intercepting the game world. One of the original ideas in the game development was to make the player's finger the protagonist, however this was discarded as Media Molecule thought resting the PS Vita on a finger might get tiring (James Spafford, personal communication, 2013). The front-facing camera on the device is used to video the player, inserting their portrait into the sun. The rear-facing camera captures the player's surroundings, glimpses of it seen at moments throughout the game. The microphone captures the player's voice to perform as the sun, and provide audio to other characters in the game (e.g. a roar). The audio-visual elements combine to make the player almost godlike, holding the game world in their hands. The affordances of this handheld, portable device create opportunities for a mobile stage of hypermedia performances that occur wherever the player is located.

Creating and sharing

In addition to developing a mediated presence of self in the game narrative, players are regularly prompted to create digitized paper items. They are presented with a green cutting board and a pencil and draw with their finger on the touch screen. Items are then cut out and used in the game, for example, a crown. In *LittleBigPlanet*, the creation and sharing of levels happens in game. In *Tearaway*, artefacts that players create exist in the physical world outside the game and are shared with other players via the official portal, Tearaway.me, or via other channels such as social media or fan-created websites. One of the official channels used by Media Molecule is Pinterest, the social media site used to curate visual pinboards of creative ideas, often craft-based including a plethora of mason jars and bunting. The paper engineering within *Tearaway* has been designed so any game object can be printed out as a template and folded and glued together by players. There is agency in how the paper is decorated: whether coloured in with pencils or printed on patterned stock. Distribution of papercraft templates shows that despite drawing on a handmade aesthetic, the new maker culture is heavily mediatized. An expanded retelling of the *Tearaway* game story, *Tearaway Unfolded* has been released exclusively for the PS4, Sony's next-generation gaming console. At the time of writing this book, Media Molecule were preparing to release another PS4 game, *Dreams*.

Dreams

Media Molecule's third title, and second title for the PS4, expands the creative tools in *LittleBigPlanet* and *Tearaway* to offer a platform where players can design 'games, art, films, music or anything in-between and beyond' (Media Molecule, 2015). Described a way to 'record your dreams', the game *Dreams* implies a broad scope of creativity, limited only by what you can dream. Pre-release presentations and video teasers hinted at how *Dreams* was intended to enable 3D design that escapes 'the tyranny of the polygon' traditionally required to build 3D objects, just as *LittleBigPlanet* did away with code to build game levels (https://youtu.be/31B9SVug1LQ). An early interview with Alex Evans, Media Molecule's technical director, and Mark Healey, the creative director, suggested that the game was a 'deceptively simple' way to share your dreams that will make you feel like a 'legendary artist' (https://youtu.be/9yrejG5rNdY). The game play is centred around creativity and community, echoing *LittleBigPlanet*'s tagline of Play, Create, Share. *Dreams* is part of a new wave of tools combining virtual reality, powerful graphics, and gestures using the PlayStation Move to allow people to explore playfully in the crossover spaces between games, virtual sandboxes, and art tools.

Commodification of creativity

Bundling each new game with a new console drives new purchases and draws players further into Sony's ecosystem of devices. The community created by *LittleBigPlanet* became a ready audience for new products, with many key members of the online communities invited by Media Molecule and Sony to product launches. This collaborative creativity is a relationship between producer and (willing) consumers.

The most recent title, *Dreams*, makes use of the PlayStation Move Controller, a motion-sensing wand with a colour-changing orb that pairs with a camera attached to the console, similar to the Nintendo Wii remote. The Move acts as a sculpting device, assisting players in sketching and building designs on screen. As with other device-based game releases from Media Molecule, it is inevitable that Sony would use the release of *Dreams* not only to push more sales of the PS4 but also to encourage sales of the Move controller.

It is easy to be impassioned by the creative possibilities provided by these games, however it must be acknowledged that there is privilege associated with the tools offered in Media Molecule's suite of games: they are only available to those with access to a PlayStation console; and the internet to access the expanded game-story and collaborative universe. The issue of quality access to digital media technologies in terms of speed and capabilities is the new participation gap in education and technology: 'what these kids [with quality access] can do at home is very different from what kids can do when they only have shared, limited, and public access to computers' (Jenkins and Bertozzi, 2008, p. 190). Buckingham (2007) notes the opportunities provided by the internet to provide a wider, authentic audience for students' work and the importance of group collaboration across digital media. As educators, how can access to these opportunities be enabled to create a level playing field in terms of developing collaborative creative skills and new media literacies? There is certainly room for games and game building in the classroom. Perhaps engagement with commercial titles, as with other forms of popular culture, offers young people a platform to learn, share, and collaborate on creative works.

Conclusion

Media Molecule's titles are interesting artefacts within the new maker culture as they provide tools for the creation of both physical and digital handicraft objects with a low barrier to entry. The creative tools afforded by the games enable collaboration, play, and performance, which are all literacies for the digital age and form part of an active digital arts culture. Fan communities act as another catalyst for the production of materials, and the distribution of knowledge about best practice. These communities play a significant role in the cycle of making, documenting, and re-making. Sony and Media Molecule's engagement with the unofficial online communities creates value and authenticity within those spaces. The success of the game and participation in related communities is due to the successful design of impetus for creativity through both the narrative, and the tools provided. The following chapter will examine how similar relationships might form between cultural institutions and their audiences.

7

The Playable Archive

Visitors, audiences, users, players

This chapter is about the performative and playful challenges that digital arts cultures present to cultural and historical memory institutions, particularly the so-called GLAM sector of galleries, libraries, archives, and museums. These organizations have long filled distinct but overlapping roles as the custodians of cultural, historical, and personal narratives. Their diverse collections reflect 'the many ways in which information [including artistic production] is created, used, valued, preserved, and disposed of by individuals, organizations, and communities in the conduct of business, scholarship, learning, and personal affairs' (Gilliland-Swetland, 2000, p. 4).

While broadly these formal institutions have focused on the physical storage of objects and records since the mid-nineteenth century, this approach has been increasingly challenged by mediatization – first by broadcast mass media (and primarily television) and then by digital networked technologies. John Hartley proposes three successive phases that have shaped cultural institutions of knowledge and relationships to their contents (2012, p. 159):

1 *Modern archives*: buildings such as museums and galleries that focused on objectivity, where *visitors* came to observe the real and the physical in what Hartley calls a mechanical relationship;

2 *Postmodern archives*: time-based and mediated primarily in the form of television broadcasts, and pitched at universal mass *audience*s for intangible but realistic representations; and

3 *Network archives*: online archives like YouTube or more broadly the internet as a platform, organized around the uncertain probability of finding material, with *users* co-creating widely accessible and potentially reusable content.

The impact of the internet and advances in computer technology generally on archival practice can now be seen in at least three key areas. First, there is a trend to digitize the modern and postmodern archives. In the case of GLAM institutions this is partly to make their objective content more searchable and accessible in mediatized form to more people, without requiring a visit to the archive in person or risking damage to fragile items in a physical collection by placing them on public exhibition. This usually means a combination of digital representations of the objects contained in the archive such as scanned documents or photographs of objects, and a related database of metadata that allows searching and linking to the digital repository. In the case of the postmodern archives, there is often also a commercial pressure as some content is seen as valuable and exploitable property that can gain income from new or nostalgic audiences. This fits with the business concept of the Long Tail (Anderson, 2004), in which many niche sales from a large archive of material combine for profit, rather than a few blockbuster hits. Former *Wired* editor-in-chief Chris Anderson identifies how the decision to release an old film or TV series on DVD (or now more likely via online services like iTunes or Netflix) used to be based on detailed estimates of likely demand for a small number of titles, but now

> That model may make sense for the true classics, but it's way too much fuss for everything else. The Long Tail approach, by contrast, is to simply dump huge chunks of the archive onto bare-bones DVDs, without any extras or marketing... In a Long Tail economy, it's more expensive to evaluate than to release. Just do it! (C. Anderson, 2004)

Young people today can readily access huge back catalogues of music, film, TV, books, and other popular media forms from digital archives – some free, some commercial, and some considered illegal in terms of copyright law. Personal data storage devices like hard drives and mobile phones are now ever-growing private and self-curated collections, containing a mix of reproduced and original works. John Potter proposes that curatorship is a form of media production that 'suggests not just writing or producing but also *collecting, distributing, assembling, disassembling,* and *moving* media artifacts and content across different stages' (2012, p. 5). Curatorship now serves as a metaphor for the performative self-representation of identity young people express through collecting, repurposing, and sharing all kinds of digital media across many different social and mobile media platforms.

Secondly, therefore, there is the broader challenge of archiving the volume of digital content now being generated within these personal and networked archives as primary source material that will serve as the future archives of many aspects of contemporary lives and cultures. Much of this content is now being distributed via online applications that are a new form of archives to rival the traditional institutions of the GLAM sector. Who owns or at least makes a claim to share in the intellectual property rights to access and use that content can be a contentious issue. Vast amounts of 'personal' data including text, images, and video that could be considered original literary, artistic, and creative works are uploaded and published by users for free to services like Facebook, Twitter, and Instagram. Hartley has described how the archival paradigm has moved historically from the modern and postmodern archives to the networked archive, which he also calls the 'probability archive', in the sense that it is 'an unreliable archive. You never know what you'll find or not find, and the archive changes constantly. A probability archive is random, complex, uncertain, indeterminate, and evolving as to its contents at any given moment' (Hartley, 2012, p. 167).

Thirdly, as the concept of digital liveness explored in Chapter 4 permeates many lives and arts cultures, there is a growing ability to capture, archive, retrieve, and even remix performances in ways not possible before the development of hypermedia spaces for artistic practice. Digital liveness makes an 'argument to view performance and documentation as interwoven cyclical states' (Read, 2014) arising inherently from the ability to record live streaming of sound, vision, and other performance data and then reuse and re-present that material 'as live' in future. Search for a popular music artist's live performances on YouTube or similar online video archives and you can invariably find official and unofficial (often via audience mobile phones) video recordings listed together. One project called Bootlegger (https://bootlegger.tv) has attempted to tap into the ubiquity of mobile devices to create crowdsourced amateur video crews at live events, enabling artists to coordinate their fans to gather and combine multi-camera footage from different angles. Bootlegger emerges from research exploring adapting professional media workflows to amateur contexts to lower the bar to entry for media production (Schofield, Bartindale, and Wright, 2015), and it illustrates the potential for an ad-hoc co-creative role for audiences in producing digital performance archives.

In addition to using cameras to record still images and video at live events for later viewing, modern audiences are now able to easily live broadcast or 'stream' to the internet via their mobile devices. The intermediality of some online and social media spaces is further enhanced by the built-in ephemerality of this live streaming, with designed time-limited availability of documented content after the live moment. For example, the application Periscope (https://www .periscope.tv) enables live video streaming from mobile devices via the Twitter (https://twitter.com) social media application, and these videos are recorded and stored in the system after the live event but generally only for twenty-four hours. While live streaming from mobile devices has been technically possible for some time, its use was hampered by a lack of social connectivity to allow discovery of the live feeds, which apps like Periscope have addressed by tapping into social media (Stewart and Littau, 2016, p. 313). The application Snapchat (https://www.snapchat.com) allows users to send images or video from mobile phones, and allows senders of content to limit viewing time to as little as one second once the recipient opens the file. This time limitation is often seen as a mechanism designed to promote both a kind of temporal privacy and a sense of living in the moment, though there is also evidence that it can give rise to suspicions in young adults' interpersonal relationships of 'destroying the evidence' of extra-relationship communications (Vaterlaus, Barnett, Roche, and Young, 2016). Snapchat can only be used on a smartphone, and content can only be sent to people connected as 'friends' on the network. The app alerts the sender if the recipient takes a screenshot of the content, and to open and view a file requires the recipient to maintain contact with the screen – theoretically to make it physically harder to take a screenshot. Of course, there are techniques and tools designed to subvert these features and allow capture of any kind of screen content as a more permanent record. Young people must now increasingly deal with the potential for what was intended as 'private' content to become part of the public and searchable probability archives of the internet.

Individual relationships with archives have moved fairly quickly in the past few decades from visitor and audience to user and co-creator. The ability to share text-based content in real time through status updates and microblogs, and then still images and video/audio live feeds has become simpler and less technically demanding for the average user of these services. It is also becoming easier to experience the rich and engaging mediatized content becoming available from both old and new archives. There is a rapid evolution from users to even more active 'players', in the sense of experiencing greater agency in participating with more open, experiential, and embodied ways of both creating and accessing archival content. As the content of archives becomes mediatized as a matter of common practice, either as online digital representations or digital-only content, they become more open to emergent and personalized journeys through the materials, with a potential for a transformation of their engagements with audiences. In addressing the context of education for example, and especially the opportunity for archives to be part of a positive and creative disruption of traditional schooling, Brad Haseman found that current curators and learning designers had some way to go in making the transition from their existing modern archive to a reimagined network archive, highlighting a need to 'move beyond understanding the archive as a reservoir of objects, digitized and ready to be consumed along a predictable pathway of knowledge acquisition. The challenge will be to design open-ended and playful experiences which are inherently unstable and inject emergence and ambiguity into the child's encounter with them' (Haseman, 2014).

Nonetheless, Haseman also identified a number of examples and areas in which at least some GLAM institutions were showing innovative transitions to a new model more aligned with a performative and playful phase in creativity-focused education. This is to be expected as the affordances of intermediality turn a range of physical and digital spaces into new sites for performative learning and cultural understandings.

Archives as hypermedia performance spaces

Many GLAM organizations inevitably maintain some focus on a more traditional role as conservators and curators of 'authentic' objects, records, and other artefacts. To an extent this holds with Walter Benjamin's (1935) suggestion that an original work of art holds an 'aura' of authenticity that mechanical copying cannot replicate, but which it can degrade. Maintaining and protecting the provenance of objects in archival collections is still seen as a specific cultural role of these institutions. However, there is also awareness that digital representations of artwork enhance its 'exhibition' value. Enabling reinterpretation and reuse of these digital artefacts reasserts the originating institution's authority and status as the physical home of the original work. For example, the Rijksmuseum in Amsterdam has received widespread recognition for the Rijks Studio project (https://www.rijksmuseum.nl/en/rijksstudio), which has made high-resolution images of more than 200,000 objects in its collection available on the web. One motivation for creating Rijks Studio was awareness that people could already find poor quality images of many works online, and this was a way to ensure there were high quality representations of the artworks openly available, so that both technical and aesthetic standards were high.

The Rijksmuseum encourages people to download the images and repurpose them as new creative works, in some ways to exploit their exhibition aura, promoting an opportunity to discover the *opportunities* of these masterpieces. In establishing the project, the Rijksmuseum's then General Director Wim Pijbes took the view that 'collage, copy paste, parody, and reproduction belong to the artistic vocabulary of all great artists', and museums should not fear allowing images of publicly significant artworks to be accessible in this way (2015, p. 2). Examples given on the Rijks Studio site show how the images can be used in applied design projects including fabric prints and stickers for clothing, furniture upholstery, wallpaper, vehicle livery, or mobile phone cases. Users are encouraged to upload and share their own designs based on the original artworks, using an online gallery system as part of the Rijks Studio website.

While creating mobile phone cases using the works of Rembrandt or Vermeer might seem to some to tarnish the integrity of the original works, it is this *potential* for any user-driven project to make use of the copyright-free digital images that illustrates the significance of unlocking the Rijksmuseum collection's digital mirror. There are always going to be tensions when the creative and performing arts are used in these interpretive ways, however examining and questioning the reification of assumed authenticity in the objective collection is a critical contribution to understanding these archives. As Anthony Jackson argues in a consideration of the use of drama conventions for interpretive performances in museum settings, 'playfulness and historical accuracy may seem poles apart. But, as most historians themselves are quick to argue, the notion of historical accuracy is itself fraught with problems. And if, in the interests of accessibility and the stirring of curiosity, factual accuracy does sometimes get compromised, this should not in itself be a cause for condemnation' (Jackson, 2000, p. 214).

The Rijks Studio project illustrates that archives do recognize a role for digital technology and the arts to come together in ways that will generate fresh, sharable content. Anyone with access to the website can play with the Rijkmuseum digital archives, which makes more of the collection visible than can be displayed physically at any time to public visitors in Amsterdam. Online visitors are not restricted to the logistical constraints of the Rijksmuseum's exhibition space or the subjective decisions of curators in determining what occupies that space. For institutions seeking to engage and serve young people who are now accustomed to personalized interactions with the Long Tail of probability archives like YouTube, searchable and browsable online archives of art like the Rijks Studio are a logical mix of representation of the 'real' object and the tools to do something with those representations. This includes bringing them into the real world as prints on physical objects, which also sits well within maker cultures. It also adds a social aspect of sharing and comparing designs online, providing a potential audience for the designs. Users are increasingly comfortable with playing a more active role in shaping both their experience in the moment and the documentation and remixing of that experience via social media in a playful, hybrid role of producer and consumer. Henry Jenkins et al. (2013) note that producing a one-size-fits-all model of materials

> imperfectly fits the needs of any given audience. Instead, audience members have to retrofit it to better serve their interests. As material spreads, it gets remade: either literally, through various forms of sampling and remixing, or figuratively, via its insertion into ongoing conversations and across various platforms. This continuous process of repurposing and recirculating is eroding the perceived divides between production and consumption. (Jenkins et al., 2013, p. 27)

Increasingly the content of archives is becoming part of this new ecosystem of spreadable media, in which 'produsers' can also be re-publishers and distributors of material by sharing links and other media, and reviewers or critics via comments and 'likes' or similar voting mechanisms. As discussed in Chapter 4, these daily engagements with digital devices and online media are often quite theatrical in nature.

Partly in response to these pressures and their effects being felt more widely across society, GLAM organizations have moved into a more 'performative turn' in the ways that their archives are exhibited and interpreted. Susan Bennett notes that although imaginative, exciting theatre has historically been cast as an antonym for museum experiences, 'theatres and museums have increasingly become symbolic and actual neighbours, sharing the task of providing entertaining and educational experiences that draw people to a district, a city, a region, and even a nation. As components of the cultural landscape, theatres and museums alike play a role in creating and enacting place-based identity' (Bennett, 2013, p. 3). Similarly, Rachel Morris notes that physical archives like museums are themselves the subjects of creative works like art, film, and literature because artists and writers recognize that

for all that they are full of solid things museums are also slippery, imaginative, conceptual places with an innate pathos and poignancy that comes from the fact that their subject is time and the different journeys that things and people make through time... So fluid is the concept of a museum that you would think that it would slip away through one's fingers – and yet it doesn't because it also has a strong and concrete existence. This double existence in both the physical and the imaginative world and their aura of poignancy means that the museums can be powerful and robust metaphors. (Morris, 2012, p. 9)

This notion of the double existence of archives like museums, present in both objective and subjective realms simultaneously, draws on dramatic conventions such as metaxis and framing discussed earlier in this book. Visitors to physical archives, or the users of online archives, can readily choose to operate in metaphorical as well as literal modes in their engagements with these knowledge institutions and their collections, creating opportunities for playful interpretations and rich learning experiences. One UK audience study found that people were motivated to visit museums for four main purposes – social, intellectual, emotional, and spiritual – and their levels of engagement increased as they moved from social to spiritual (A. McIntyre, 2007, p. 27). Museums however tend to prioritize the intellectual, with their educational and knowledge-building roles such a fundamental aspect of museology. Morris notes that 'whilst most museums are happy to respond to the need to educate their visitors they are in general less comfortable satisfying the other three motivations' (2012, p. 10). That may be beginning to change with greater awareness of the potential for physical and virtual archives to act as hypermedia spaces, in which objects and digital liveness can co-relate to produce mutually affective and transformative experiences. Chiel Kattenbelt's descriptions of intermediality, in which he proclaims that 'personally, I do not speak any longer about arts *and* media, as in, for example, theatre *and* media, but only as media' (2008, p. 21) could equally be applied to designing social, intellectual, emotional, and spiritual experiences with the archives. When viewed *as* media, the archive becomes even more performative and 'playable'.

Further understanding of intermediality is a critical part of the transition from modern and postmodern archives. Increasingly, GLAM institutions are at risk of being outperformed in innovation, popularity, and importance by popular archives operating natively in hypermedia spaces like the web and mobile networks and able to leverage the affordances of more participatory technology such as YouTube, Flickr, and Facebook. One area of cultural practice that illustrates the combination of digital liveness and archives as a site for creative practice is around the form of computer game-based film production known as 'machinima'.

Archives of play:
From speed runs to Twitch TV

Digital liveness emphasizes not only performance in new and mediatized forms but also a greater possibility for recording and replaying it in iterations further and further removed from the original. Clair Read notes creation of a cycle of performance and documentation, 'as streamed performances have the ability to be recorded as live whilst streaming live, mediatization seemingly encourages performances to be documented; by enabling the documents of the recorded or streamed versions of the performance to in turn become working documents themselves, currently (and confusingly) named live streamed "performances"' (Read, 2014).

One example of arts practice that illustrates the pairing of performance and documentation in digital liveness is that of machinima, a televisual animation genre that emerged from demonstrations of elite game play in early 3D first-person computer games such as *DOOM* released by US developer id Software in the early 1990s. Machinima now commonly describes this hybrid of digital performance and televisual art form grounded in the use of video game software. The term can be seen as a mashup of early attempts to describe the form such as 'machine cinema' or 'machine animation' (Newman, 2008, p. 144). Video game developers have produced increasingly sophisticated real-time graphically rendered virtual worlds for their products, and some players and artists have found ways to take advantage of these procedural tools to create animated movies of their own.

Leading video game historian Henry Lowood emphasizes that 'machinima is at its heart not only about performance but also about documentation: (1) it is founded on technologies of capture through which in-game assets and performances are redeployed and reworked, and (2) it creates historical documentation that captures aspects of the spaces, events, and activities through the lens of the player's view of the game world' (Lowood, 2011, p. 4). The extensive online archives of machinima to be found in YouTube or curated collections (e.g. https://archive.org/details/machinima) illustrate how the practice relies on being able to document and repurpose the in-game performances created in these hypermedia spaces.

In its early forms, machinima relied on the game engine to both record and play back this captured performance. The *DOOM* game engine gave rise to prototypical archives of live in-game performance that served as demonstrations ('demos') of elite or unique gameplay. These demo files could be distributed and then replayed by other players with their own copy of *DOOM*, creating a player community that operated around a growing context for spectatorship, and in turn 'the result was nothing less than the metamorphosis of the player into a performer' (Lowood, 2006, p. 30).

These game demos challenge the notion that performance cannot be saved, recorded, and shared. In *DOOM* the player's in-game performance was captured – digitally recorded – as sequences of interface input (e.g. keyboard and mouse commands), and stored as binary data. If the player moved their character forward and fired a weapon, the character's changing coordinates in the 3D game space and the player's command actions were recorded and stored as data in the demo file. When the demo file was downloaded from an archive and replayed, the software engine drew on the data to replicate the same conditions and actions, manipulating the game world and the characters to replay the action according to the stored parameters. Unlike watching a movie of the action, replaying the demo was more akin to re-experiencing the game, in the game engine, through the eyes of the original player. In this way, machinima has its roots as a metagame experience driven by fan culture, one example of which continues in the form of 'speed runs' in which players seek to record the fastest completion of a game or game level. These serve an instructional purpose, with players able to experience a game through the eyes of an elite or highly creative player, but they are also vastly entertaining to watch for the skills and creative problem-solving displayed by the speed runner. There are archives of speed runs that are continually updated with new game titles (e.g. the Speed Demo Archives at http://speeddemosarchive.com/), and fans hold regular speed run events that take place before live and online audiences.

In time, the machinima community moved from these demo files that needed to be replayed in the proprietary game engines, and developed tools to convert them into movie files. This allowed the fan base to expand attention beyond pure gameplay and to consider post-recording production decisions such as alternative and external camera positions (called 'recamming'). All machinima inherently require real-time rendering of the original source content within the game software, including the original performance, whatever the level of post-production included in the final product. The key to machinima is this creative use of the game engine that procedurally generates the graphics, physics, settings, props, effects, lighting, avatars, camera views, and sounds of the game. On-screen content changes in response to player input, and in some games there may be multiple players interacting in and with the same virtual space simultaneously. This sense of digital liveness, both in terms of the game world being generated on-the-fly and the procedural responsiveness to human player/performers, is what makes machinima different to pre-rendered digital animation. Machinima's use of the software engine to generate the on-screen content in real time is another example of intermediality. The procedural production affordances of the computer create a hypermedia space that combines game media, performance, post-production elements such as video and sound editing, and digital distribution through online publishing channels.

Game engines are generally not designed for this form of moviemaking, though some contain tools that make it possible. Game designers themselves often wish to produce machinima as part of the testing and promotion of their product. Machinima films fit within a model of fan culture and often pay homage to, or build upon, the existing storylines and characters presented in the game titles. It is reasonable to assume that most machinima makers are typically fans/players of the games they use to create their works, and even if a machinima maker chooses to buy a particular game title as a production platform rather than as a game, inevitably a certain amount of deep gameplay and skill development will be needed in the beginning to understand and leverage its machinima capabilities. The different affordances of the game engines adopted for machinima are reflected in the different types of performances made possible, as evident in machinima archives. Cameron and Carroll (2011) have noted that some games allow relatively easy puppet-like control over on-screen performances, some are preferred for the combinations of scripted bot performances and human-controlled avatars they allow, and some titles deliberately include machinima-like capture and playback tools as part of the game experience. Just as a film director might prefer to work with certain equipment or particular crew members, machinima producers also have preferred games.

Machinima is also now influenced by the broader real-time performance possibilities created by live streaming. In the game community one popular source of live game play content is Twitch TV (https://www.twitch.tv/), a service owned by Amazon. Twitch combines televisual and social media aspects, with a channel producer or 'streamer' able to broadcast combinations of live feeds from within a game environment overlaid with audio (and usually video) commentary as they participate as a player. Audience members or 'followers' can engage with the streamer through text commentary feeds, and the interplay and responses can in turn be reflected in game actions or the live commentary. Some followers may also be nominated as moderators in a stream, taking on additional administrative work. While there are major game tournaments broadcast through Twitch, with their own expert commentary teams and presentation styles that would be familiar to viewers of live sports broadcast on television, generally Twitch streams are from single player/presenters. Streamers often post extensive equipment lists that would rival a small television production company (all with convenient links to purchase the same equipment via the Amazon online store), thus promoting their technical expertise and helping to guide other potential producers towards establishing their own Twitch streams.

The streams function as communities with a dual emphasis on the content and participation. The streamer may generate and control the high-fidelity broadcast content, but the followers and moderators can access and contribute the low-fidelity chat (Hamilton, Garretson, and Kerne, 2014, p. 1316). The stream is both an online fan community and a hypermedia space where multimodal creation of audio, video, game play, and text takes place. While the chat might be ephemeral, Twitch does generate an archive of the broadcast stream that it calls a Video on Demand (VOD) archive. Twitch encourages streamers to use the VOD service as a marketing tool for their streams, and automatically records and stores the VOD content for a period of time before deletion. Streamers can also produce shorter highlight clips from the default VOD recordings, and these are kept indefinitely. Thus Twitch facilitates both short-term archiving of the streams by default, and encourages production of self-curated highlights that form the more permanent archive. In this sense there is a return to the earlier days of machinima history, where the content being captured was focused on expert game play and demos rather than cinematic narratives. The VOD capabilities of services like Twitch illustrate a means of documenting and curating live, co-created digital performances combining commentary, game play, and chat.

Whatever form it takes, the growing online archives of machinima will be a record of game performance, rather than game play or the game industry. While there are also efforts to document game productions and preserve video game hardware and software, the machinima archives will document performances in the hypermedia spaces defined by digital games, and will be 'not a repository devoted to the history of game design, technology, or business – events that transpired outside of game worlds – but to the history of what players have done *inside* digital games' (Lowood, 2009).

Towards playable archives

Digital media technologies and the arts practices emerging from them challenge traditional views of the archive, especially the weight of authority or aura of authenticity GLAM institutions enact through preservation and control of access to materials. Increasingly, modern and postmodern collections are adding or creating new digital representational collections, for example the Routledge Performance Archive (https://www.routledgeperformancearchive.com), increasing the possibilities for opening access and allowing users to find new ways of searching, viewing, experiencing, and reusing the archive content. The 'probability archives' powered by the internet as a source of both original and existing materials add further possibilities and challenges. Whether born from transforming existing archives or emerging organically from network platforms, these digital archives are hypermedia spaces that hold the potential for performative, playful, and affective engagements with user/players. The archives themselves can be portals to 'playable' spaces, just as a theatre stage, heritage sites, or physical GLAM space can be used for drama, games, and other creative and educational activities.

One example of research around more performative – and overtly playable – interactions with archival content is the work described in Chapter 5 around *Beowulf* and other canonical texts held by the British Library. This project explored how to engage with these texts to connect library spaces with digital game spaces. *Beowulf* was considered a good choice as subject for three reasons (Burn, 2015). First, the only copy of the *Beowulf* manuscript was already the subject of a leading example of the digitization of rare and fragile archival content, in the form of the Electronic Beowulf project (http://ebeowulf.uky.edu/), which combines high-resolution images of the original text with translations and a number of tools to assist in scholarly study of the text. The Beowulf game project extended the British Library's history of digital adaptation of the poem into forms of game narrative and dramatic action. Secondly, the *Beowulf* poem belongs to a narrative tradition that has been one of the major influences on video game design, via a lineage that includes sword and sorcery fantasy tales, monsters, heroes, weapons, and settings drawn from Old English and Scandinavian sagas and the work of author/scholars like J.R.R. Tolkien. For the Anglo-Saxon scholars involved in the project, the adaptation of *Beowulf* into a video game provided new techniques for reinterpreting the poem, and connecting it to contemporary popular cultural contexts. Thirdly, *Beowulf* is a popular text in translation for secondary schools at Key Stage 3 in the UK, and the use of games and drama in the project enabled multimodal approaches to learning that could assist students to make connections between an archaic form of narrative and their own contemporary gaming cultures.

One of the key elements of that project is the development and use of *Missionmaker: Beowulf*, video game design software that enables the creation of 3D first-person games using characters and settings matched to the Anglo-Saxon text of *Beowulf*. A previous version of Missionmaker had already been used to enable young people to design game experiences around Shakespeare's *Macbeth*, in a collaborative project with Shakespeare's Globe Theatre in London. The Globe is an example of a blend of theatre and history, and serves as a major tourist, education, and entertainment site in the city. Creating a game evokes a number of decisions that might not be triggered by more traditional approaches to the text. For example, young people creating games in *Missionmaker: Beowulf* needed to consider the narrative in terms of designing puzzles to be solved by the player, or whether characters encountered in the game will respond as allies, enemies, or neutrals according to sets of conditional rules. As the software gives them the authority as game designers to transform literary properties into game narratives, *Missionmaker: Beowulf* allows users to choose to engage with elements of the text authentically, or they can explore new possibilities.

Digital archives are well positioned to be 'living' archives of performance that can expand to capture and re-present more content as desired. This makes them well suited to the cycle of performance and documentation that now marks the era of digital liveness and intermediality. This effect is evident not just in digital arts cultures, but also in traditional performing arts disciplines that may once have been considered immune to the transformative influences of digital media on aesthetics and practice. For example, Whatley notes that a digital archive of dance like Siobhan

Davies RePlay (http://www.siobhandaviesreplay.com) is not only a collection of those traces left behind (often moving images) of what is generally considered to be an ephemeral and embodied art form, but 'in the same way that a dance work only really exists in the moment that it meets the audience, the digital archive similarly exists only when it is made public, can be retrieved online, and can be found by the user' (Whatley, 2013, p. 172). This is an example of Hartley's meaning of the term 'probability archive', and it emphasizes that the uncertainty of finding and using the digital material can preserve the intangibility of the original content, such as a dance performance. Digital archives are inherently procedural and rely on live interactions with users to generate representations of the data: 'much like live performance, it both exists and does not exist' (Whatley, 2013, p. 165).

The procedural powers of digital media lend great affordances to capturing, replaying, manipulating, and sharing the content of archives in new and exciting – playful – ways. Intermediality comes into effect, turning the networked archive into a hypermedia space for multimodal reconstruction of narratives. These new playable archives will contain not just information about the past, but the potential for future content as well through user/player co-creation and the generation of even more data for the archive. Derrida and Prenowitz's (1995) notion of the 'unknowable weight' of the archive describes both the 'weightlessness' of a digital archive that does not require physical storage for materials and the sense that the possibility of generating and receiving new digital content by interacting with user/players means the archive content is never static and never fully knowable.

Dark play ... risks and responsibilities for playable archives

As outlined in Chapter 1, although playfulness as part of the drama framework is used in this book for viewing digital arts cultures, it is not assumed that all play is co-operative and with universally positive intent. 'Dark play' (Schechner, 2002) is one of the potential risks associated with the development of more playable archives, in which some participants might consciously or subconsciously subvert the playful frame. Many GLAM organizations are high-profile cultural icons and significant tourist sites, and so possible reputational and ethical risks that might impact on an institution's 'brand' and credibility are not taken lightly. While the term 'play' might evoke a sense of good natured exploration and healthy fun it must be recognized that, like many human social activities, play can represent a spectrum of behaviours, and mean different things to different people.

The increased use of online and mobile technologies to create these new and exciting ways to engage with audiences does also lead to questions about privileging access to those that can afford it. Also, and this is related to problems with 'dark play' in some respects, there can be difficulties around representation of diverse views and opinions in online spaces. Some online cultures are seen as being over-represented by certain demographic groups, which can lead to issues of exclusion or worse. This is sometimes reflected in the weight given to material evidence in traditional archives, which as Anna Farthing has noted 'means that well-documented characters from history are represented in considerable detail, as protagonists, while the illiterate, undocumented, unrepresented masses are sketched in like a chorus of supporting artists' (2009, p. 100). Although talking about drama in museums, Farthing's observations could easily apply to the design of digital interactions with archive content as well.

In the enthusiasm for more participatory and co-creative opportunities afforded by digital media there should also be recognition of the risks associated with user-generated content and personal identity. Researcher danah boyd notes one of the hidden risks of the 'networked public' spaces inhabited by young people, where the persistence and searchability of digital content in the networked archives increases the probability that material may be captured, stored, searched, retrieved, and re-published in other contexts (2007). Game demos and speed runs are also a form of personal data footprint that people leave behind. In one well-known early example, it is still possible to find and download *DOOM 2* demo files created by the expert player known as NoSkill, who in real life was American Christopher Crosby. NoSkill died in a vehicle accident in late 2001; however, it is possible to view the completion of game maps from 1995 and 1996. It can be eerily like inhabiting 'the shell of the ghosts of players' (Lowood, 2006) – seeing the game experience through their eyes.

Conclusion

As seen throughout this book, the cultural landscape is increasingly both mediatized and enacted at many personal levels through daily engagements with technologies and devices. Many people now carry around in their smartphones, for example, personal archives of relationships, productions, and encounters. Helen Nicholson argues that all 'archives, however personal, partial or incomplete, allow us to both re-construct and re-embody the images and narratives of the past, and in ways that allow for new forms of cultural and artistic expression' (2012). This is a new form of self-curatorship that John Potter argues is a form of media literacy that encompasses a range of collecting, producing, and sharing skills in highly performative modes across multiple platforms (2012). Although the two domains of performance and archive are often understood as opposed to each other with 'one representing the fleeting and ephemeral, the other signifying stability and permanence' (Bennett, 2013, p. 9), those ontologies have become less clear-cut in recent years. In the liquid postnormal world infused with digital liveness the archives are no longer just about what objects can be physically stored, just as performance is not bound by traditional notions of theatre and social ritual. While 'theatre's ephemerality as exhibition' (Bennett, 2013, p. 5) is often seen as making it difficult if not impossible to document or archive, the increased mediatization of live performance, for example, the emergence of live streaming as part of the technological repertoire of hypermedia, introduces new possibilities for archiving and re-presenting performance.

The challenge is that while museum audiences may recognize and understand the imaginative, playful, and poignant powers of the archives they visit and engage with, not all of these institutions are yet willing or able to tap into those desires for affective participation with the archive content. However, the performative turn in archives is now being shaped by the transformative powers of networked digital technologies towards the playable archive.

8

Coding and Creativity

One of the core themes of this book is that a purposeful mashup of disciplines such as drama, learning, media, and technology can and does produce hybrid creative and artistic responses to the world, and in ways more powerfully transformative than the individual disciplines themselves. Such an interdisciplinary approach between performing arts and essentially science-based fields like computer engineering does not always come easily in formal education settings such as schools. This is not a new situation born out of digital media; for example, English chemist and novelist C.P. Snow's famous 1959 Rede Lecture despaired at what he saw as a growing chasm with arts and humanities on one side and the sciences on the other, since 'the clashing point of two subjects, two disciplines, two cultures – of two galaxies, so far as that goes – ought to produce creative chances. In the history of mental activity that has been where some of the breakthroughs came' (1961, p. 17). Disparities between art and science continues to be a source of tension within formal education despite growing evidence that blending of the Science, Technology, Engineering, and Mathematics (STEM) subjects with the

Arts (to produce STEAM) produces more creative problem-solving approaches in both the arts and sciences.

As is often the case when merging new technologies into existing practices, there is no one-size-fits-all when it comes to blending arts and digital media. Nicholas Negroponte in his book *Being Digital* (1995) observed that when computers and art first meet, the signature of the machine can sometimes be too strong and the 'technology can be like a jalapeño pepper in a French sauce. The flavor of the computer can drown the subtler signals of the art' (1995, p. 223). In the excitement of exploring the possibilities of new technologies like 3D printing, the Internet of Things, visual coding, virtual reality and 360-degree videos, drones, and robotics, it is not surprising that activities and resources will focus on mastering the technical rather than artistic aspects, at least in the early stages. Negroponte famously described the emerging digital revolution as a shift from atoms to bits, for example, a shift from the atoms of physical media like a newspaper to a digital equivalent consisting of data. Once creative work becomes about bits, the artistic outputs are inherently manipulable, remixable, and shareable. However, as Negroponte noted at that time and as observed at different moments in this book, some arts are initially more at home in hypermedia spaces than others. For example, musical performance has found ready affordances and opportunities in digital media that were not so readily accessible by dance and live drama. The documentary power of digital media and the subsequent creation of performance archives is one consequence of intermediality. Interestingly, the Maker Movement and related Digital Do-It-Yourself cultures show a shift towards hybrid creative practices in which bits and atoms converge. For example, 3D printing is a process of taking the bits of digital design files and printing out the atoms in a physical object.

Whether working in digital or hybrid arts, it is clear that the basic building blocks of creativity are made from computer code, whether it is made visible and accessible to users or not. In broad terms, 'digital fluency requires not just the ability to chat, browse, and interact but also the ability to design, create, and invent with new media ... . To do so, you need to learn some type of programming' (Resnick et al., 2009). Learning coding or programming is an important step, but learning creativity *through* coding is the path to wider innovation with many forms of digital technology. This chapter considers the understanding and application of programming languages – which here is collapsed into the term 'coding' – as a way of generating creative and artistic work that can converge with physical objects and live performance in hypermedia spaces.

Thinking about computational thinking

One of the more immediate outcomes of the STEAM trend in both formal and informal educational settings has been a growth in opportunities for young people to learn computer coding, either as part of the formal school curriculum or via after school code clubs or self-paced online lessons. In the UK, school pupils from ages five through to fourteen now engage with a computing curriculum that includes programming principles. The Australian national curriculum has recently introduced a technologies subject covering a similar age range. In January 2016 the then US President Barack

Obama announced in a weekly address that computer science 'is a basic skill. Right along with the three Rs', to help address the shifting economy and the concerns of educators and business leaders (2016). Many governments around the world have enacted similar changes to the school curriculum. In the developed world at least, the political rhetoric surrounding these changes inevitably points to preparing students to meet the challenges of an increasingly technological world of work, citing concerns for future employment and a need to support innovation in business and industry. However, a problem remains that this push for 'coding across the curriculum' is still conceived primarily as advanced mathematics or a foundation for applied computing to meet the needs of science and employers, rather than also as a springboard for creative and social pursuits within contemporary and equally demanding and innovative digitally based arts cultures.

Some educators do recognize that computer coding is also part of a creative design skill set, enabling young people to exert greater agency and creative skills towards using procedural methods to generate artistic output. To help avoid these new computing curricula being seen as just an assembly line for coders, there has been increased use of the term 'computational thinking' to try and connect the teaching of underlying technical skills with goals of promoting logic, problem-solving, and creativity within the cultural setting of ubiquitous digital media technology. This aligns with notions of computational thinking espoused by researchers such as Seymour Papert, whose work in *Mindstorms: Children, Computers, and Powerful Ideas* argued for constructionism as a learning approach in which a learner constructs a meaningful product with technology (1980). Papert was concerned that computers, although often seen as offering improvements to home and business life, could also be powerful teaching machines with the potential to change thinking and access to knowledge. This meant that the computer could easily be used to programme the learner through what he considered instructionist approaches. Instead, Papert proposed constructionism as a form in which the learners would programme the computer and not the reverse.

Computational thinking is a slippery term, with definitions ranging from instructing students in coding languages to theoretical approaches to logic and creativity. Drawing on Papert's writing about computational thinking, Lorena Barba argues that there is a risk that 'opportunities are missed to empower young people to change their world through computational thinking, and instead simply training them to be better manipulators of code rather than forgers of powerful new ideas' (2016). She argues that although Papert's definition of computational thinking emphasizes developing understanding of the technology through use, by working on projects and solving problems as they arise, this approach is sometimes watered down to coverage of broader theoretical problem-solving. In formal education this is often the result of limited time and resources to devote to project-based learning, and drama educators would be familiar with similar constraints in school settings. There is a problem with making computational thinking too abstract and analytical instead of considering it as a lens for thinking about the world and for taking action, using digital media technology to tackle real problems. Tom Igoe, one of the co-founders of arduino.cc which develops the Arduino prototyping tool described later in this chapter, also argues that programming a computer needs to be seen not just in terms of coding languages (the input) but in terms of what you can do with computers such as generating and manipulating media like images, games, and music (the output). Igoe argues that young people shouldn't just 'learn to program in order to get a good job. Learning to think computationally can give you a new way to understand and describe your world. Learning to program can make you a more expressive person' (Igoe, 2016). Similarly, computer engineer Basel Farag emphasizes that 'coding is not the new literacy', and it is a relatively low-level skill compared to developing computational thinking that encourages problem-solving, creativity, and empowerment for young people making use of digital media technology as a form of self-expression (2016).

Approaches to coding and creativity that focus on learning through producing a working project fit in with views that learning through making and tinkering is a valuable and effective way to combine technical and craft skills with creative expression, problem-solving, and even collaboration and entrepreneurship. Coding can be a trial and error approach that allows participants to learn from their own mistakes, and to benefit from the breakthroughs and examples of others. This includes an element of agency and empowerment for learners and creators that fits with the 'produser' approach to shift from media consumer to media producer, and the sharing of experiences and products. This trend is evident in the recent history of using computer games in educational settings. The so-called serious games movement, partly springing from a games industry looking for new markets in addition to purely entertainment titles, saw resurgent interest in the use of contemporary gaming technology for formal education and training. While there are examples of use of commercial games or specifically designed educational titles serving a need, some educators have realized there is greater value in engaging people in the process of designing their own games. If digital games are a dominant media and art form for the twenty-first century, or the Ludic Century as games designer Eric Zimmerman has suggested, then it is a new digital literacy to enable people to create game products:

> Games alter the very nature of cultural consumption. Music is played by musicians, but most people are not musicians – they listen to music that someone else has made. Games, on the other hand, require active participation. Game design involves systems logic, social psychology, and culture hacking. To play a game deeply is to think more and more like a game designer – to tinker, retro-engineer, and modify a game in order to find new ways to play. As more people play more deeply in the Ludic Century, the lines will become increasingly blurred between game players and game designers. (Zimmerman, 2013)

When it comes to games as learning environments, *making* the game is sometimes a more critical learning activity than *playing* it (Kafai and Burke, 2015). In summarizing research on serious games Yasmin Kafai and Quinn Burke found that much discussion revolved around the use of commercial games in educational contexts, or the design of games to teach standard curricula like math ematics or science, including some projects that use games as part of a 'learn to code' activity. However, there is an emerging field that looks at game design as a learning strategy for addressing a range of topics, such as classic literature. These are part of a 'paradigmatic shift toward constructionist gaming' that is propelled by developments such as the broader initiatives to promote computational thinking, a need to broaden participation in computing, and the wider emergence of the maker or digital do-it-yourself culture among young people (Kafai and Burke, 2015, p. 314). The biggest shift towards game design as a learning approach may come from within the gaming industry and gaming cultures, with many popular games now routinely including level and character creation or modification as a central feature. Examples of the multimodal learning and creative opportunities these products enable in the examination of video games like *LittleBigPlanet* as discussed in Chapter 6 for example, or the examination on machinima and in-game recording of performance in Chapter 7.

A connection with multimodal literacy and computer games also echoes some of the work around affinity spaces already discussed elsewhere in this book. It fits within the concept of connected learning that is built on three foundational aspects of equity, full participation, and social connection (Ito et al., 2013). Connected learning is a valuable set of properties for considering the connections between coding and creativity as part of the wider body of evidence highlighting the importance of art in education. This draws attention to the need to perceive coding as a potentially creative rather than purely functional approach to self-expression through computational thinking and the production of performative forms of digital media. As one possible way forward in researching this area, Ito et al. have identified what they consider as three core properties of connected learning that serve as markers of the powerful creative learning experiences that are possible. Firstly, connected learning experiences leverage the affordances of digital tools to produce a wide variety of mediatized cultural content in experimental, iterative, and active ways.

Secondly, new media enables social and mobile communities that can emerge, grow, and thrive around shared purposes, especially those driven by shared passions and interests. The affinity space concept highlights how the technological tools associated with these spaces creates new possibilities for cross-generational, cross-cultural, and interdisciplinary creativity and learning, often beyond the boundaries of formal educational settings but increasingly those borders are becoming more porous as educators realize the powerful potential. Thirdly, the opening up of access to learning and creative endeavours via open networks built on online and mobile platforms is providing ways to make activities in this space more visible and shareable.

This chapter will return to the concept of computational thinking, and in particular a framework developed by Karen Brennan and Mitchell Resnick (2012), drawing on their experiences as part of the team behind the *Scratch* programming tool. To provide better context for considering that work, the chapter will firstly outline some examples of the tools and technologies that are being used in the pursuit of coding and creativity, starting with *Scratch*.

Scratch

One of the most popular programming tools for use with young people is *Scratch*, developed by MIT Media Lab's Lifelong Kindergarten research group (https://scratch.mit.edu/). The core audience is eight- to sixteen-year-olds, with a peak among twelve-year-olds. *Scratch* is a web-based graphical tool that allows users to snap together graphical programming blocks on the screen to create sequences of computer code to mix together graphics, animations, photos, music, and sound in interactive sequences like games. As shown in Figure 8.1, the programming blocks are designed to only fit together in ways that make syntactical sense from a programming point of view, helping users to learn different types of controls, inputs, outputs, and Boolean logic that are considered a basic building block in computational thinking concepts.

The development team emphasize that the name *Scratch* encourages a sense of tinkering and handcrafting by iteration, similar to the way hip-hop artists make music by 'scratching' vinyl records back and forth on the turntable. It is meant to be a messy

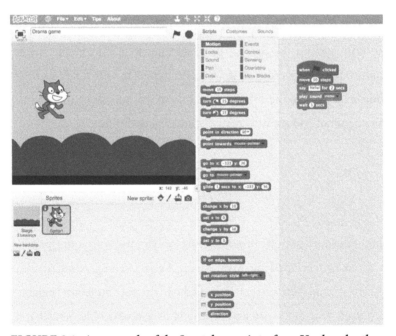

FIGURE 8.1 *An example of the* Scratch *user interface. Used under the Creative Commons Attribution Share-Alike License.*[1]

and highly interactive space for young people to tinker with ideas, and to snap together code, and to see the results immediately by running the code. There are three core design principles for *Scratch*: to make it more tinkerable, more meaningful, and more social than other programming environments. This concept of tinkering is a strong ethos within the broader maker movement. The idea of iterative design and playful experimentation is a direct connection to some of the conventions of drama and role-based work in education. Prototyping is a way of blending existing knowledge and technology to explore what could be – it is a form of exploring the world through a hands-on approach by combining the 'what is' and the 'what if'.

The ability for users to find meaning in their work is part of *Scratch*'s design. The software is intended to allow users to explore many different types of projects according to their needs and interests, such as stories, games, simulations, and animations. It is also possible for individuals to personalize their projects by importing original media elements such as music clips and photos, and to create graphics. In this way *Scratch* provides an opportunity for users to work on projects that are meaningful to them, and therefore they are more likely to get more deeply engaged and explore deeper computational aspects as they work.

Notably, part of the *Scratch* design is the sharing and reuse of projects via a website, and the creation of discussion around *Scratch* programming. This is to generate a social aspect to using the software, which not only helps to generate interest and an outlet for creativity but also provides a support network for users to find help when needed. The website promotes sharing, collaboration, and critique of works. Work on the website is covered by a Creative Commons license to promote this aspect of the site.

Publishing or performing work before an audience is a valuable aspect of many learning approaches, particularly when it comes to arts-based practices. The inclusion of publishing, sharing, and critiquing tools within *Scratch* is a core educational element that helps to make it a valuable tool for arts educators, not just those interested in using it to promote mathematical or computational curricula. The design team have noted a number of emergent behaviours around the social aspect, including a sense of pride when a project is adapted and remixed by others (Resnick et al., 2009). Initially some Scratchers were upset and felt their ideas were being 'stolen'. This led to creation of a design feature to link back to the original project when copies are made, to ensure that credit is given to the originator, and to promote the open source nature of the *Scratch* site and the projects created within it. In this sense *Scratch* is an example of a coding tool that is built from the beginning to allow not just functional programming skills in a specific computer language, but rather to allow young people to tinker and build in creative and collaborative ways.

Minecraft

Minecraft is another popular example of game software that allows significant creation and modification of content by the user as a fundamental mechanic within the game itself. *Minecraft* is considered a sandbox game because players create by building and manipulating objects within the game space. Noted for a low-resolution textured cube aesthetic that is visually reminiscent of early computer games, it has been widely used in formal education settings for a range of learning areas including STEM or STEAM.

Players can choose to play Minecraft in either creative or survival mode. In creative mode the player receives unlimited resources to enable them to enjoy crafting and building within the world. In survival mode the player will encounter problems and monsters that they must overcome by finding and using resources appropriately. Minecraft also accommodates both individual and group play, and an ability to explore maps created by other players.

Minecraft is the focus of third-party manuals and guides (the game itself was notoriously light on instructions and documentation), and has an extensive network of fans and community resources available for novice and expert players. Niemeyer and Gerber (2015) place Minecraft within an ecosystem of metagaming where youth engage in a range of multimodal practices to produce content like walkthrough guides and machinima movies to express both their skills and their passion for the game. The materials they produce are a form of what Thomas Apperly and Catherine Beavis (2011) call a 'paratext', the surrounding materials that frame engagement with *Minecraft* itself but also give meaning to the diverse acts of multimodal creation around it. There are many thousands of hours of video clips showing viewers how to achieve complex crafting sequences within the game. Players have built complex simulations of real-world sites using the tools created within the game. There are numerous Twitch TV channels for dedicated *Minecraft* fans to watch live in-game streams and interact with commentators. Niemeyer and Gerber are interested in the paratexts around *Minecraft* as a possible guide to how creation of these types of texts might be incorporated into formal education settings. Again, framed with the DIY maker culture this highlights the power of engaging students with creative acts that they can control and pursue in terms of their individual passions and shared affinities.

Arduino

Since the days of using cheap computers in classrooms, for example, the 1981 Acorn BBC Micro project (discussed later in this chapter), some have recognized the importance of connecting software coding with manipulation of hardware and objects to do something with the code, and measure its effects in the real world. One example is the creation of Papert's Logo programming language to manipulate small robotic 'turtles', which continue to be used today. Current examples include the Sphero, which is a small robotic ball that can be programmed and manipulated through code using an interface similar to *Scratch*. Another is the programming of small flying or driving drones, such as the Parrot. Commercial toy manufacturers such as Lego have also drawn on the work of Papert and others to create programmable combinations of hardware and software such as the Lego Mindstorms kits.

More recently, and in keeping with a general trend towards utilizing relatively cheap components which can be extended and modded by the addition of modular components or code, there are examples of open source hardware and electronic prototyping that can also be used with block programming tools based on systems like *Scratch*. The Arduino is an example of an open source prototyping platform that uses circuit boards, micro controllers, and other components to allow a wide range of inputs from sensors and actions, and to output a variety of modes such as an LED light, posting content to the web, or activating a switch. Developing out of work at the Ivrea Interaction Design Institute it was intended as a tool for students who lacked a specific background in electronics and programming, but could enable them to build and programme a range of projects such as scientific instruments, robots, or musical devices.

Raspberry Pi

Another hardware platform popular for creative and educational applications is the Raspberry Pi. Developed by the Raspberry Pi Foundation, a registered charity in the UK, the aim was to create low-cost but high-performance computers for fun and education. The Raspberry Pi is often compared with the Acorn BBC Micro project of the 1980s, which aimed to make low-cost computers available for children and young people to use in the early boom of personal computing and education.

The Raspberry Pi hardware is a roughly credit card-sized single motherboard computer featuring components to allow connection to a monitor, screen, power supply, and the internet. A number of accessories have become available for use with the device, including cameras, and an interface with external sensors and equipment including the Arduino. The Raspberry Pi primarily uses open source Linux software to operate, including a version specifically modified for use on the device.

The appeal of the Raspberry Pi in arts and education settings is partly its stripped bare hardware aesthetic. Contemporary personal digital devices like smartphones, tablets, and personal computers are increasingly designed as 'black boxes' that do not require or allow users to tinker with the hardware components. The Raspberry Pi and similar devices are clearly intended to allow experimentation and modification, and users are required to plug in accessories and cables to ports on the motherboard to add basic functionality. The intention is not to turn every user into a computer engineer, for as Clive Beale, director of educational development at the Raspberry Pi Foundation, argues: 'We don't teach music in school to make everyone a concert violinist … what we're saying is, "this is how these things work, it's good for everyone to understand the basics of how these things work. And by the way, you might be really good at it"' (Gardiner, 2014).

BBC Micro

The BBC Micro was a series of computers and other hardware built by the Acorn Computer company for the British Broadcasting Corporation, as parts of the BBC Computer Literacy Project. The intention was to build and distribute microcomputers that could be used to complete projects that would be discussed and broadcast in a BBC TV program. It is estimated that at one point about 80 per cent of British schools had a BBC Micro. The next generation of the BBC Micro, the micro:bit, was released in 2015 and was given to every school child in Year 7 or equivalent (age 11 or 12) for free, whereas the earlier computer cost hundreds of pounds (Kelion, 2015). Students can code using a number of languages available via the BBC micro:bit website (microbit.co.uk), test the code, then write the code (or 'flash' it) onto the micro:bit via USB. Students can also send their code to the micro:bit from the micro:bit smartphone app using Bluetooth. The BBC micro:bit can be connected to other units such as the Raspberry Pi or Arduino to expand its computing power. Head of BBC Learning, Sinead Rocks, suggests: 'We happily give children paint brushes when they're young, with no experience – it should be exactly the same with technology' (BBC, 2015).

Computational thinking concepts

As mentioned earlier, Karen Brennan and Mitchell Resnick (2012) have drawn on their work with the *Scratch* team to draft a framework for considering computational thinking. They distinguish between three elements: computational concepts, practices, and perspectives. Those can be examined in more detail in terms of their connection to creative and performative use of digital media.

Brennan and Resnick identify seven common programming concepts that are common to many coding languages, but which can transfer to other contexts. They identify sequences, which are the individual steps or instructions that specify the behaviour or action to be produced when the code is run. Loops are a repetitive mechanism for running the same sequence multiple times. Events are when one thing causes another thing to happen, which is an essential concept in creating interactive media. Parallelism describes an ability to run different sequences of instructions happening at the same time, which is now a part of most modern computer programming languages. Conditionals, the ability for decisions to be made based on certain conditions to support expression of multiple outcomes, are another key interactive media concept. Operators enable the coder to perform numeric and text manipulations. Data involves storing, retrieving, and updating values, for example keeping score in a game.

Computational thinking practices

Brennan and Resnick interviewed and observed young designers and noted that framing computational thinking around concepts alone would not be a complete representation of their learning and participation. In observing design practices of young people they identified four main sets of practices: being incremental and iterative, testing and debugging, reusing and remixing, and abstracting and modularizing (2012, p. 7). These sets of practices can translate to similar activities in a variety of arts-based creative processes, including some forms of improvised performance and drama. Incremental and iterative approaches to a project fit with devised and sometimes messy projects to be found in theatre rehearsals and drama work. Small parts of a plan or design might be prototyped and tested and the design adapted based on that experience. It might occur in small stages over time, rather than as an intensive period of work. Testing and debugging can involve a trial and error approach to critical problem-solving, or it might be a structured approach, for example, a checklist of things to test. This can also be where users draw upon the skills, knowledge, and experiences of others in the community to help identify and solve problems. Reusing and remixing is considered a key part of digital arts cultures, and reflects the intermediality of much of this creative work as it might draw upon and mashup elements or existing work in new and interesting ways. Building upon the work of others can be seen as a skill in itself, as it requires some discernment as to which projects provide the best launching point for a new project. Abstracting and modularizing is the building of something large by putting together collections of smaller parts. These can all be seen as a core practice in a range of design and problem-solving concepts.

Computational thinking perspectives

In addition to identifying concepts and practices, Brennan and Resnick (2012) found that young designers working with *Scratch* would talk about an evolving understanding of themselves, which could describe a shift in their perspective towards computational thinking. Expressing ideas through interactive media played a central role, as it marks a shift from simply seeing media as something to be consumed towards something that can be designed for self-expression. They also found that users formed new perspectives on connecting with others as part of the work on computational design using *Scratch*. This was seen as an opportunity for 'access' to people both as sources of knowledge and advice but also as collaborators and, significantly, as an audience for the work being produced. Finally, Brennan and Resnick found that users developed a questioning perspective that encouraged them to not simply accept obvious design affordances and limitations in the computational systems, and to question why the technology worked the way it did. This can help to make a more general connection between young people and the technology they see around them in the world, and to not take for granted that it just works or that it works in their best interests.

Conclusion

This chapter has examined some examples of combining coding and creativity in ways that often teach basic computational skills and even particular programming languages, but also leave the door open for more individual and creative explorations of what can be done, what problems can be solved, and what can be manipulated and changed in the real world. Many of the tools considered in this chapter tap into digital media in both software and hardware and make use of social and connected experiences that are enabled largely through networked technologies. They are part of the hands-on maker movement that emphasizes the pursuit of experiential and meaningful projects that invite collaboration, sharing, critiquing, and remixing.

The next chapter looks at combinations of play, performance, and technology in built environments like cities and towns. In a form of digital citizenship, people are increasingly being encouraged to explore applications of coding and creativity to both reclaim and transform urban spaces, as well as transform the lives of the citizens that live in them.

9

The Playable City

In mid-2016, many streets and parks were filled with people playing a game that has prompted questions about the occupation of urban spaces, and even what spaces are appropriate for play. That game was *Pokémon Go* (Niantic, 2016), a highly popular location-based augmented reality game played on a mobile phone with the aim of catching – and battling – animated creatures called Pokémon ('pocket monsters'). Not all of those who encountered *Pokémon Go* players were pleased to see them. As Gallagher and Neelands noted in 2011, 'The city is contested space; urban, a contested term. The city, like a play, is a space where everything means more than one thing. It is an objective thought and a subjective experience, a charged and symbolic thing, as well as a real, material, lived, reality' (p. 152). This contested space offers considerable scope for play and creativity. Bogost proposes that it is precisely because cities are real spaces with real people going about their lives that these bounded and bordered spaces can be reimagined and reconfigured in ways that seem fun or fictional (2016, p. 88). Some of the activities and technologies described in this chapter illustrate ways that play and creativity are happening in the urban environment, from forms of pervasive games to do-it-yourself interventions, and even the repurposing of government data.

Pokémon Go and play in urban spaces

Pokémon ('pocket monsters') are animated creatures that trainers (the players) capture and train to battle against each other. The Pokémon property has been franchised for more than twenty years and spans media such as video games, board games, trading cards, toys, an animated television series, and films. *Pokémon Go* is the first smartphone augmented reality game of the franchise, and requires players to traverse the streets to catch Pokémon, which can be spotted by viewing the world around them through their mobile phone screen and camera. To describe the game briefly in its current form: after creating an in-game avatar, a map is generated of a player's surrounding environment that contains game elements called Pokéstops, a place corresponding to a physical location in the real world, where they can collect digital game objects on their phones such as Pokéballs (an in-game tool used to capture Pokémon), Pokémon eggs, and potions and revives (in-game tools used to nurture a Pokémon's health). The map also displays Pokégyms, again corresponding to a physical location, where players can go to participate in game-based battles with other players. These game elements are usually located at public points of interest such as parks, art installations, or memorials. The map-based data are drawn from a previous augmented reality and location-based game, *Ingress* (Niantic, 2012), where players battle in one of two factions to gain control of landmarks which are then linked together to form part of a larger territory for their faction. Part of the gameplay included players entering information about landmarks using the *Ingress* app. These types of games are called pervasive games, a form of play that moves gaming away from the fixed screen and back into the physical world (Montola, Stenros, and Waern, 2009).

Pokémon Go has been lauded for encouraging physical activity more than most video games (e.g. Pokémon eggs could only be hatched after a user had walked several kilometres – and this could not be readily cheated by using a vehicle, as the GPS tracking is set to capture movement at walking speed). It is also claimed that the game has encouraged rediscovery of local environments and helped to change ideas about the use of public spaces:

> Pokémon Go extends the concept of property ownership to its geo-located virtual turf. A physical public space that it designates a Pokegym – such as the Sydney Opera House – can 'belong' in game to one of three teams... at a deeper level, allowing players to collectively 'own' a site's virtual territory drives affiliations with some physical locations – such as those Pokegyms held by a player's own team – over others. (Abboud, 2016)

Discourse about *Pokémon Go* includes a questioning of which spaces are appropriate for incorporating into augmented reality gameplay. Statements from prominent memorial sites around the world such as the Australian War Memorial, the National Holocaust Museum in Washington, DC (USA), and Auschwitz (Poland) all discouraged visitors from using the app at those sites (Bromwich, 2016). Police forces used social media and even electronic road messages to remind players not to trespass on private property or drive a vehicle while in pursuit of Pokémon. At the height of its popularity the game also raised safety concerns, as players traversed the urban landscape fixated on their phone screen (sometimes late at night) and it was suggested that the game could be used for organized crime by finding players and leading them into secluded areas where they could be robbed (Stringer, 2016). The game has also drawn large groups of players together in spaces not generally seen as open or playful, or designed to accommodate large crowds, which can also be problematic. In the suburb of Rhodes in Sydney, Australia, crowds of players congregated at a small park that was the intersection of three Pokéstops. The players were blamed in media reports for causing traffic jams, environmental damage, litter, and excessive noise. Players claimed that they were moved on by police and some were issued with fines for loitering (Lemon, 2016). The fact that many of the players are young people taps into community concerns about youths seemingly just 'hanging out'. As Goggin (2017) notes, 'rightly so, users, gamers, researchers, urban planners and designers (especially those in city and municipal government), are thinking about the implications for *Pokémon GO* in terms of rights to the city, and other claims of "spatial justice"' (p. 12). Critics of the game also raised privacy issues, as play is dependent on the provision of specific geo-location-based data. *Pokémon Go* is certainly not the first mobile app or game to make use of augmented reality, or maps, or location-based data, but it was the first to bring it into mainstream popular culture on such an international scale.

Come Out and Play, and Hide and Seek

Come Out and Play is an annual festival held since 2006 where public spaces are filled with games and playful experiences. The festival has been held in New York and San Francisco, and in Amsterdam as part of the European PICNIC creativity and innovation festival in 2007. The festival turns cities into giant playgrounds and is 'a forum for new types of public games and play by bringing together players eager to interact with the world around them and designers producing innovative new games and experiences' (Come Out and Play, 2016).

In recent years, the festival has had multiple parts: Family Day, including games for children and families; Field Day, a collection of new field games and sports; and After Dark, a street-based arcade held in the evening. The games at Come Out and Play have engaging names like *Bacon versus Zombies*, *A Game of Foams*, and *PacManhattan*. Some games use mobile or fixed technology, and some games are based around physical play. In the search for high-resolution graphics and realism in video games, organizers and participants alike suggest that 'the most photorealistic, socially networked 3D environment you can play a game in is real life' (Fleetwood in Krotoski, 2008). The shared social experience of 'city sized fun' helps players rediscover and reclaim the urban spaces around them.

After attending the first Come Out and Play festival in New York in 2006, Alex Fleetwood, an independent producer, produced a spin off event in 2007 at London's South Bank, the Hide and Seek festival. In an interview with *The Guardian* he said, 'our aim was to create an environment where anyone who wanted to could experiment with making games, and where adults were invited to play together in public' (Fleetwood in Krotoski, 2008). From there, he became director of a games studio of the same name, working in the site 'where games meet culture' (Hide and Seek, 2013). A significant urban work developed by Hide and Seek was *99 Tiny Games*, as part of the London 2012 festival that coincided with the 2012 'big' games: the Summer Olympics. *99 Tiny Games* was a collection of small, quick to understand games spread through the city via large stickers in public spaces such as bus stops, parks, and town squares. As described by Hide and Seek at the time, 'players will be tested on everything from wits to creativity to cooperation to determination, all within immediate reach of their home, workplace, or favourite pub' (2012). These site-specific games draw from the popularity of board or parlour games as a place for shared social experiences. *99 Tiny Games* and Come Out and Play move physical games beyond the private lounge room to a more open environment where they become both private and public performance.

Hide and Seek created a spinoff of *99 Tiny Games* via a successful crowdfunding campaign on Kickstarter to develop a Tiny Games iPhone app. Like the *99 Tiny Games* embedded in London, each game in the app has short and simple instructions to facilitate play. The app user is first asked to input their location: at home, on a walk, at a road, at a pub, in a queue, or at work. If you are in a queue, is it a short queue, long queue, or waiting room? Some games can be played alone, or with others. Players might be prompted to use props around them such as magazines, newspapers, or drink coasters. An example of a two-player game in a waiting room might be to each name a colour, and then race to look around the space to find a place or object where those two colours are touching. This simple game gives players a new frame through which to look at the space they are in.

The combination of mobile technology such as the *Tiny Games* app and the physical world creates new forms of play by making it possible to carry a pocketful of games and create a playful experience almost anywhere. As Fleetwood suggests, 'perhaps the designer's role, which was always about creating this sense of a magic circle within the simulated world, will be to broaden that circle to encapsulate whole social spaces' (Fleetwood in Stuart, 2013). Unfortunately the Hide and Seek studio closed at the end of 2013 due to funding issues; however their alumni continue the creative production of different modes of play.

Smart Cities

The phrase 'Smart Cities' has gained momentum in recent years at a policy and government level. Definitions of smart cities have covered a broad scope of attributes including social inclusion, educational attainment, and environmental sustainability (Caragliu, Del Bo, and Nijkamp, 2011; Hollands, 2008), but in practice the term now almost exclusively refers to the use of information and communication technology in urban spaces. It is important for artists and educators to consider the implications and possibilities of these technology-driven changes to urban environments, as this is likely to be the world inhabited by significant percentages of the world's population. The United Nations has forecast that two-thirds of the world's population will be living in cities by the year 2050 (United Nations,

2014). There is an opportunity to shape, reflect on and critique what it means to live, work, and play in these spaces before and as they emerge.

This networked city aligns with the idea of the Internet of Things, where everyday objects are connected to the internet using basic computer chips. The classic example of the Internet of Things is a smart fridge that can notify you when you have run out of milk, and order more milk for you. Examples of other Internet of Things products pitched at home consumers include devices that enable you to have coffee made before you wake up, turn off a lamp after you leave in the morning, and turn on heating before you arrive home in the evening. This transmission of data has been tested over the electricity grid to enable households with 'smart' appliances to use energy more efficiently (Carrington, 2016).

Online shopping behemoth Amazon sells 'Dash' buttons that enable users to order household items over the internet at the press of a single button. The branded button is attached to a single product, for example, washing powder, and can be placed anywhere in the household, such as on a washing machine. The idea is that when an Amazon customer notices they are running low on washing powder, they press the Dash button to order more over the internet without needing to unlock their smartphone or sit at a computer. This simplifies the process of acquiring the new product. The Internet of Things can be searched using Thingful.net, a search engine that can be used to find connected things close to you – for example, a home-made Arduino weather station. A search of things around us while writing this chapter shows Raspberry Pis, personal weather stations, energy metres and carbon footprint calculators, and boats.

Searching Amsterdam, the Netherlands, shows more Raspberry Pis, personal weather stations, and boats; electric cars in a car share scheme; wikibeacons, a crowdsourced map of Bluetooth beacons; and webcams. The concept of a Smart City is built on the principles of the Internet of Things, where bicycle racks, lamp posts, and traffic lights are all networked and are responsive to citizen needs via sensors. Some of these technologies are already here: for example, the bicycle service reporting button on Transport for London's bicycle share scheme. The movement of citizens can be tracked based on their use of public transport, for example, London's Oyster Card, or simply by their mobile phone, a tracking device that many of us carry with us everywhere. It is no surprise that governments are increasingly evaluating ways to use data and technology to manage cities and their citizens more efficiently.

The utopian vision of a smart city cannot be without criticism. Connecting different channels of data together is potentially lucrative for technology companies as they create both software and hardware to sell to local government. *Guardian* journalist Steven Poole asks 'what role will the citizen play? That of unpaid data-clerk, voluntarily contributing information to an urban database that is monetised by private companies?' (Poole, 2014). Similar concerns now pervade many daily engagements with technology, in which people are increasingly asked to provide a range of personal data that can ultimately be commodified in ways they do not readily foresee. It has become a truism in the world of 'free' online services that 'If you are not paying for it, you're not the customer; you're the product being sold'[1] in terms of the information provided willingly or unknowingly through online activities.

How open is 'open'?

Concerns over data mining highlight the complexity of intellectual property, licensing, and privacy issues operating within digital arts cultures. Central to many of the practices described in this book is the concept of 'open sourcing', which is quite common in computer software and prototype digital hardware development. Code and plans are made available with no or only limited restrictions on modification and use. As considered in Chapter 6 for example, commercial game developers have recognized that embracing a player/co-creator model can generate a community of interest around a game franchise like *LittleBigPlanet* by co-opting some of the principles of 'modding' and sharing common in the open source community. The complexity of open licensing is reflected by a recent research project that investigated open education practices in Australian universities. The Open Education Licensing project team produced the Continuum of Openness[2] to illustrate the various combinations of legal, technical, and accessibility levels can range from fully open to closed and highly proprietary.

A common request is that any improvements or changes are kept in the open domain, so that others may continue to benefit from modifications. Open access to data is now a vital aspect of the open source approach. The Open Data Institute in the UK endeavours to make some of the data collected by cities and councils open to the public and suggests that open data is:

- helping government to make public services more efficient;

- driving innovation and economic growth by revealing opportunities for businesses and startups to build new services;

- offering citizens insights into how central and local government works, improving public trust and boosting political engagement; and

- helping government and communities to keep track of local spending and performance. (http://theodi.org/roadmap -uk-2015)

Civic hacking: Making and digital art on an urban scale

Open data sets like those described above have driven the civic hacking movement, where this data is used by grassroots groups of coders and designers to develop apps or websites to help interpret this data to provide transparency, accountability, and improved access to government services. The term hacking is often associated with breaching closed security systems, however, in these communities it is a method of creative problem-solving by repurposing open data. In the UK, mySociety (mysociety.org) is an example of one such group of not-for-profit civic hackers. Their Better Cities work has developed software that enables easier ways to report maintenance issues, ways to show users who their local council or member of parliament is, and maps of transport options based on time rather than distance. They suggest that their work will 'empower citizens, open channels of communication and help planners to make the right decisions' (mySociety, 2016). Some examples of similar organizations are Hack the City (UK, hackthecity.net); Open Culture Data (Netherlands, opencultuurdata.nl); Code for America (codeforamerica.org); and Code for Australia (codeforaustralia.org). Increasingly governments are taking notice of the opportunity to collaborate with civic hacking organizations through events such as GovHack (Australia and New Zealand), UKGovHack (UK), and National Day of Civic Hacking (USA). These events often have a top-down approach, and a large constituency of participants are often public workers or civil servants that are employed in design and technology development roles.

Civic hacking also develops from data that are not available. Born from Internet of Things meetups in Amsterdam and New York City, Air Quality Egg is an Arduino-powered, egg-shaped device that uses an array of sensors to measure and aggregate local air quality data. The group behind the device realized that government weather bureau data are often sampled from distant sensors and broadly applied to regions, and so they developed the Air Quality Egg with the aim of generating a more localized measuring network. Air Quality Egg is an open source project but was also launched on crowdfunding platform Kickstarter, as a way to assess its viability for mass production and distribution. The project was successfully funded, and began creating fully assembled consumer-ready eggs as well as kits for do-it-yourself enthusiasts. Air Quality Egg was included as a highlight in Kickstarter's 2012 year in review (Kickstarter, 2012).

As discussed in Chapter 8, a combination of coding skills and creative thinking skills can empower and enable more participation in a range of new forms of media and culture. A combination of basic coding and data scraping – collecting content found on websites and adding it to a database, for example – can lead to playful interventions in cities. One playful example was the unofficial Twitter account of the Tower Bridge in London, @twrbrdg_itself. No longer active, the account used a software agent or bot to automatically publish tweets when the bridge was opening and closing, and which vessel was passing under it. These data were obtained from the bridge lift schedule on the Tower Bridge website. Using the first person in the structure of tweets, for example, 'I am opening for the HMS Puncher, which is passing up riverstream' personified the bridge and created a sense of playfulness.

Another initiative to inspire civic hacking, and also an example of how technology can be used to model possible future scenarios in a playful way, is *Maker Cities* (makercities.net), the massively multiplayer game created by the Institute for the Future, a not-for-profit research and future-thinking institute in Palo Alto, California. The *Maker Cities* game encourages the submission of ideas 'about how the maker movement might impact society at large: how we learn, govern, eat, and live'. The maker movement is a technology-influenced do-it-yourself culture, enabled by technology that enables anyone to be a designer and fabricator, from open source electronics to 3D printing. Chris Anderson of *Wired* declared makers as the frontrunners of a new industrial revolution (2012).

The online collaborative *Maker Cities* game requires players to

1 **IMAGINE + ADD** Imagine an idea for your city in 2025 and add your future (idea) to the map.

2 **SUPPORT** Other players support your future and you support others' futures. After 2 supports, a future moves to the refine stage.

3 **REFINE** Other players refine your future and you refine others'; after 6 refinement suggestions, a future moves to the make stage.

4   **MAKE** Now anyone can make a prototype (drawing, photo,
    video) and upload it to the game to help bring any future
    to life!

The game also includes weekly challenges to inspire thinking around specific issues such as health. Makerspaces, or Fab[rication] Labs are popping up in cities around the world. These are places where people come together to access work space and tools such as 3D printers, laser cutters, and machining tools (Hirshberg, Dougherty, and Kadanoff, 2016). The maker movement holds public events, called Maker Faires, to showcase projects and share work with the wider community. These events, along with themed hackathons (like the National Day of Civic Hacking) and meetups encourage collaboration and creative problem-solving.

Institute for the Future suggests that gaming is 'the best way to imagine creative responses, shift our thinking, rekindle optimism and move towards action'. The director of Game Research and Development at Institute for the Future is Jane McGonigal, whose work focuses on using games to solve real-world problems. She has designed games that get players to examine global issues like poverty, hunger, and climate change. Games like *Maker Cities* tend to be called serious games, a form of gaming that is not necessarily for entertainment, but for learning, training, or social change. As previous research has shown, serious games share many parallels with models of applied drama that pursue similar purposes. Carroll and Cameron (2009) have outlined the shared features of video game and drama approaches that seek to engage participants with solving real-world problems by placing them in a role as trainee professionals, within real communities of practice. Makerspaces are of interest to educators due to their function in encouraging self-directed learning, and multidisciplinary thinking (Educause, 2013). The *Maker Cities* game aims to harness grassroots creativity and production to commission ideas for future urban living.

The umbrella of maker culture also covers the revival of handmade crafts such as knitting that use social and participatory media to create a broad sense of meaning and shared purpose (Gauntlett, 2011). These extend to interventions in the urban landscape such as guerilla knitting or yarnbombing, where public objects are covered with knitted wool, for example, a telephone box cosy as knitted by Knit the City (knitthecity.com); guerilla gardening, where flowers are planted (without permission) on traffic verges, or vegetables in vacant lots (guerillagardening.org); and projects such as Jan Voormann's Dispatchwork (dispatchwork.info), where Lego is used to patch up cracks in buildings all over the world. Each of these interventions reminds us of the presence of people in urban environments and makes cities brighter places.

Playable Cities

In response to the smart city movement, and around the time that the *MIT Technology Review* proclaimed 2013 as the year of the Internet of Things, Watershed, the creative digital media arts centre in Bristol, UK, developed the Playable City Awards to commission work from across the globe that encourages playful interventions of urban infrastructure. They describe the Playable City as a city where 'people, hospitality and openness are key, enabling residents and visitors to reconfigure and rewrite its services, places and stories' (Watershed, 2013). Encouraging residents and visitors to engage with public spaces in a playful way reconnects them with the city, and engages them personally, rather than treating them as a passive data clerk in a smart city. Since the Playable City project was established in the UK it has now expanded to Recife in Brazil and Tokyo in Japan. The first Playable Cities conference, Making the City Playable, was held in Bristol in 2014 and showcased the Playable City projects, looking towards growing discussion and community around effecting change through play.

The first winner of the Playable City Awards in 2013 was a project titled 'Hello Lamp Post'. Hello Lamp Post combined two ideas: memories created when walking through a city, and making use of the individual identifier codes on lamp posts (or other objects, such as post boxes) for a playful purpose, rather than for maintenance and administration. To play Hello Lamp Post, people needed to find a unique identifier number and send a text message containing it, for example, 'Hello Lamp Post #325' to the Hello Lamp Post phone number. After sending a message, they would receive a message back from the object containing a question which can be responded to, for example, a post box might ask 'Does being here remind you of anything?' Answers were collected and published on the Hello Lamp Post website (http://hellolamppost.co.uk/conversation) including, 'That it's time to go to work not dawdle talking to post boxes', 'Yes, I remember sitting here with friends watching the olympic torch pass by', 'That life is fleeting', 'That I'm hungry', and 'Being near home'. This created an interesting archive of playful interactions and memories with objects including lamp posts, cranes, and telegraph poles.

The awards have since included *Shadowing*, where street lights play back the shadows of passers by at night, recorded with an infrared camera; and Urbanimals, a project that draws on motion sensor/time of flight technology from games (e.g. Xbox Kinect, PlayStation Move) to project interactive creatures into the urban landscape. Finalists in 2016 included Dance Step City, a projection of dance steps onto footpaths to inspire playful movement; Happy Place, a reinterpretation of street signs as experiences activated when a passer-by smiles at them; Im[press]ion, an installation of pin screens that connect strangers in different locations; Make Your Rhythm, where bus stops are turned into musical instruments; Mischievious Footprints, an animation of footprints that documents the movement of people across the city; Paths, a sound and light installation activated by cyclists; Stop, Wait, Dance Walk, where music and lights turn crossing the road into a playful experience; and the Conversing Circuit, an interactive map installed in a bus stop that emits light and sound.

Advances in mobile and wireless technology have made pervasive games an increasingly popular form of play and participatory performance. UK artist group Blast Theory are renowned internationally for their design of 'groundbreaking new forms of performance and interactive art that mixes audiences across the internet, live performance and digital broadcasting' (Blast Theory, 2016). Blast Theory's work is often described as pervasive gaming, but the scope of their urban location-based work could also be described as site-specific role play, or interactive art installations. As noted by Carroll, Anderson, and Cameron in 2006, Blast Theory use technology as a way of reappraising the arts and transforming whole communities. Notable urban-based work from Blast Theory includes: *Can You See Me Now?* (2001), a chase game where street-based players equipped with global positioning system (GPS) devices chase online runners; *Uncle Roy All Around You* (2003), where online and street-based players collaborate to find Uncle Roy; *Rider Spoke* (2007), where participants cycle around a city and find a hiding place to record a message for someone else; *A Machine to See With* (2010), a role-based cinematic crime drama; *I'd Hide You* (2012); and *Too Much Information* (2015), an audio walk around the streets of Manchester.

Blast Theory's work often acts as a cultural counterpoint to many aspects of technology such as surveillance culture. Many of their performances are location-based and use GPS mapping technology. Their role-based pervasive games give participants a new frame through which to view the urban landscape. In many works, strangers are connected through a shared experience both online and within the streets. Some games prompt players to interact with passers-by, for example, by asking for directions. The everyday nature of this interaction protects the passers-by who are not aware that a game is being played. As with other forms of site-specific theatre and play, as Baudrillard (1983) argues, some simulations will always seem real to someone. As discussed by Montola et al. (2009), there are certain people, such as police officers, who do not have the luxury of treating things like games. As fun as these immersive experiences in built environments might be for some, as with applied drama the framing and consideration of both participants and stakeholders needs to be considered.

Conclusion

Combining play, performance, and technology in built environments leads to new forms of creativity, and performative and playful explorations of real and augmented spaces. Citizens are increasingly being encouraged to interact with and act upon different forms of technology to engage with their cities and towns in new ways. This ranges from the development of applications to interpret and make better use of transport services to becoming an active and local monitoring station to improve upon the gathering of air quality data. Connecting grassroots groups of people with similar needs, problems, or interests with relevant services provided by government – often at a local level – can develop interesting partnerships. This is becoming a way of navigating growing urbanization and the smart cities movement. Playful methods to consider and act through the consequences of future scenarios is another way in which citizens can help shape the spaces in which they live and work. Play is a way to both reclaim and transform urban spaces, as well as transform the lives of the citizens that live in them.

10

Making Research in Intermedial Spaces

The reflections throughout this book on the role of research in intermedial spaces are influenced by the growing need to design research projects and methodologies that fit around the distinct practices and cultures within these spaces. One of the most prominent movements to make practical these aspirations is the Digital Humanities movement. While notoriously difficult to define (Gardiner and Musto, 2015), it features collaboration that is frequently international, and the leveraging of computer-based technologies for research in the humanities. While there are specific features of research into intermediality that are drawn out in this chapter, the inquiry in these spaces could easily fit under the digital humanities umbrella.

Like much contemporary research, this kind of inquiry is by its very nature interdisciplinary, and it consequently attracts all the challenges

This chapter in part revisits a discussion relating to research in Michael Anderson's *Masterclass in Drama Education: Transforming Teaching and Learning* published by Continuum in 2012. The discussion of research approaches in this chapter focuses more directly on intermediality.

and opportunities of that form of research. Social innovation through researching opportunities for enhanced learning and civic engagement is a key role of research. Not only is this because it is intellectually intriguing or academically satisfying but also because there is a sense that the forces of postnormality need to be addressed. Chaos, complexity, and contradiction (Sardar, 2010) will reshape the nature and possibilities of learning and artistic practice. As with most changes in communities, there is the likelihood that commerce and other external interests will take the lead if educators and practitioners cannot. If that reshaping process is to be democratic, inclusive, and ethical, it is worth considering how to design research that leads to outcomes that make a difference for diverse communities, rather than leaving it to 'the market' to determine priorities and solutions.

This chapter will examine the realities of doing research that relates to live performance, mediatization, and education. It will consider some models and methodologies that are suited to interdisciplinary research. These will be accompanied by some practical examples where practitioners are working in partnership with researchers to deliver evidence-based understandings to extend and support development in this area. The chapter begins by discussing the role and place of interdisciplinary research.

Interdisciplinary research

Long-standing and often fruitless discussions in universities and research centres that have encouraged interdisciplinary research now at last seem to be coming into season. The fluid circumstances of the early twenty-first century are encouraging researchers to leave their disciplinary silos to share understandings across fields. This increasingly common approach to designing research in many fields moves beyond the cliché of the individual genius researcher, and focuses on the establishment of teams of research collaborators who are formed around the needs of the project. Research that connects with intermediality in the arts and education can see project teams that feature:

- teachers
- teaching artists
- artists and creative workers
- education, sociology, or performance researchers
- curators and archivists
- participants as co-creators and co-researchers

Generally, the aim of these teams is to collaborate to make sense of intermediality in the types of hypermedia spaces discussed in this book, analyse the works produced in them, and expand understandings of the nature of audiences/participants/produsers. For instance, in the Playing Beowulf project described in Chapter 5, the researchers and teaching artists in the team frequently interchanged roles based on the day-to-day needs of the project. In addition, the nature of what was being researched also changed throughout the week of the project workshop. On any one day the researchers may have been considering performance-making process, pedagogical practices, the integration of technology and performance, the impacts of computer-based technologies on learning, or the role of identity play in adolescents when performance making. This constantly shifting process demanded by emergent performance-driven practice makes research in these spaces inherently interdisciplinary.

In researching intermediality there are first-order questions to ensure that the research is focused and relevant, which will now be examined in more detail.

What and/or who are we researching?

In some ways interdisciplinarity requires research approaches and methods that simultaneously take account of the complexity of chaotic systems and allow work within them. The confusion and complexity of postnormality demands flexible research approaches and collaborative researchers. The fluid world intensifies the difficulty of the research undertaking, and this creates an extra pressure for researchers to clearly understand the 'what' and the 'who' of the research. In a recent project Peter O'Connor and Michael Anderson worked with young Indigenous Australian students, using Applied Theatre as Research (ATR) methods to understand and design a new education programme (O'Connor and Anderson, 2015). These ATR methods are discussed later in this chapter. This Young Mob project employed performance, video materials and video making, music, and dance to create fictional frames within which the participants/ co-researchers provided insights into the design of the programme. In essence this methodology was devised for and shaped by the project rather than being taken from the researchers' standard methodological toolkit and applied to the project. This kind of methodological flexibility is critical when considering intermediality.

On the Young Mob project, the research team were determined from the beginning to include participant voice in the research project. As a result, the research output did not conform to what many might recognize as 'traditional'. Taylor's description of what he calls the rebellious and revolutionary turn away from 'scientism' in drama and arts educational research points to the adoption of critical positions to acknowledge and accommodate 'the transformatory capacity of the artform to release us into new forms of experiencing, new modes of rendering' (1996, p. 11). How researchers choose to represent and render research outcomes can remain in synch with the artforms and arts cultures being examined. In addition, part of the 'release' possible in these approaches is from power relationships that require objectification of the research subject. Carroll argues that 'in drama research the participants are knowing subjects within their cultural context and they can construct dramatic narratives about the world drawn from their personal experience and imagination' (1996, p. 76). The Young Mob participants/co-researchers were not positioned as passive subjects but rather they were active participants in designing, making, and delivering the research. The analysis of the data was undertaken by the research team but the intent, and for the most part the practice, of the research blurred the lines between disciplines, participant/researcher, and traditional/ innovative research methodologies. While this approach did have its own challenges it responded directly to the research question that sought to understand the needs of Indigenous young people as constructors and initiators of their own futures.

The Young Mob project highlights some of these challenges and also the opportunities in this kind of research. The blurring of audience, researcher, participant, and art maker (the 'who' of the research) is the kind of mashup of roles that researchers in these spaces frequently face. This demands researchers have a collaborative and flexible approach to the needs of all of those involved in the research in whatever role(s) they take.

There is also a blending of the 'who' and 'what' of the research. In the Young Mob research O'Connor and Anderson were examining imagined futures through arts-based methods. While researchers frequently set out to create categories or containers within a project, this is not always possible in this kind of research. The cultural identities of the Indigenous young people in this research, the research process itself, and the proposed outcomes were indivisible. The cultural identity of the young people and their aspirations for the future fed directly into the programmes they designed for the NGO funding the research. This kind of research, which prototypes learning processes, must involve the 'who' and 'what' simultaneously to ensure the research conclusions are meaningful and applicable to the participants and to those commissioning the research. This leads to the 'why' of the research.

Why are we researching?

The next question that arises is why is research actually being conducted in these spaces? Ultimately researchers are attempting to create meaning through the convergence of different practices to create new ways of doing education and the arts. There are several answers to the why question, which can be distilled into three categories:

a) the prototyping of new approaches

b) to understand the effectiveness of these approaches for participants/audience, and

c) to describe and analyse practice

The Playing Beowulf research project described in Chapter 5 examined all three. In the process of prototyping a practice-based intermedial pedagogy the researchers also needed to understand how that pedagogy impacted on student learning. It is of course possible to conceive of research projects that address only one of the above. For instance, the trial of a virtual reality programme may mostly be about understanding effects on the distance/audience. Similarly, the development of a new performance may be predominantly about design. That said, the role of effects and prototyping are rarely separated and even when one predominates the other is usually present.

Why does it matter (who cares)?

The 'who cares?' question is about impact, and is relevant to all research. However, finding the audiences and stakeholders impacted by these intermedial research projects, and making them care, is a significant challenge. These kinds of research projects by their very nature do not speak only to one audience but rather they engage with multiple research stakeholders including but not limited to educators, artists, and cultural organizations such as galleries – making the relevance sometimes difficult to 'sell'. Any approach that blends disciplines necessarily blends audiences. In the Beowulf project a key institutional partner, the British Library, was also a key audience for the research outcomes though the researchers could see relevance for educators, games designers, policymakers, and many other areas of industry and practice. Actually engaging those audiences can be a task almost as difficult as the research itself. This difficulty can lead to research projects speaking primarily back to the funders, sometimes in a virtuous circle seeking to attract further funding for another layer of research, and at risk of failing to fully engage with audiences beyond the virtual and literal walls of the academy.

Methodological choices

This chapter is going to provide a survey of the options and choices that are available to researchers in intermedial spaces. The 'traditional' methodologies of quantitative and qualitative research have not been excluded, and it is not suggested that the only way to engage with this kind of research is through 'cutting-edge' or emergent methodologies. It is possible, feasible, and in some cases wise to use traditional research methodologies depending on the nature of the research problem and the audience for the research. The discussion that follows is divided into three main sections: quantitative methods, qualitative methods, and emergent methodologies in their application to intermedial research. These include design-based research, action research, and Applied Theatre as Research. The division of the chapter into these sections is intended to provide a relatively easy path through the explanation of methods so that researchers in these areas might have a starting point. The methods suggested here are not the only approaches possible in intermedial spaces, though they do favour educational research. In the fields of performance studies, sociology, anthropology, and museum studies there are a multitude of research methods that can be drawn upon. The methods chosen here reflect the authors' experiences with research in intermedial spaces.

In reality, the divisions between 'types' of research can be messier and more arbitrary than accounted for here. There has been a strong debate between positivist and interpretive paradigms of research; however, there is now an established view that merges qualitative and quantitative methods and will hopefully embrace more innovative or emergent methodologies. You will notice that the discussion here is situated in educational research. This is done for two reasons: (a) because that is the authors' area of expertise and (b) for the most part educational research is intrinsically applied and often it is interdisciplinary. Before breaking down the methodological options there is discussion on how to choose methods for these kinds of spaces.

Finding methodology:
Rejecting false dichotomies

There has been a strong and useful argument in education about how to examine research questions. Habitually the arguments have usually fallen into a dichotomy: the qualitative versus the quantitative. As Carroll argues (1996, p. 74), researchers should be mindful that all methodologies are human constructions and have inherent flaws and biases. Acceptance that there is no 'clean' or 'objective' methodology creates the freedom to discuss a more focused design problem: what methodology will suit the needs of the question? In some cases, it will suit the research question to run a quantitative analysis, in other cases a more complex design will produce more insightful outcomes. Sometimes both will be required to adequately explore an issue, while in other circumstances an artist-led approach may be required. The approaches discussed here might be implemented over a series of sessions, or as a short-term or cross-sectional study that allows researchers to examine many cases over a short period of time. Other research projects may take a number of years in a longitudinal study. Longitudinal studies examine 'features of people or other units at more than one time' (Neuman, 2006, p. 31). The longitudinal design is relevant to learning in these spaces as it allows examination of the possibility and significance of change (or no change) over time. Time allows consequences to take place. The length of the study usually corresponds to the nature of the question, the available resources, and the space and media available to report the outcomes of the question. One of the most long-standing methods to consider first is quantitative research.

Quantitative research:
Findings with 'hard edges'

Quantitative methodologies do have a role to play in educational and digital arts research. They can provide an overall summary of simple information such as 'How many students have used technology in performance making in school?' or 'Does learning with technology and performance improve understanding of coding?' When delving into the complexities of the learning experience qualitative methodology is a natural choice. As Elliot Eisner points out (1978, p. 201) in exploring the complexities of educational research, there is little to be gained in reducing the 'human mind to a single score'. Conversely, the qualitative method attempts to 'adumbrate its complexities, its potential, and its idiosyncrasies' (1978, p. 201). Within the double speak that sometimes passes for discussion in bureaucracies there is often a call for findings with 'hard edges'. What this means is findings that can show significance in a statistical way. For instance: X% of students achieved higher technology scores as a result of making a performance.

There is of course an inbuilt discrimination in a call for hard-edged data as it presupposes that anything relevant can be demonstrated in a quantitative way. The complexity of learning is difficult to reflect with quantitative methodologies, and the complex nature of intermediality makes this even more difficult. Creative practices in these spaces are so heavily based in experience, intuition, and human interactions that much of research depends on understanding and interpreting the lived learning experiences of performers, participants/audiences, and teachers. This kind of research does not always come with 'hard edges'.

To adequately engage with research in this area, qualitative approaches can record and analyse the richness of what goes on in learning and particularly learning in these spaces by capturing their complexities. Whichever methodologies are chosen, the audience for that research needs to be acknowledged, understood, and accounted for in the research. If one aim (as researchers) is to advocate a case to policymakers, perhaps researchers will need to speak the language of quantitative research to make the point. If striving to describe the complexities inherent in intermedial spaces and learning, researchers could continue using existing and new methodologies where they suit the research question and are able to describe the multidimensional nature of experience and learning. Many questions that could be explored in intermedial spaces will require a portmanteau or *bricolage*[1] approach to research that engages with several methodologies to answer several sometimes complex questions, and this can be considered now in terms of mixed methods.

Mixed methods approaches

A mixed methods approach to research can examine a large set of questions in the middle ground between qualitative and quantitative methods, and this is used frequently in interdisciplinary research. Johnson and Onwuegbuzie (2004, p. 15) argue mixed method research occurs 'where the researcher mixes or combines quantitative and qualitative research techniques, methods, approaches, concepts or language into a single study. Philosophically, it is the "third wave" or third research movement, a movement that moves past the paradigm wars by offering a logical and practical alternative' (p. 17). For example, this approach could allow a researcher to use a survey to examine why certain groups of audience/participants do not engage with intermedial spaces in a museum. The results of this survey may lead to conclusions that suggest further analysis. In the analysis of these survey results you might undertake a cluster analysis that groups variables. Maybe your variables are audience/participants' access to technology, audience/participants' engagement in intermedial learning and attitudes to technology. Perhaps for the sake of this example, the survey found a group of audience/participants with low engagement in intermedial learning despite good access to technology. This is a potentially very interesting finding. The problem is, however, the quantitative analysis tells us that the correlation exists but does not tell us why. To examine why, the researcher needs to use a qualitative approach such as interview or case study of those within this group. This approach has the potential to provide the quantitative measurement that museum curators, exhibit designers, and policymakers crave and the qualitative responses that many educators require to explain the complexity of engaging with these kinds of spaces. Johnson and Onwuegbuzie (2004) argue that this method has the potential to unify elements of educational research and examine research questions that cannot be examined by qualitative or quantitative research alone: 'by narrowing the divide between quantitative and qualitative researchers, mixed methods research has a great potential to promote a shared responsibility in the quest for attaining accountability for educational quality' (2004, p. 24). There are however some questions that are suited to qualitative methods alone. The remainder of this chapter now explores methods that are qualitative or emergent.

Qualitative approaches

Qualitative research has had a 'distinguished place in the human disciplines' since the 1920s and 1930s (Denzin, 1994, p. 1). The growth and development of qualitative research paralleled the need for a more powerful and naturalistic research method than positivism (Eisner, 1978, p. 202). Bruner (1990, p. 130) argues that 'neither the empiricist's tested knowledge nor the rationalist's self-evident truths describe the ground on which ordinary people go about making sense of their experiences'. Qualitative research allows researchers to delve into the layered complexity of lived human experience. Research in intermedial spaces often requires methodology that allows for the complexity and idiosyncrasies that are inherent in a process of collaborative creativity. The depth of analysis possible in qualitative research is not available in more reductionist methodologies. As Grady (1996) argues, to deal with the complexity of human experience research should be undertaken from an informed position, which allows the researcher to 'choose challenging rhetorical and methodological tools that allow us to focus on the complexities of the practice of theory in practice' (Grady, 1996, p. 70).

Eisner defines qualitative methodology as 'that form of inquiry that seeks the creation of qualities that are expressively patterned, that seeks the explication of wholes as the primary aim, that emphasizes the study of configurations rather than isolated entities, that regards expressive narratives and visuals as appropriate vehicles for communication' (1978, p. 198). His identification of qualities that are expressively patterned reflects the central significance of identifying the quality of the learning experience through its features. This approach seeks to analyse each specific context to create broader understanding, learning, and experience around intermediality. Denzin and Lincoln (2005, p. 3) also argue qualitative research has the power to transform as it has immediate relevance to its community. They argue that qualitative research is 'a situated activity that locates the observer in the world ... qualitative research involves an interpretive, naturalistic approach to the world. In other words, qualitative researchers study things in their natural settings, attempting to make sense of, or to interpret, phenomena in terms of the meanings people bring to them' (2005, p. 3). Qualitative approaches fit well with research that seeks to transform learning or practice rather than just depict or reflect current practice.

Case study

A case study is defined as 'the study of the particularity of and complexity of a single case, coming to understand its activity within important circumstances' (Stake, 1995). Exploring teachers' experience of designing learning for intermedial spaces can potentially provide a rich, deep, and complex picture for analysis. Although generalizations are unable to be made as a result of that analysis, it is an insight into a process. To use a filmmaking analogy, case study can tell a story through a 'close-up' on the context of the learning experience, the 'mid-shot' context of the intermedial space (museum, school, makerspace, stage), illuminated by the 'wide-shot' of engagement of the students or participants in intermedial spaces for learning and creative practice.

Participants in these kinds of research are themselves specific and unique 'cases' who have their own constructed realities. Having several 'cases' affords the researcher the opportunity of making comparisons and contrasts that may lead to a better understanding of the wider world of experience and learning in intermedial spaces. The information drawn for comment from these cases will obviously reflect the research question or as Stake argues: 'my choice would be to take from the case from which we feel we can learn the most' (1995, p. 243). Consequently, when material is chosen from the interview transcripts and developed into narratives, material should be selected that is most appropriate to the themes and sub-themes of the research. So for instance how do audiences/participants understand intermediality and how can it be recruited to enhance learning or participant engagement? Interviews are a common strategy for collecting data for case studies.

Interviews

Interviews provide a way to discover the attitudes, recollections, and understandings about a certain research topic in some depth. The aim of this strategy is to engage in a conversation that creates mutually constructed meaning. The most useful research interview is the semi-structured interview. In the semi-structured interview, the participant and the researcher both have input into the process. This type of interview is more honest, morally sound, and reliable, as it treats the respondent as an equal and allows them to express personal feelings and therefore presents a more 'realistic' picture than can be uncovered using traditional methods. As Fontana and Frey (1994, p. 373) argue 'forgetting the rules [of traditional interviewing] ... allows research subjects to express themselves more freely, and thus to have greater voice both in research process and in the research report' (1994, p. 368).

Often these types of interviews begin with a discussion about the process that encourages the participants to negotiate the interview as it progresses. The participants have the right not to answer the questions, to ask questions of the researcher, and to add their own observations of the process. At any stage they can terminate the interview. Video can be used to record the interview that captures the non-verbal features of the discussion (Fontana and Frey, 1994, p. 371) that may be significant in the data analysis process.

Problems still remain with this more informal style of interviewing. This approach supports the idea of a discussion although the interviewer's first task is to listen. As Ely comments (1991, p. 67): 'LISTEN, LISTEN and LISTEN MORE'. Even though there is a collaborative element, the first priority is to listen to the story. To do otherwise is to reinforce the old hierarchy of the researcher and the 'researched'. Researchers have to resist the temptation to add their own commentary on the situation they are researching. The conversational style of this interaction facilitates this kind of response. The research methodology, however, is attempting to reflect the participant's experiences and not the interventions of the researcher. Researchers of (and in) intermedial spaces may find emerging methodologies suit their research questions more effectively.

Emergent methodologies

Participatory action research

Participatory action research (PAR) comes closest to the ideal of praxis: practice and action as research. PAR typically involves the use of qualitative interpretative modes of inquiry and data collection by participants (designers, teachers, curators, or artists), often with the assistance of full-time researchers, with a view to helping participants make judgements about how to improve their own practice: 'the emphasis is "practical", that is on the interpretations that teachers and students are making and acting on in the situation' (Kemmis and McTaggart, 2005, p. 561). The focus for participatory action researchers is on improving the situations in which they are situated. There has been some criticism that this method, founded on the progressivism of the 1970s and 1980s, has fallen short of its ambitious aims of changing the world. In response to this criticism Kemmis argues that participatory action researchers 'may not have changed the world but they have changed their worlds' (Kemmis and McTaggart, 2005, p. 600). This research method is suited to intermediality research as it allows those engaged in their design and delivery to constantly refine and reimagine what might be possible using the affordances of different creative and learning spaces. Additionally, PAR holds the promise of enriching practice through the research of it.

In PAR, action researchers devise a research question that relates directly to their practice such as 'how can a national library create an intermedial space that will engage participants/audience in the story of colonisation?' The action researcher would then (perhaps with the assistance of another researcher) design an intervention (a group of focus experiences around colonization) and then put it into action (implement the experiences with audiences/participants). As the experiences take place, data are collected perhaps through interviews, participant journals, or observation to reflect what is going on in the intervention. The concluding reflection provides an in-depth examination of the learning process that may then be linked to advances in theoretical discussions that relate to learning or intermedial performances.

Design-Based Research

A relatively new research method, Design-Based Research (DBR) was developed specifically for use in educational settings. DBR is informed by both action research practices and experimental laboratory research. Like action research, it is a grass-roots approach; the research focus is specific to the particular site in which the research is taking place. However, like laboratory research DBR follows a structure of design, collection, and analysis that incorporates theory building and testing. Essentially, DBR can be 'characterised as an inter-disciplinary mixed method approach conducted "in the field" that serves applied and theory-building purposes' (Reimann, 2011, p. 37). DBR was developed to make education research more relevant for teaching practices by linking theory and practice more strongly to educational research (Reimann, 2011). This linking is achieved in DBR through the development of research projects with local relevance and the implementation of research in authentic settings. Wang and Hannafin (2005) characterize DBR projects as:

1   Pragmatic – they are usually intervention orientated and designed to take place in real-world settings.

2   Grounded in theory and research – unlike other forms of practitioner research, DBRs must evolve from an interpretive framework and/or instructional theory.

3   Flexible, iterative, and interactive – the research should be modified based on reflection from participants and findings from data collection.

4   Integrative – the research needs to fit in with, and be part of, the school community.

5   Contextual – the elements of the research (interpretive framework, methodology, design) need to be appropriately aligned and the research as a whole needs to work within the wider context of the school and system.

Often a DBR focuses on a single issue that has local relevance to the research site, such as the potential learning impact of intermedial spaces – this has relevance to the local spaces and the design of intermedial learning generally. DBR can also have relevance to educational research and practice more generally. Therefore, DBR projects can be roughly characterized as informed by broader theory, but emerging from a specific local issue. DBRs in the field of education are generally teacher-led, with teacher learning central to the design (Bannan-Ritland and Baek, 2008). A community of educational leaders and researchers can be brought in as needed for support. Often academic researchers act as 'critical friends' and offer to help with planning, documenting, and disseminating the research. DBR is also an effective method for studies that wish to understand a phenomenon or test the effectiveness of a theory in multiple sites. For example, if taking the earlier example of intermedial spaces being used for the understanding of colonization, the sites might be a classroom, a library, an art gallery, and a museum. Teachers/curators/facilitators/artists in multiple sites may be provided with a common set of approaches to designing and implementing the experience. The research team support practitioners by providing them with guidance on intervention design, data collection, and analysis. Each site then produces a report of their intervention. Collectively, these reports form the data for the wider study.

Unlike other research methodologies (such as experiments, discourse analysis, case studies), DBRs do not have a specific method; rather they follow a framework or philosophy of ongoing data collection (Reimann, 2011) and therefore each project is unique. However, the DBR process generally consists of four elements:

1   Informed planning and implementation of a project;

2   continual trialling and 'taking stock' where the project is modified or redesigned according to ongoing data collection;

3   evaluation of local impact upon completion of the project; and

4   evaluation of the potential for broader impact in the education field more generally.

Like action research, DBR takes place in cycles, with a focus on testing and revising the study as necessary during the process rather than at the end. Incorporating the four elements listed above, and acknowledging that all DBRs are different, Reimann (2011, p. 40) suggests three main phases and typical activities of a DBR process. They are as follows:

Phase 1 – Preparing the experiment

- Clarifying goals
- Documenting starting points
- Outlining an envisioned learning trajectory

Phase 2 – Experimenting to support learning

- Collecting data in cycles of design and analysis (as discussed above and similar to the action research process)

- Applying interpretive frameworks
- Formulating and testing domain-specific theories

Phase 3 – Conducting retrospective analyses

- Outlining the rationale for the interpretive framework and methods in light of the data and results
- Establishing trust in the findings (ensuring and highlighting the rigor of the study)
- Ensuring repeatability
- Ensuring generalizability

It is in this last phase that a major distinction between action research (and other forms of practitioner research) and DBR are evident. Although grass-roots, DBR as a method is concerned with making a difference to wider systems – local studies that have global impact. As a result, a major phase in the work is ensuring the results of the local 'test' can be replicated and distributed. Therefore it is key that the study is explicit, trustworthy, generalizable, and repeatable. Another recent emergent approach is Applied Theatre as Research.

Applied Theatre as Research

Theatre techniques can be effectively integrated throughout research processes. Researchers also recognize that forms of theatre making can be a complete research methodology, rather than just a tool employed within another approach (Belliveau and Lea, 2011; Gallagher, 2011;

Norris, 2009). As ways of learning, there are many commonalities between performance, learning, and qualitative research (Henry, 2000). Both require:

- a sensitive and self-reflexive response to the environment
- a willingness to improvise and to take risks
- the employment of multiple roles and changing settings
- a willingness to engage with narrative

Furthermore, both engage with:

- tacit knowledge involving affect and intuition
- personal and social realities
- metaphors and symbols to communicate meanings
- ways of knowing which people use in their everyday lives. (Henry, 2000, p. 51)

Specifically, both Helen Cahill (2006) and Diane Conrad (2004) argue there are many similarities between PAR and applied theatre. Applied theatre, like PAR, often involves a process of inquiry, based on a topic, theme, or problem relevant to the participants (Nicholson, 2005; Prendergast and Saxton, 2009; Prentki and Preston, 2009; Thompson, 2006). The Young Mob project referred to earlier in this chapter is an example. Cahill observes that both traditions 'are centrally concerned with dialogue, praxis, participatory exploration and transformation' and involve 'collective processes of enquiry, action and reflection' (2006, p. 62). In both processes the relationship between the researcher/practitioner and participants is a collaborative one. Applied theatre, then, like PAR, has the potential to be an affective methodology for research with young people.

As Wyn and White argue (1997), young people tend to be excluded from problem-solving activities relating to their own affairs and are commonly pathologized or glamorized in health and education discourses. Once relegated to the role of object of research, young people can only with difficulty be seen as the source of solutions (Cahill, 2006, p. 63). What Applied Theatre as Research (ATR) achieves, which most other research methods do not, are emotional and aesthetic, multi-modal (aural, oral, kinaesthetic and symbolic) forms of interaction and representation (Cahill, 2006, p. 63). Reflecting on her experience of using drama to research with urban high school students, Kathleen Gallagher notes how 'led by art, researchers, teacher, and students moved differently: We created an experiment in research that changed the terms of engagement' (Gallagher, 2011, p. 328; Gallagher, 2007). She found that researching through drama made possible different modes of communication, conduct, and embodiment (Gallagher, 2008). She also argues that this approach gives participants as co-researchers the opportunity for 'self-representation', whereas in other methodologies it is the researcher who represents the research participants:

> This is theatre as methodology, theatre as a mode of devising a meta-world; to collaboratively and artistically frame a 'real' research problem or context in order to peer inside it. Engaging youth in research – theatrically – provides a robust environment for questioning, as the work deals in metaphor, or recreates 'real life' situations in which collaborators are able to more freely experiment with alternative strategies and perspectives in testing the validity of their own theories and insights about the world. (Gallagher, 2011, p. 328)

In much applied theatre, topics, themes, or problems are explored through drama with a group of people. Participants can take on many roles: planning, acting in role, reflecting and critiquing out of role, and presenting their work. Applied theatre might involve the participants working directly with an experience or issue from their own lives, or they might work analogously through a fictional frame. Either way, the theatre forms used are designed to create a safe and critical distance from a subject (Fels, 2011; Fels and Belliveau, 2008; Gallagher, 2011). A variety of theatrical traditions might be used in this way: researching, writing, and performing a scripted play (Norris, 2009); verbatim theatre and storytelling (Anderson and Wilkinson, 2007), participatory improvisation (Fels, 2011; Gallagher, 2011); contemporary performance art (Hughes MacNamara, and Kidd, 2011); forum theatre (Boal, 1983); process drama (Heathcote, 1984); or site-specific performance (Hughes, et al., 2011; Ledgard, 2007; MacNamara and Rooke, 2007). Applied theatre can engage people in identifying problems, considering diverse issues, experiences, and perspectives, and imagining or enacting possible solutions for future. Given the emphasis placed on the complex and confusing nature of the postnormal world, it should now be considered how to ensure credibility of the research being undertaken in the spaces.

Validity, reliability, and credibility

Validity reflects the extent to which research is 'sound, cogent, well grounded, justifiable or logically correct' (Schwandt, 2001).

If research is credible, it should be trustworthy so that it truly reflects the authentic voice of the participants and resonates with others who will be engaged by the research. Many qualitative methodologies seek to remove the traditional 'researcher' and 'researched' status. This partnership can be maintained by ensuring that the research participants feel that the research undertaken with them reflects what they feel they wanted to communicate as part of the process. Giving research participants an opportunity to respond to their contribution ensures the reliability and the credibility of the research. Research participants may ask for changes to the research and even though the researcher may disagree with these sentiments, the participants have the right to be represented in ways that they feel are valid. Naturally this requires negotiation on the part of the researcher and the participants but the voice and wishes of the participants are central to the validity of the research. The credibility of the research lies in the authenticity and clarity of the research participants' voices and their transferability, creating knowledge that leads to a deeper understanding of the research question.

Crystallization

There are some useful measures of credibility here but one of the most useful is crystallization. Along with the authenticity of research participants' voice is an important part of the developing reliability of qualitative research. Triangulation is a well-known method that employs a variety of data sources in a study (Janesick, 1994, p. 214). It is a useful term but does suggest limitation. The crystallization method has greater scope to validate the data. Laurel Richardson (1994) says the 'central image for "validity" for postmodernist texts is not the triangle – a rigid, fixed, two dimensional object. Rather, the central image is the crystal, which combines symmetry and substance with an infinite variety of shapes, substances, transmutations, multidimensionalities, and angles of approach. Crystals grow change, alter but are not amorphous' (1994, p. 522).

Crystallization seems more able to describe several approaches to validating the research data. The process also reflects the possibility of several reflections from the same source, in other words several interpretations from the one interview, narrative, or case study. The researcher's interpretations may be only one of the many interpretations possible. For instance, if your study examined teachers' experience of the classroom through narratives, you might use several methods of validation for the narratives. First, the teachers in the study could validate the narratives (one facet of the crystal) by reading and responding to the narratives, indicating whether they are a valid reflection of their experience. At any point they could negotiate changes and make additions to the narratives. This validation allows the authentic voices of participants to emerge and ensures the researcher's style or voice does not overwhelm the participants' voices. Another facet of this crystallization process might be to bring in other researchers to analyse interviews, narratives, and case studies and suggest other interpretations of the data.

Finally, this chapter on making research acknowledges some of the ethical issues that arise in all research (and research in intermedial spaces is no exception).

Ethical considerations

No discussion of research can or should omit the ethical challenges that face researchers. Education presents some especially challenging ethical dilemmas, as research participants are often young children or young adults. Those serious about researching practice must accept that there are some ethical questions to be reconciled and resolved during research. Undertaking research within a space that involves students or teachers requires ethical clearances. This has a twin purpose. It lets a system (such as university or school) know what the researchers are doing and allows others to peer review the ethical robustness of the planned research. While there are whole devoted to the ethics of research in education, this section will deal with a critical issue that is pertinent to work in mediatized spaces: anonymity and confidentiality.

Anonymity and confidentiality

Researchers take different views about anonymity in educational research. Punch argues, 'there is strong feeling among most fieldworkers that settings and respondents should not be identifiable in print and that they should not suffer harm or embarrassment as a consequence of research' (1994, p. 93). Other researchers, such as Shulman (1990, p. 11), take a different view, claiming that participants' voices should be recognized. However, she also points to the consequences and implications of revealing participant identities that may single them out for ridicule and oppression.

Her study into the attitudes of teachers in classrooms left her participants potentially vulnerable as 'teachers rarely leave the scene [of research]. They must bear the burden of their written words, for they remain participants long after they complete their roles' (Shulman, 1990, p. 14).

Anonymity often empowers research participants to speak out about their experience of other teachers, colleagues, or supervisors in ways that would be impossible if they were identified publicly (Shulman, 1990, p. 11). Pseudonyms are useful for the research participants, participants' schools, and any other person who could be identified or identify others. Broad geographical areas can be used to identify and contextualize the location of the research participants. It is sound advice to take the safe course and make the participants anonymous. Participants may decide that they would like to associate themselves with the research but that should be left up to them.

Conclusion

This chapter presents the beginning rather than a comprehensive summary of engagement with issues around intermedial spaces and research. The nature of the liquid world and the interdisciplinary nature of this emergent field ensure that research in this area will constantly feature innovation, adaptation, and agility. For example, the shape of the Beowulf performance devising process changed from hour to hour as discussed in Chapter 5. The research parameters required the research team to be similarly agile as one performance approach was abandoned in favour of a hybrid of others at times.

One way to remain flexible is to engage with traditional and emergent research and not to eschew either. Researchers have seen much fruitless discussion over which methodology is best. More importantly when ask about researching into intermedial spaces: 'what and/or who are we researching?'; 'why are we researching?'; and 'why does it matter (who cares)?' before engaging with the methodology. A clear understanding of research intentions will drive questions, and will make the outcomes of research useful for audiences. Research in this area is critical to understanding the potential affordances and risks these new spaces present. Moreover, this emergent field requires theory-building research that assists in growth, development, and further invention of knowledge and practice. Research is not the only way to understand the prospects for this area but it is one critical way that can help create the future and understand the potential of intermediality.

11

The Future of Making/
Making the Future

Reflections

You will have noticed by now in this book that we have sought to imagine what's possible as well as what currently is. In 2006 two of us – working with our late colleague Professor John Carroll – described some trends we felt would be relevant to drama educators working with technology. Our book *Real Players* (2006) brought together the performance world of educational drama and the real-world digital environment inhabited by many young people. We were making a case for drama educators to make use of the tools these spaces afforded, and also consider how drama might be a way to critique technologies and develop electronic literacies. These six speculative statements were outlined in the concluding chapter of *Real Players* (2006, pp. 157–168), and we will briefly reflect on them before taking another 'predictive punt' at the future of digital drama, education, and making.

The future is participatory

We noted in 2006 that digital developers had tapped into a DIY online media trend that enabled and relied upon input from users. This predated the widespread use of social media services like Facebook, Instagram, and Twitter as content sharing platforms and coincided with the emergence and rapid adoption of media self-publishing sites such as YouTube and Vimeo for videos and Flickr for photographs. In the commercial entertainment world there was also a clear trend towards the exploitation of a dramatic property (Sutton, 2012) across many media forms, and we used Disney's *Lion King* as an example of a story told across animated film, stage adaptations, video games, and assorted commercial and fan-produced paratexts. We suggested this was leading to an approach to narrative and performance in which 'students will learn to create works that are not attached to any particular medium' (2006, p. 161). This was a similar theme to the concept of transmedia storytelling, which Henry Jenkins defined as the art of world making so that 'to fully experience any fictional world, consumers must assume the role of hunters and gatherers, chasing down bits of the story across media channels, comparing notes with each other via online discussion groups, and collaborating to ensure that everyone who invests time and effort will come away with a richer entertainment experience' (2006a, p. 21). An example of this distribution of story across different media channels is apparent in the Star Wars franchise, where the world and the stories in it can be found in movies, books, TV series and web specials, video and board games, comics, toys, and other media. Some of these channels are considered official story 'canon' by producers and fans, others are simply encountered as part of the expanded universe of official and fan production around the canonical texts. There are many similar narrative franchises that could be considered as examples of transmedia productions, such as Star Trek, The Hunger Games, Harry Potter, James Bond, and Doctor Who. Many of these also have vibrant and creative fan production cultures associated with them, often gravitating to online affinity spaces affording the development of digital literacies.

The future is about communities

Extending the notion of participation, which implies collaborative or shared experiences, we noted that digital networked media afforded the emergence of loosely determined communities around common interests regardless of real-world social, geographical, and political boundaries (2006, p. 162). We strongly framed this around the context of communities of practice, following the work of Lave and Wenger (1991) in describing them as contexts for situated learning. However, we suggested that digital media was transforming them into something else, allowing more role-based and dramatic 'as if' learning, in conjunction with authentically framed or commissioned project work. This drew together ideas such as the drama convention of mantle of the expert with digital games and simulation work such as 'epistemic games'.

Although we saw that digital media was changing the nature of communities of practice, at the time we did not make a connection with the concept of 'affinity spaces' (Gee, 2004), which focuses attention on the physical, virtual, or blended spaces where people interact around a common interest or endeavour. The term was originally used to describe online sites organized around popular video games, where fans created and shared a range of information and media artefacts (Duncan and Hayes 2012, p. 3). Affinity spaces are now more broadly recognized by researchers as sites, or networks of multiple sites linked through social media, built around all manner of shared passions and common endeavours (Curwood, Magnifico, and Lammers, 2013; Lammers et al., 2012).

The future is always on

We observed that the pervasive nature of contemporary digital networked media led to a world in which we are permanently interconnected to each other and to news, social, and information services. In terms of the performative nature of digital media we noted that 'if we are always "on", we are also always potentially "live" and ... Liveness becomes a valuable commodity in itself' (Carroll, Anderson, and Cameron, 2006, p. 163).

We have expanded considerably in this book on the notion of digital liveness, and its connection to the everyday performativity inherent in our use of digital media. Services like Periscope and Facebook have enabled live video streaming from mobile devices, and social interactions are increasingly televisual in these spaces. The term 'live' has also become a consumer brand, and is even used to promote the experience of viewing theatre 'as live' through satellite broadcasts from theatre venues to cinema audiences, as in the UK's National

Theatre Live. This brings shows to audiences who might not be able to obtain tickets or travel to the performance venue. This is increasingly accepted as an alternative way to experience theatrical performances, because as Auslander (2014) suggests liveness comes from distance, which inherently produces a form of (dramatic) tension:

> in all cases liveness is the experience of having an active connection to an event taking place now, but somewhere else, whether that somewhere else is miles away or only inches away. In all cases the live connection feels as if it could abolish distance but never actually does, and indeed cannot, since liveness like theatre posits itself in distance.

The future is about trust

We noted that increasingly we are required to make informed judgements about the veracity and quality of information we are receiving online (Carroll, Anderson, and Cameron, 2006, p. 164). This is now one aspect of what we have described in this book as a digital literacy, and it is made even more significant by increased awareness of the threats to privacy, collection of data from our digital footprints, and the rise of state surveillance of digital spaces.

Generations of young people engage with even more powerful procedural tools that track, combine, and mine data with increasing efficiency. There remains a role for drama educators and arts practitioners to work with young people to explore these issues, using opportunities to promote digital literacies. We must all consider the implications of working within digital spaces that may be provided by proprietary companies wishing to access content or metadata from those using those spaces. One project that seeks to investigate these issues is Share Labs' Facebook Algorithmic Factory (https://labs.rs/en/), an experiment in combining journalism, digital art, and data visualization to explore potentially hidden and exploitative practices operating within social media. This type of online resource could easily form the foundation of deeper drama or art-based learning, especially when coupled with mashup tools like Mozilla's X-Ray Goggles or C&T's Prospero discussed in Chapter 1.

The future is mobile

We recognized at that time, just predating the release of major smartphone models like the first iPhone in 2007 and tablet devices like the iPad in 2010, that mobile telephones were becoming a ubiquitous personal media device. We also noted significant ownership of basic mobile devices even in relatively poor nations, which were moving to mobile internet as a way of overcoming the need for expensive wired infrastructure. We concluded that 'precisely because it is always with us, and that it is always on, the mobile telephone is potentially one of the most powerful transformative agents for drama and learning available to date' (2006, p. 164).

What we did not appreciate fully was that mere ownership of mobile devices, even the latest models of smartphones, does not map automatically and easily to 'mobility' in a wider sense of movement towards better social and economic standards for individuals. Working with young people defined as NEETs (not in education, employment, or training) in the UK city of Leeds, Thornham and Cruz found that as objects, mobile phones are constantly played with and shared – always at hand or in the hand – though they 'are also smashed and broken and never entirely fixed' (2016, p. 5). Government departments and agencies regularly penalized the young people in this study by not providing mobile-friendly portals to their services and administration. The mobile literacies of these young people as expressed in their use of tools and functions did not translate into 'the right kind' of mobility when engaging with systems and processes, which serves as a reminder that 'mobile phones are not free from sociocultural, political and economic power structures, and any mobility or agency they may offer the user is momentary, contentious, negotiated and ambivalent' (Thornham and Cruz, 2016, p. 12).

The future is more accessible

Notwithstanding this form of 'immobility' that digital technologies do not automatically or universally erase, we noted that the digital divide exists but that mobile technologies and other advances were helping to give access to information and communication in some of the poorest and remotest areas of the world. There are many ways in which have and have-not divides can exist around young people and digital technology. For example, one recent study by the Pew Institute noted that although a high number of young people now have access to a mobile phone, there remains a distinction between smartphones and 'basic' handsets with fewer features (Lenhart, 2015). In digital storytelling projects with young people, Crystle Martin and Mimi Ito (2015) found that a percentage of young people were unfamiliar with some phone features or unable to make use of apps and services like Instagram and Snapchat that others are finding powerful tools for connectivity, creativity, and identity formation and maintenance. Now, as we first proposed in *Real Players*, there remains an opportunity for drama educators to humanize technology by working on aspects of human-to-human interaction in these forms of communication, performance, and media sharing (2006, p. 167).

There were of course many ideas and suggestions in *Real Players* that did not develop in the ways we speculated that they might. Some of the tools and services mentioned were superseded by even newer technologies and applications. It is always difficult to predict how particular services and brands will evolve, or even if they will still exist even a few years down the track despite dominating the market or being the trend leader for a period. However, as we jump forward another decade or so, we now once again look for some signs of the near future that may hold fresh interest or significance for those working in the intermedial spaces generated by drama, education, technology.

The future is mobile making

You probably only have to look around you now to confirm that mobile devices have become part of the fabric of everyday life. Once seen as something to be controlled or even banned from many formal settings, they are now being accommodated in schools, universities, and workplaces through so-called Bring Your Own Device (BYOD) models of providing wireless access, software apps, and cloud computing services. To some extent this could be a case of giving up the fight to control use via policies that learners and workers will clearly ignore or sidestep if they feel they are unfair or not appropriately applied (Kuznekoff, Munz, and Titsworth, 2015). There is still growing evidence that these devices can truly be distractions in classrooms, with a negative impact on learner performance when students engage with content that is not relevant to the class activity (Berry and Westfall, 2015). While that might seem an obvious outcome of not paying attention in class, it is difficult to shake off an entrenched belief that young people are born to multitask efficiently with technology, despite substantial evidence to the contrary that it's not as universal as the 'digital native' meme of the early 2000s suggested (Kennedy, Judd, Churchward, Gray, and Krause, 2008). A belief in their multitasking prowess is probably strongest in young people themselves. When interacting with people who have always had access to these mobile devices at the heart of their social, personal, and now working lives for finding content and communicating, it is difficult to deny them access in the workplace and educational settings where these activities are also common. Also, web or software services are becoming more (or only) usable from a mobile device, and so it is not always efficient or practical to ban or control their use if they are regularly the right tool for the task at hand.

Having these powerful computing and media devices accessible in some settings does open up new possibilities for creative and playful learning, including incorporation into drama and multimodal learning and performances that make use of intermediality. In particular, we see ways in which mobile devices are used not just as a bring-your-own channel for consuming educational content or completing learning tasks already developed around ICT curricula based in computer labs. Rather there is an opportunity to pursue a hybrid of media making and performance that these devices now allow. Cameron and Wotzko (2015) have explored opportunities for using mobile devices in educational settings that can draw upon well-understood drama conventions, while making use of the new creative affordances of the devices themselves. Some forms of applied theatre and process drama, operating as a way to enable learning across the curriculum, can function well within this hybrid performance and media space. In addition to generating or refreshing well-known dramatic conventions to accommodate contemporary mobile technology, a further opportunity remains to use these devices as production tools with their own already established existing workflows, practices, and creative cultures. Smartphones, tablets, and even some media players and game consoles now feature the tools and functions of a multimodal production platform that is closely tied to the performative and social personas of each individual owner or user.

Drama educators and practitioners are now well established in using digital storytelling in both formal and informal settings to examine young peoples' expression of self and identity generated through combinations of performance and creative practices in multimodal digital platforms (Wales, 2012). Exploring this blend of oral storytelling, digital media and performance (Chung, 2007) through a 'mobile making' approach is a variation of the method that engages with the tools increasingly at hand – literally, *in* the hands of most participants. As noted earlier in this chapter, that is not to assume that all devices are equally capable or that individuals are universally adept in their use for media production and performance.

That is precisely why an integrated media and performance approach to education or working with young people with these devices can be a critical aspect of creativity in arts education.

More broadly, as discussed throughout this book the evolution of digital and online technology has encouraged participatory cultures accessible to young people where 'fans and other consumers are invited to actively participate in the creation and circulation of new media content' (Jenkins, 2008, p. 331). Engagement with this participatory culture continues to enable the audience to move on a sliding scale from consumer to producer of media content, or 'produser' (Bruns, 2008), much like how drama encourages the move from audience to participant or 'spectactor' (Boal, 1995). In the example of the live performance devised by young people around the story of *Beowulf* described in Chapter 5, the presence of mobile devices was unavoidable. Many of the family and friends forming the live audience for the performance used their mobile phones to capture images and video of the show. This is the norm in many performance settings where the use of cameras and phones is allowed. However, the research team also used a mobile phone to live stream the performance to colleagues in London via Periscope, and this also potentially made it available to anyone who happened to come across the link in Twitter and other means for finding live Periscope broadcasts.

The presence of mobile devices among performers and their audiences is therefore one sign that the future continues to be mobile in the sense of integration into a range of aspects of our lives. Not only will events be recorded for later review or sharing – sometimes publicly, sometimes in our own personal archives – but now increasingly these performances will also form part of a live stream of daily lives, and potentially as many different live streams as there are audience members with mobile devices. Periscope and similar apps allow for viewers to comment and 'like' streams in real time, adding an element of critique, feedback in the moment that is an expansion of the possibilities of participation.

The future is more participatory

Henry Jenkins et al. in 2009 described a participatory culture as one with

> relatively low barriers to artistic expression and civic engagement, strong support for creating and sharing creations with others, some type of informal mentorship whereby what is known by the most experienced is passed along to novices, members who believe that their contributions matter, and members who feel some degree of social connection with one another – at least, they care what other people think about what they have created. (2009, pp. 5–6)

More recently, Jenkins in conversation with danah boyd and Mimi Ito recognizes that there are still many barriers to full participation, or that participatory media forms can come and go. He shifts towards a more relative discourse that tracks the continued movement towards a *more* participatory culture that is 'a set of ideals, a kind of social structure we are collectively trying to achieve, a collection of aspirations about what a better cultural configuration might look like' (Jenkins, Ito, and boyd, 2015). Participatory cultures can be an avenue for ugly practices to occur as well as those broadly considered positive or beneficial to many. Jenkins et al. discuss that participatory spaces and tools are not in themselves platforms for negative behaviour, but that it is the development of shared purposes, cultures, and practices that can help to shift towards the more positive and transformative outcomes for those engaging in these spaces. This has the potential to provide a strong connection with those working in drama and the arts seeking an applied or critical approach to education and other aspects of society. It equally recognizes that it can take significant work and risk to challenge dominant forces and practices in many aspects of society. It is also not to say that participatory cultures require pure like-mindedness or an unbending crowd mentality to operate effectively, however there is a sense that the social and connected aspects of working in these spaces are what make them truly powerful and potentially transformative. Rather than concentrating on the individualized and personalized experiences of digital media which can border on narcissism, we suggest there are opportunities for more participation in connected and shared human experiences made possible through digital arts practices.

The future is about spaces

Young people now move between formal and informal settings for learning, creativity, identity formation, and play. The nature of intermediality as a mode of production, enacted and embodied in hypermedia spaces combining multimodal literacies, is enabling a resurgence of making culture based on both formal curricula and personal passions and interests. There have been attempts to describe the learning and mentoring processes operating within these group cultures, for example, labelling them communities of practice or 'groups of people who share a concern or a passion for something they do and learn how to do it better as they interact regularly' (Wenger, 1998, p. 1). This connects with French cybertheorist Pierre Lévy's idea of 'collective intelligence' (2000), where there is too much information about a topic for one person to know so the knowledge is both shared and pooled within a community. Jenkins suggests this 'knowledge space' is realized by online fan communities where 'consumption has become a collective process' (2006a, p. 4). James Gee (2004) calls this informal learning environment an 'affinity space'. Gee considers affinity spaces an alternative notion to communities of practice and suggests labelling a group of people as a community of practice is problematic due to varying levels of engagement within the group. Gee suggests that if we start with spaces, 'we can then go on and ask to what extent the people interacting within a space, or some sub-group of them, do or do not actually form a community' (2004, p. 89). Affinity spaces are enabled by the networked digital technologies like the web, but can operate in a hybrid physical/ online mode. By definition these spaces are about the range of projects they accommodate, and many of these are not purely online pursuits, though ultimately they may be mediatized in some form to be published, shared, and critiqued by the people operating together in the space or even by outside audiences. Gauntlett points to Csikszentmihalyi's approach to creativity that rejects it as solely an individual pursuit, and 'instead, observes how the thing we call creativity emerges from a particular supportive environment' (2011,

p. 14). The quantity of multimodal production that has emerged from fan cultures associated with affinity spaces demonstrates how these spaces can be conducive to creativity.

While in 2006 we suggested that 'community' was one likely element of the future worth noting, the concept of affinity spaces refines this to reflect that not everyone engaging in these shared projects and spaces considers themselves as belonging to a community. The concept of community as we broadly experience it in our daily lives suggests borders, hierarchy, and social processes of acceptance and exclusion. Affinity spaces take on many of the underlying principles of a community of practice, but better accommodate that people will dip in and out of these spaces and their activities without any sense of joining a group with shared goals or values. As Devane argues, the loosely knit social relations in schools and workplaces often challenge conventional interpretations of community, and the 'anonymous and ephemeral social ties commonly found on Internet sites render it nearly incoherent' (2012, p. 165).

One of the sticking points with adoption of the community of practice concept by organizations and schools is the difficulty of designing an effective replica of the properties seen in these groups when they emerge organically. The notion of creating a space for creative project work to evolve around the shared interests of an open community of people does seem more achievable in terms of a facilitated approach. The maker space movement is more appealing to many artists, educators, and participants in this regard, based on the intention to provide a well-equipped space that can be inhabited in different ways by different people who can come and go and work individually or collaboratively as desired.

A greater sense of the role played by mobile media in creating, coordinating, and engaging with these affinity spaces is likely to arise, as these devices are not only a platform for communication, collaboration, and the consumption and production of content in their own right; they are also a means by which many people make use of online media and social networking portals to pursue their passions. As with communities of practice, it is tempting to consider ways to harness these affinity spaces in the service of formal educational structures. However, Duncan and Hayes argue for a '"middle path", considering digital media and online interactions not for how we should manage them or necessarily accommodate them within existing educational structures, but for what they tell us about the forms of learning and literacy that are already instantiated within the use of these media' (2012, p. 3).

The future is about places

Another trend we see as holding great potential interest in the near future concerns the resurgence in virtual reality technology. In particular, the move into consumer markets of headsets, apps, and still and video cameras that can capture high-resolution 360-degree content is driving new interest in creating and sharing more immersive mediatized engagements based on 'place'. For example, both YouTube and Facebook have developed specific workflows for publishing 360-degree video content. This is backed up by the other activities of these companies in recent years, for example, Google (the owners of YouTube), have worked to develop affordable and accessible virtual reality (VR) headsets that make use of mobile telephones – the Google Cardboard, for example. Facebook purchased the Oculus VR company in 2014, and although designed primarily for the virtual game market, the Oculus Rift headset technology is finding wider application as part of a wave of consumer VR headsets hitting the market. Steam, primarily an online games distribution service, is a key hub for promoting and distributing both commercial and independent VR game titles. In 2016 it announced its Destinations channel as a way of promoting and enabling sharing of virtual experiences that invite a new way of experiencing presence in a 'place'.

All of these technologies require educators and arts practitioners to give greater attention to firstly the hypermedia spaces where young people are engaging with each other while pursuing cultural practices, enabling new forms of mash-up performance, play, and identity exploration; and secondly, to how young people are starting to reconceive and re-mix the concept of space or place itself through the use of digital forms of representation of 360-degree video and procedurally generated VR worlds. This also forms a key element of the notion of digital liveness that will continue to emerge and develop as a fundamental aspect of many entertainment, education, and creative engagements with real and virtual objects and spaces.

The future is quantified

Learning analytics is now seen as a fundamental use of technology in educational settings, driven by the realization that as more and more aspects of education are facilitated or tracked through online and software applications, it becomes possible to make use of that data to create both individual and group learner profiles. While the claim behind the technology is that it will enable positive institutional and educator responses to learner needs, for example, by identifying 'at-risk' students or monitoring progress towards learning aims, there are those who perceive that it also enables surveillance and potential discrimination.

Learning analytics is a subset of a wider phenomena described as 'big data', which is the collection and analysis of huge data sets generated in all sorts of contexts, and then mined by powerful algorithms to identify previously hidden patterns or trends. Increasingly, big data is being used not just to analyse past trends but to predict future outcomes or behaviours. Like learning analytics, while proponents of big data claim it is merely a science of analysis and prediction that can be used for efficiencies and benefits, there are clearly concerns about the ability to identify individuals and their habits and preferences. For example, it is known that companies like Google and Facebook are able to track individuals as they search and browse information on the web, and generate profiles that archive past activity as well as predict likely future outcomes such as political stance or health status. The fact that much of this big data application is opaque to many users further adds to the sense of risk and exploitation associated with this aspect of our digital lives. It is partly with these types of concerns in mind that we had already forecast 'trust' as a key element of the future for young people in 2006.

We have entered an area of what some have described as the 'quantified self' (Wolf, 2009), or 'lifelogging' (Selke, 2016), where we use all types of media recorders and digital trackers to measure, record, archive, and even share aspects of our personal lives. A common example from the consumer market is the rise of fitness trackers, wearable devices that constantly monitor a range of activities like steps walked, stairs climbed, pulse rates, and even sleep patterns. Apps and services to control or in some cases replace these wearable devices are increasingly built into mobile devices. Modern smartphones include GPS, compasses, accelerometers, and other probes allowing tracking of movement, speed, and location. Some of these devices can track your jogging route onto a map and share it with your friends or publish it openly on the web. Again, this raises concerns about privacy and safety. In the world of big data, this type of fitness information can potentially be shared not just with friends but with health providers or insurance companies who might use it to make assessments of current and future health risk (Lupton, 2016). As Selke notes, 'the real *lifelogging* innovation is the data collection that usually goes unnoticed in daily life' with sensors now constantly collecting data without any decisions required by the individual.

However, there are also performative and creative opportunities made possible by these quantified self-technologies, particularly in the sense that they are a physical connection to our real bodies as we move through physical space. In terms of digital storytelling, combining wearable cameras with biometric data can turn the real world and the real body into components of a multimodal performance. There is a playful response to fitness trackers, for example, in the sense of what might be termed the '*qualified* self', where people use the data generated to make explicit their awareness and reflections on this type of data tracking. There are examples of people deliberately running certain routes and tracking this onto a map to produce images, such as the penises logged by San Francisco runner Claire Wyckoff (Parkinson, 2014).

In terms of the digital identity experimentations discussed in Chapter 3, the quantified self can be regarded as another way for young people to create their own digital archive of biometric and other data, similar to the personal archives discussed in Chapter 7. Also, the emphasis placed on using some data as a motivator or measure for self-improvement means that lifelogging is a way of projecting an individual's 'best self' into the future. Lupton (2016) suggests that 'self-tracking data practices can be understood as self-narratives and the performance of selfhood'. Data must be interpreted and assessed, and then it can be used and shared to present a reflexive narrative of the self.

Conclusion

Digital arts cultures can operate as a partnership of drama strategies, technologies, and media education to help young people investigate realistic visions of the future. A high level of mobile device ownership is not yet matched by even distribution of functionality and user experience. However, combinations of media and data tracking now increasingly common in everyday life illustrate both the risks and potential creative aspects of emerging forms of multimodal production. There is an opportunity to continue shaping these digital arts cultures in more participatory ways, tapping into desired social structures and shared aspirations.

Although we have proposed some possible futures here, we do not suggest that digital media and networked technologies are the only forces that will shape the worlds inhabited by young people. At a functional level, as Steve Dixon observes, 'the technology may still seem extraordinary...but "digital" no longer denotes the future or the magical, merely another tool and facility' (2007, p. 652). What is more 'magical' is the hypermedial nature of spaces for performance, enabling combinations of modes of expression and exploration, and created somewhere between the real and the technological. This is of significance to our social and cultural institutions that must now deal with a form of porosity enabled by digital – and especially mobile – technologies that enable knowledge, experiences, and interactions to seep through institutional borders and barriers.

Our consideration of the future has now set the scene for the final chapter, where we draw a set of conclusions about drama and digital arts cultures.

12

Conclusion

The easy sentiment of the counter-digital

Through this book we have referred to drama and digital arts cultures as a mashup of human acts and technological affordances. These can be more broadly framed as a call to *act* together within and upon the world, engaging through and with technology to understand, enact, and engage with fluidity and precariousness. One of the great strengths of drama is its ability to confront and engage difficult topics and events, using role protection and distancing conventions, for example, to protect participants and create opportunities for affective, critical and transformative learning and understanding. The potential for drama in arts and education contexts to confront the postnormal world and its emerging contradictions, chaos, and complexities continues to offer ways for us to understand and react to the emergent realities, but especially for young people whose brave new world this will be.

As we argued earlier in this book, we do not see drama and technology as binary opposites. They are two elements that can combine to produce new and complex hybrid forms that are part of learning and living as we move forward together in a more liquid world. We have given examples of technology opening up hybrid spaces for drama, education, and artistic endeavour that combine physical and mediated tools and experiences in increasingly seamless and effortless ways. We hope that the mashup of art forms, learning, and approaches to research we have considered within the theoretical context of intermediality show that drama and the digital can blend in productive and creative ways, enabling either new spaces for art and education or at the least an interdisciplinary bridge between different streams of practice.

To illustrate the power of this approach, we can reflect on the journey through this book in terms of Bill Blake's summary of 'the easy sentiment of the counter-digital ... [that] relies on simplified distinctions between the mediated and the real, the technological and the homemade, the universal and the local, the overstated and the unspoken, the endless looping and the organically harmonious, the ridiculously pretentious and the authentically purposeful' (Blake, 2014, p. 25).

The mediated and the real

A common theme that runs throughout this book is that the performing arts have become increasingly mediatized, while at the same time digital art forms have rediscovered the performative nature of creativity. In the frame of digital liveness, we have considered how drama and its conventions for performance and learning are an essential part of the interdisciplinary, hypermedia landscape of digital arts cultures. We believe that is well signposted by the concept of intermediality, which will rightfully be a critical area for ongoing research in arts and education.

The mediated and the real are not distinct ontological propositions, but are liquid and complex systems. As a response to the postnormality of our world, intermediality represents an evolving (both in terms of lived experience and technological development) and reconfiguring system of mediatized performative practices. These can admittedly be difficult for both participants and observers to easily navigate, particularly in institutional settings like schools, universities, and museums. However, rather than simple distinctions between the mediated and the real, the challenges and opportunities of the future can be considered in terms of new mashup experiences. As we have considered in this book, digital liveness blends the mediated and the real. It expands our creative and educational boundaries beyond time, space, and even the assumption of human-only social presence in our daily engagements with entertainment, information, and educational institutions and events.

The technological and the homemade

Blake (2014) notes that counter-digital sentiments around the theatre tend to fall towards a heavily craft-based or 'artisanal' response that emphasizes collaboration, live interaction, and intimacy. In this book we have provided examples, such as in the handmade aesthetics used in popular digital games by Media Molecule mentioned in Chapter 6, that even the idea of craft and the handmade is now heavily mediatized. Although making and working with digital media content is often seen as the opposite of more physical and material forms of artistic work, the more recent 'maker culture' is less definite about these boundaries. Making with digital fabrication equipment like 3D printers, laser cutters, and electronic prototyping platforms, such as Arduinos and Raspberry Pis, is in many ways still seen as embodied, technologized, but artisanal art work. Gauntlett (2011) argues that working with digital and online media is still a 'hands-on' approach to doing and making, and we feel that in this sense embodied presence remains strong even in heavily mediatized forms, or even procedural forms of expression enacted through game design or coding using *Scratch* or *Minecraft*. Design, whether through physical products or computer code, is still a human act of creativity. Many of the specific tools or games considered in this book tap into digital media, as software and hardware, and make use of social and connected experiences that are enabled largely through the networked technologies present in digital arts cultures. They are part of the hands-on maker movement that emphasizes the pursuit of experiential and meaningful projects that invite collaboration, sharing, critiquing, and remixing. Also, to reflect more broadly on technology being seen as an external force, and distinct from something that might be made 'in the home', we considered the concept of playable cities as a model for combining play, performance, and technology in built environments. This suggests new pathways to both real world and digital citizenship. Creativity, playfulness, performance, and digital liveness are all ways that citizens can both reclaim and transform built environments, as well as transform the lives of those that live in them.

The universal and the local

We have seen how many of the features of the liquid world we now inhabit, with its postnormal features of chaos, contradiction, and complexity, are generated in the collisions of global and local cultures. We can no longer see clear distinctions between those things that will impact on us all and those that are only of interest or concern to a smaller group. The portmanteau term of 'glocal' is sometimes used to capture this merging of global and local. This is not always a smooth or mutually beneficial process, and the resulting friction is often justifiably characterized in negative terms, because it is true that it produces the rapid changes that are often considered problematic for those caught up in the shifts. We have examined how this is especially the case in education, and also suggested that institutional constraints and siloed disciplines can contribute to the impacts of these changes. However, in this book we have tried, without gratuitously advocating the role of technology for its own sake, to suggest how playful experimentation with cultural assets including the technologies and affordances of digital networked media can help to mitigate some of the negative effects of postnormality.

We have also considered how notions of the universal and the local can begin to blend when considering approaches to researching intermediality. We have noted that all participants in this type of research will be individuals with their own cultural identities and constructed realities, and as such will be unique cases. However the interdisciplinary and collaborative processes suitable for research projects in intermediate spaces will provide opportunities for making comparisons and contrasts that may lead to a better understanding of the wider world of experience and learning. The nature of our fluid world and the interdisciplinary nature of this emergent field ensure that research in this area will constantly feature innovation, adaptation, and agility. This requires us to engage with both traditional and emergent research, forming a clear understanding of our research intentions, and taking a wider and more universal view to the potential audiences and stakeholders for what might initially seem to be a local or specific case for research.

The overstated and the unspoken

In formal education settings such as schools and universities, resources are being committed to digital technology infrastructure. Investment in technology is not new, but the ratio of budget spent on digital systems as opposed to say physical buildings and teaching staff is shifting in favour of large-scale digital 'solutions'. Technology investment by educational institutions has generally been 'based on what they believe students need, want, and already have' (Oblinger and Oblinger, 2005, p. 1.3). Increasingly, and often as a budgetary rather than a purely pedagogical concern, focus has shifted to what learners may already have in terms of both technology and the digital skills or literacies to work and learn with them. Consequently, it has become attractive to assume that new generations of students are more self-sufficient than their predecessors with digital media. It was easy to view young people as digital media savants, and believe that new technology is the domain of the *next* generation. Marc Prensky (2001) gave rise to some of the most evangelical claims that students were 'Digital Natives', while their teachers were, for the most part, 'Digital Immigrants', leading in turn to an academic 'moral panic' around the need for radical changes (Bennett, Maton, and Kervin, 2008). It has generally become more widely recognized now that these generalizations about young people's acuity with technology are often overstated (Anderson, Carroll, and Cameron, 2009, p. 8). Concerns about the limitations of young people's digital literacies, and articulation of productive and helpful ways to address gaps and even negative practices, are no longer the unspoken or specialist concerns of the few.

While often overstating the digital literacies and practices of young people, there has been a risk of silencing the creativity and innovation they display in these spaces. It is perhaps convenient to dismiss the often playful explorations of digital technology exhibited by young people outside of formal settings as time wasting or disruptive when transferred to classroom or workplace. We have discussed in this book how digital arts cultures are highly performative and playful, and reflective of many types of identity play that may not even be visible or understandable to people outside those cultures (especially adults). We need to keep working towards a greater appreciation of both the overt (overstated) and less visible (unspoken) presentations of self in performative mediatized spaces to inform both our classroom and applied drama practices and enhance our perspectives of new media and entertainment forms.

The endless looping and the organically harmonious

In this book we have provided examples of digital media, especially procedural code, increasingly becoming intertwined with live performance in ways that can blur the ontological nature of the 'performer'. In our discussion of the Beowulf Sydney Project, for example, we described how a group of young people and teachers experimented with possible ways of integrating different live and digital elements in performance. They developed a more sophisticated understanding of live and digital drama, a blended creative endeavour framed by given rules, mechanics, and conventions.

We have also considered ways in which digital media's performance and archiving affordances are changing our view that live performance is the realm of the physical and organic. Procedural media with its looping code sequences and algorithmic computations can be used for real-time performance, as seen in machinima and game 'speed-run' demos, for example. This sense of digital liveness, both in terms of the game world being generated on-the-fly and the procedural responsiveness to human player/performers, is what makes machinima different to pre-rendered digital animation. Similar archives of dance or dramatic performance, such as, National Theatre Live, are renegotiating the boundaries of code and live presence on the spectrum of experiencing and researching performance.

The ridiculously pretentious and the authentically purposeful

There is a temptation to evaluate many aspects of arts and education as falling more into one of these two 'easy sentiments', if we treat them as descriptive categories. To some extent it is a very subjective view as to where some of the theories and practice we have described or proposed in this book are grounded. Our goal has been to consider how the cultural landscape is increasingly both mediatized and enacted at many global and personal levels, and it is inevitable that some will regard our mashups of drama, technology, and education as hyperbole or not applicable to their own settings. Others (we hope) will see that digital arts cultures can operate as a partnership of drama strategies, technologies, and media education to help young people purposefully investigate and purposefully create realistic visions of the authentic future.

NOTES

Chapter 1

1   The 'Hack the News' screenshot used in this book is taken from https://mozilla.github.io/webmaker-curriculum/WebLiteracyBasics-I/session02-hackthenews.html. More resources are available at the Mozilla Learning Network (https://learning.mozilla.org/), which provides a central hub for tools like X-Ray Goggles, and a range of learning activities around learning to code and make web content.

2   Other projects have combined drama conventions like Newspaper Theatre with relatively common technologies such as PowerPoint slides and classroom audio/visual equipment (Boland and Cameron, 2005) and Twitter (Wotzko, 2012).

Chapter 2

1   The Programme for International Student Assessment (PISA) was developed and administered by the Organisation for Economic Co-operation and Development (OECD).

2   See, for example, the online repository of theatre performances at National Theatre Live: http://ntlive.nationaltheatre.org.uk/.

Chapter 3

1   The relevant issue of *The New Yorker* is now online; however, a subscription is necessary to view the content. Although the image is copyright, it can be readily found in a Google search. It was also reproduced in a *Washington Post* article on the twentieth anniversary of its publication, which is available online at http://wpo.st/bBNo1.

2 The Kardashians are a US 'celebrity' family featured in the reality TV show *Keeping Up with the Kardashians*: http://www.eonline.com/shows/kardashians

3 lonelygirl15 was a series of YouTube video blogs from a teenage girl, Bree, that ran from 2006 to 2008. Although framed as if they were real blogs from a real teenager, the series was revealed to be fictional.

4 The term 'vlog' is a portmanteau of 'video' and 'blog'. It is a monologue to camera, traditionally filmed using a webcam.

5 Instagram does not require a profile representing your real self; however, as Facebook owns the platform, a user's accounts are often connected.

Chapter 5

1 For consistency we have used the term 'students' instead of actors or participants here because the intent of this project was predominantly pedagogical. It is also less confusing than describing the same student as a puppeteer, game maker, actor, and so on. In this project most students took on multiple roles. It also leaves room for the possibility of co-construction of pedagogy and performance, which was the initial intent, and to some extent the outcome of the project.

2 The Sydney team comprised Professor Michael Anderson, The University of Sydney (research co-ordinator), Phil Relf (puppetry and South Sydney Council), Dr David Cameron (digital gaming and researcher), Phil Glen (digital video), Celina McEwen (researcher), and Howard Matthew (ATYP coordinator).

3 ATYP is the pre-eminent theatre for young people in Australia and runs school holiday workshops in theatre and acting for students from 4 to 18.

4 For consistency we have used the term 'teachers' to cover the facilitators, academics, teaching artists, and researchers who were involved in the teaching on this project.

5 Missionmaker is the game-design tool used to create the game sequences that were incorporated into the performance.

6 There are several freely available examples on the web, and the storyboard we used is at: http://www.storyboardthat.com/storyboards/rebeccaray/heroic -journey-beowulf.

Chapter 8

1 *Scratch* is developed by the Lifelong Kindergarten Group at the MIT Media Lab. See http://scratch.mit.edu.

Chapter 9

1 This quote is most often attributed to MetaFilter user blue_beetle: http://www.metafilter.com/95152/Userdriven-discontent#3256046
2 See http://www.oel.edu.au for more information on the Open Education Licensing project, and the Continuum of Openness.

Chapter 10

1 Denzin and Lincoln call the qualitative researcher a Bricoleur, or one who produces a bricolage, that is a pieced-together, close-knit set of practices that provide solutions to a problem in a concrete situation (1994, p. 2). As the Bricoleur analogy suggests, qualitative methodology is 'multi method in focus' (Denzin and Lincoln, 1994, p. 2). It is now important to explore the research question and then elucidate the bricolage that has been constructed to fit the question.

REFERENCES

Aarseth, E. J. (1997). *Cybertext: Perspectives on ergodic literature*. Baltimore, MD: Johns Hopkins University Press.

Abboud, R. (2016). Public space versus Pokémon Go. *Architecture AU*. Retrieved from http://architectureau.com/articles/public-space-versus-pokemon-go/

Adams, T. (2014). Golem, the clay man with a message to subvert our Christmas tech-fest. *The Observer*. Retrieved from http://www.theguardian.com/stage/2014/dec/21/golem-clay-man-with-a-message

Allard, J., & North, R. (2014). *Beowulf and other stories: A new introduction to Old English, Old Icelandic and Anglo-Norman literatures*. Abingdon: Routledge.

Alrutz, M. (2015). *Digital storytelling, applied theatre, & youth*. London: Routledge.

Anderson, C. (2004). The long tail. *Wired*. Retrieved from http://www.wired.com/2004/10/tail/

Anderson, C. (2012). *Makers: The new industrial revolution*. New York, NY: Crown Business.

Anderson, M. (2012). *MasterClass in drama education: Transforming teaching and learning*. London: Continuum.

Anderson, M. (2014). The challenge of post-normality to drama education and applied theatre. *Research in Drama Education*, 19(1), 110–120.

Anderson, M. (2015). Drama, creativity and learning. In S. Schonmann (Ed.), *International Yearbook for Research in Arts Education 2015: The wisdom of the many – Key issues in arts education* (pp. 235–240). Munster: Waxman.

Anderson, M., & Cameron, D. (2013). Drama and learning technologies: To affinity spaces and beyond. In M. Anderson & J. Dunn (Eds.), *How drama activates learning* (pp. 226–244). London: Bloomsbury.

Anderson, M., Carroll, J., & Cameron, D. (Eds.). (2009). *Drama education with digital technology*. London: Continuum.

Anderson, M., & Jefferson, M. (2016). Teaching creativity: Unlocking educational opportunity. In P. O'Connor (Ed.), *The possibilities of creativity* (pp. 151–170). Newcastle upon Tyne, UK: Cambridge Scholars Publishing.

Anderson, M., & Wilkinson, L. (2007). A resurgence of verbatim theatre: Authenticity, empathy and transformation. *Australasian Drama Studies*, 50, 153–169.

Apperley, T., & Beavis, C. (2011). Literacy into action: Digital games as action and text in the English and literacy classroom. *Pedagogies: An International Journal*, 6(2), 130–143.

Auslander, P. (1999). *Liveness: Performance in a mediatized culture*. London; New York, NY: Routledge.

Auslander, P. (2002). Live from cyberspace: Or, I was sitting at my computer this guy appeared he thought I was a bot. *Performing Arts Journal*, 70, 16–21.

Auslander, P. (2012). Digital liveness: A historico-philosophical perspective. *PAJ: A Journal of Performance and Art*, 34(3), 3–11.

Auslander, P. (Writer). (2014). *On Liveness: Pre/During/Post* [Videorecording]. Retrieved from http://bcove.me/63yl0hym

Baker, S. A. (2011). The mediated crowd: New social media and new forms of rioting. *Sociological Research Online*, 16(4), 21.

Bannan-Ritland, B., & Baek, J. (2008). Teacher design research: An emerging paradigm for teachers' professional development. In Anthony E. Kelly, Richard A. Lesh, & John Y. Baek (Eds.), *Handbook of design research methods in education* (pp. 246–262). London: Routledge.

Barba, L. A. (2016). Computational Thinking: I do not think it means what you think it means. *medium.com*. Retrieved from https://medium.com/@lorenaabarba/computational-thinking-i-do-not-think-it-means-what-you-think-it-means-6d39e854fa90#.vizrrik9s

Baudrillard, J. (1983). *Simulations* (P. Beitchman, P. Foss, & P. Patton, Trans.). Cambridge, MA: MIT Press.

Bauman, Z. (2000). *Liquid modernity*. Cambridge: Polity Press.

BBC. (2015). The BBC micro:bit. *Make it digital*. Retrieved from http://www.bbc.co.uk/programmes/articles/4hVG2Br1W1LKCmw8nSm9WnQ/the-bbc-micro-bit

Belliveau, G., & Lea, G. (2011). Research-based theatre in education. In S. Schonmann (Ed.), *Key concepts in theatre drama education* (pp. 332–338). Rotterdam: Sense Publishers.

Benjamin, W. (1935/1968). The work of art in the age of mechanical reproduction (H. Zohn, Trans.). In H. Arendt (Ed.), *Illuminations*. New York, NY: Schocken Books.

Bennett, S. (2013). *Theatre and museums*. New York, NY: Palgrave Macmillan.

Bennett, S., Maton, K. A., & Kervin, L. (2008). The 'digital natives' debate: A critical review of the evidence. *British Journal of Educational Technology*, 39(5), 775–786.

Berry, M. J., & Westfall, A. (2015). Dial D for distraction: The making and breaking of cell phone policies in the college classroom. *College Teaching*, 63(2), 62–71.

Blake, B. (2014). *Theatre & the digital*. Houndmills: Palgrave Macmillan.

Blast Theory. (2016). Our history & approach. *Blast Theory*. Retrieved from http://www.blasttheory.co.uk/our-history-approach/

Blau, H. (2002). The human nature of the bot: A response to Philip Auslander. *Performing Arts Journal*, 70, 22–24.

Blizzard Entertainment. (2004). *World of Warcraft.* Irvine, CA: Author.

Blizzard Entertainment. (2010). *Starcraft 2: Wings of liberty.* Irvine, CA: Author.

Boal, A. (1979). *Theatre of the oppressed.* London: Pluto Press.

Boal, A. (1995). *The rainbow of desire.* London: Routledge.

Boal, A. (1998). *Legislative theatre: Using performance to make politics.* London: Routledge.

Boal, A. (2015). *Rainbow of desire.* London: Routledge.

Bogost, I. (2016). *Play anything: The pleasure of limits, the uses of boredom, and the secret of games.* New York, NY: Basic Books.

Boland, G., & Cameron, D. (2005). *Newspaper Theatre: Applying performance-based learning to journalism education.* Paper presented at the Journalism Education Association conference, Surfers Paradise, November.

Bolter, J. D., & Grusin, R. A. (1999). *Remediation: Understanding new media.* Cambridge, MA: MIT Press.

Bolter, J. D., MacIntyre, B., Nitsche, M., & Farley, K. (2013). Liveness, presence, and performance in contemporary digital media. In U. Ekman (Ed.), *Throughout: Art and culture emerging with ubiquitous computing* (pp. 323–336). Cambridge, MA: MIT Press.

Bolton, G. (1986). *Towards a theory of drama in education.* Harlow: Longman.

Bower, J. L., & Christensen, C. M. (1995). Disruptive technologies: Catching the wave. *Harvard Business Review, 73*(1), 43–53.

boyd, d. (2007). Why youth (heart) social network sites: The role of networked publics in teenage social life. In D. Buckingham (Ed.), *MacArthur Foundation series on digital learning: Youth, identity, and digital media volume.* Cambridge, MA: MIT Press.

boyd, d. (2014). *It's complicated: The social lives of networked teens.* New Haven, CT: Yale University Press.

Brennan, K., & Resnick, M. (2012). *Using artifact-based interviews to study the development of computational thinking in interactive media design.* Paper presented at the annual American Educational Research Association meeting, Vancouver.

Bromwich, J. E. (2016). Where Pokémon should not go. *New York Times.* Retrieved from http://www.nytimes.com/2016/07/13/technology/where-pokemon-should-not-go.html

Bruner, J. S. (1990). *Acts of meaning* (Vol. 3). Cambridge, MA: Harvard University Press.

Bruns, A. (2006). Towards produsage: Futures for user-led content production. In Fay Sudweeks, Herbert Hrachovec, & Charles Ess (Eds.), *Cultural attitudes towards communication and technology 2006,* 28 June–1 July, Tartu, Estonia.

Bruns, A. (2008). *Blogs, Wikipedia, Second Life, and beyond: From production to produsage.* New York, NY: Peter Lang.

Buckingham, D. (2007). Digital Media Literacies: Rethinking media education in the age of the Internet. *Research in Comparative and International Education*, 2(1), 43–55.

Buckingham, D. (2008). Introducing identity. In D. Buckingham (Ed.), *Youth identity and digital media*. Boston, MA: MIT Press.

Burgess, J., & Green, J. (2009). *YouTube: Online video and participatory culture*. Cambridge, UK: Polity Press.

Burn, A. (2013). Computer games on the playground: Ludic systems, dramatized narrative and virtual embodiment. In R. Willett, C. Richards, J. Marsh, A. Burn, & J. C. Bishop (Eds.), *Children, media and playground cultures: Ethnographic studies of school playtimes*. Basingstoke: Palgrave Macmillan.

Burn, A. (2015). *Playing Beowulf: Gaming the library*. Retrieved from https://darecollaborative.net/2015/03/11/playing-beowulf-gaming-the-library/

Cahill, H. (2006). Research acts: Using the drama workshop as a site for conducting participatory action research. *NJ: Drama Australia Journal*, 30(2), 61–72.

Cameron, D., & Carroll, J. (2009). Lessons from applied drama: Conventions to help serious games developers. In O. Petrovic & A. Brand (Eds.), *Serious games on the move*. Vienna: Springer.

Cameron, D., & Carroll, J. (2011). Encoding liveness: Performance and real-time rendering. In H. Lowood & M. Nitsche (Eds.), *The machinima reader* (pp. 127–142). Cambridge, MA: MIT press.

Cameron, D., Carroll, J., & Wotzko, R. (2011). *Epistemic games and applied drama: Converging conventions for serious play*. Paper presented at the Digital Games Research Association, Hilversum, the Netherlands.

Cameron, D., & Wotzko, R. (2015). Hold the phone: Drama education and mobile technology. In M. Anderson & C. Roche (Eds.), *The state of the art: Teaching drama in the 21st century* (pp. 149–169). Sydney: Sydney University Press.

Cameron, J. (Writer). (1984). *The Terminator* [Motion picture].

Caragliu, A., Del Bo, C., & Nijkamp, P. (2011). Smart cities in Europe. *Journal of Urban Technology*, 18(2), 65–82. doi:10.1080/10630732.2011.601117

Carrington, D. (2016). An energy first as UK successfully transmits data via national electricity grid. *The Guardian*. Retrieved from https://www.theguardian.com/environment/2016/oct/11/energy-first-as-uk-successfully-transmits-data-via-national-electricity-grid

Carroll, J. (1986). Framing drama: Some classroom strategies. *National Association for Drama in Education Journal*, 12(2), 5–7.

Carroll, J. (1996). Escaping the information abattoir: Critical and transformative research in drama classrooms. In P. Taylor (Ed.), *Researching drama and arts education: Paradigms and possibilities* (pp. 72–84). London: Falmer Press.

Carroll, J. (2002). Digital drama: A snapshot of evolving forms. *Drama & learning: Melbourne Studies in Education, 43*(2), 130–141.

Carroll, J. (2004). Digital pre-text: Process drama and everyday technology. In C. Hatton & M. Anderson (Eds.), *The state of the art: NSW perspectives in educational drama.* Sydney: Currency Press.

Carroll, J., Anderson, M., & Cameron, D. (2006). *Real players? Drama, technology and education.* Stoke-on-Trent: Trentham Books.

Carroll, J., & Cameron, D. (2005). Playing the game: Role distance and digital performance. *Applied Theatre Researcher, 6*, 1–11.

Carroll, J., & Cameron, D. (2014). Social media networks and the 'unthinkable present': A users' perspective. In R. Stocker & T. Bossomaier (Eds.), *Networks in society: Links and language* (pp. 167–200). Singapore: Pan Stanford.

Carroll, J., & Xu, R. (2012). *Time of flight: Biodigital feedback and performance design.* Paper presented at the Performance: Visual aspects of performance practice, 2nd Global Conference, 2011, Prague.

Causey, M. (2006). *Theatre and performance in digital culture: From simulation to embeddedness.* Abingdon: Routledge.

CEDA. (2015). *Australia's future workforce?* Committee for Economic Development of Australia, Melbourne.

Chan, V. (2015). *Facebook reports fourth quarter and full year 2014 results.* Retrieved from https://investor.fb.com/investor-news/press-release -details/2015/Facebook-Reports-Fourth-Quarter-and-Full-Year-2014 -Results/default.aspx

Cheung, C. (2000). A home on the web: Presentation of self on personal homepage. In D. Gauntlett (Ed.), *Web studies: Rewiring media studies for the digital age.* London: Arnold.

Cheung, C., & Huang, J. (2011). *Starcraft from the stands: Understanding the game spectator.* Paper presented at the Proceedings of the SIGCHI Conference on Human Factors in Computing Systems.

Christiane, P. (2005). Intermedia in the digital age. In H. Breder & K.-P. Busse (Eds.), *Intermedia: Enacting the liminal* (pp. 36–50). Dortmund: Dortmunder Schriften zur kunst.

Chung, S. K. (2007). Art education technology: Digital storytelling. *Art Education, 60*(2), 17–22.

Coleridge, S. T. (1817). *Biographia literaria; or, Biographical sketches of my literary life and opinions.* New York, NY: Published by Kirk and Merein.

Come Out and Play. (2016). About. *Come Out & Play.* Retrieved from http:// www.comeoutandplay.org/about/

Conrad, D. (2004). Exploring risky youth experiences: Popular theatre as a participatory, performative research method. *International Journal of Qualitative Methods, 3*(1), 12–25.

Corti, K., & Gillespie, A. (2015). A truly human interface: Interacting face-to-face with someone whose words are determined by a computer program. *Frontiers in Psychology*, 6. doi:10.3389/fpsyg.2015.00634

Couldry, N. (2004). Liveness, 'reality', and the mediated habitus from television to the mobile phone. *Communication Review*, 7(4), 353–361.

Craft, A. (2002). *Creativity and early years education*. London: Continuum.

Craft, A. (2003). *Creativity across the primary curriculum: Framing and developing practice*. London: Routledge.

Csikszentmihalyi, M. (1990). *Flow: The psychology of optimal experience* (1st ed.). New York, NY: Harper & Row.

Curwood, J. S., Magnifico, A. M., & Lammers, J. C. (2013). Writing in the wild: Writers' motivation in fan-based affinity spaces. *Journal of Adolescent & Adult Literacy*, 56(8), 677–685.

Cutica, I., Iani, F., & Bucciarelli, M. (2014). Learning from text benefits from enactment. *Memory & Cognition*, 42(7), 1026–1037.

Darling-Hammond, L. (2004). Standards, accountability, and school reform. *Teachers College Record*, 106(6), 1047–1085.

Davis, S., Ferholt, B., Grainger Clemson, H., Jansson, S.-M., & Marjanovic-Shane, A. (Eds.). (2015). *Vygotskian and sociocultural approaches to drama, education and research*. London: Bloomsbury.

Denzin, N. K. (1994). Introduction: Entering the field of qualitative research. In Norman K. Denzin and Yvonn S. Lincoln (Eds.), *Handbook of qualitative research*. Thousand Oaks, CA: Sage.

Denzin, N. K., & Lincoln, Y. S (Eds.). (2005). *The Sage handbook of qualitative research* (3rd ed.). London: Sage.

Depoorter, D. (2015). *TinderIn*. Retrieved from http://driesdepoorter.be/tinderin/

Derrida, J., & Prenowitz, E. (1995). Archive fever: A Freudian impression. *Diacritics*, 25(2), 9–63.

DeVane, B. (2012). Whither membership? Identity and social learning in affinity spaces. In E. R. Hayes & S. C. Duncan (Eds.), *Learning in video game affinity spaces* (pp. 162–185). New York, NY: Peter Lang Publishing.

Dixon, S. (2007). *Digital performance: A history of new media in theater, dance, performance art, and installation*. Cambridge, MA: MIT Press.

Duncan, S. C., & Hayes, E. R. (2012). Expanding the affinity space: An introduction. In E. R. Hayes & S. C. Duncan (Eds.), *Learning in video game affinity spaces* (pp. 1–22). New York, NY: Peter Lang Publishing.

Dunn, J., & O'Toole, J. (2009). When worlds collude: Exploring the relationship between the actual, the dramatic and the virtual. In M. Anderson, J. Carroll, & D. Cameron (Eds.), *Drama education with digital technology* (pp. 20–37). London: Continuum.

Eco, U. (1989). *The open work* (A. Cancogni, Trans.). Cambridge, MA: Harvard University Press.

Educause. (2013). *7 Things you should know about maker spaces*. Retrieved from https://net.educause.edu/ir/library/pdf/eli7095.pdf

Eisner, E. W. (1978). Humanistic trends and the curriculum field. *Journal of Curriculum Studies*, 10(3), 197–204.

Ely, M. (1991). *Doing qualitative research: Circles within circles* (Vol. 3). London: Psychology Press.

Erikson, E. (1968). *Identity, youth and crisis*. New York, NY: Norton.

Eriksson, S. A. (2011). Distancing. In *Key concepts in theatre/drama education* (pp. 65–71). Rotterdam: Sense Publishers.

Facer, K., Joiner, R., Stanton, D., Reid, J., Hull, R., & Kirk, D. (2004). Savannah: Mobile gaming and learning? *Journal of Computer Assisted Learning*, 20(6), 399–409. doi:10.1111/j.1365-2729.2004.00105.x

Farag, B. (2016). Please don't learn to code. *TechCrunch*. Retrieved from http://social.techcrunch.com/2016/05/10/please-dont-learn-to-code/

Farthing, A. (2009). Audio drama and museums: Informal learning, drama and technology. In M. Anderson, J. Carroll, & D. Cameron (Eds.), *Drama education with digital technology*. London: Continuum.

Fels, L. (2011). A dead man's sweater: Performative inquiry embodied and recognised. In S. Shonmann (Ed.), *Key concepts in theatre/drama education*. Rotterdam: Sense Publishers.

Fels, L., & Belliveau, G. A. (2008). *Exploring curriculum: Performative inquiry, role drama, and learning*. Vancouver: Pacific Educational Press.

Fischer, G. (2004). *Social creativity: Turning barriers into opportunities for collaborative design*. Proceedings of the eighth conference on Participatory design: Artful integration: interweaving media, materials and practices, July, Volume 1 (pp. 152–161). ACM.

Fish, W. J. (2016). 'Post-Truth' politics and illusory democracy. *Psychotherapy and Politics International*, 14(3), 211–213. doi:10.1002/ppi.1387

Flanagan, M. (2009). *Critical play: Radical game design*. Cambridge, MA: MIT Press.

Flintoff, K. (2009). Second Life/simulation: Online sites for generative play. In M. Anderson, J. Carroll, & D. Cameron (Eds.), *Drama education with digital technology* (pp. 202–221). London: Continuum.

Florida, R. (2014). *The rise of the creative class – revisited: Revised and expanded*. New York: Basic books.

Fontana, A., & Frey, J. (1988). Interviewing: The art of science. In Norman K. Denzin and Yvonn S. Lincoln (Eds.), *The handbook of qualitative research* (pp. 47–79). Thousand Oaks: Sage.

Frasca, G. (2001). *Videogames of the oppressed: Videogames as a means for critical thinking and debate*. Atlanta: Georgia Institute of Technology.

Frey, C., & Osborne, M. (2013). Improving technology now means that nearly 50 percent of occupations in the US are under threat of computerisation. *LSE American Politics and Policy (USAPP) Blog*. Retrieved from http://blogs .lse.ac.uk/usappblog/2013/09/30/computerisation-50-percent-occupations -threatened

Fryer, N. (2010). From reproduction to creativity and the aesthetic: Towards an ontological approach to the assessment of devised performance. *RiDE: The Journal of Applied Theatre and Performance*, 15(4), 547–562.

Funtowicz, S., & Ravetz, J. R. (1991). A new scientific methodology for global environmental issues. In R. Constanza (Ed.), *The ecological economics* (pp. 137–152). New York, NY: Columbia University Press.

Funtowicz, S., & Ravetz, J. R. (1993). Science for the post-normal age. *Futures*, 25(7), 735–755.

Gallagher, K. (2007). *The theatre of urban: Youth and schooling in dangerous time*. Toronto and Buffalo: University of Toronto Press.

Gallagher, K. (2008). The art of methodology: A collaborative science. In K. Gallagher (Ed.), *The methodological dilemma: Creative, critical and collaborative approaches to qualitative research*. Oxford: Routledge.

Gallagher, K. (2011). Theatre as methodology or, what experimentation affords us. In S. Shonmann (Ed.), *Key concepts in theatre/drama education*. Rotterdam: Sense Publishers.

Gallagher, K., & Neelands, J. (2011). Drama and theatre in urban contexts. *RiDE: The Journal of Applied Theatre and Performance*, 16(2), 151–156.

Gardiner, B. (2014). Adding coding to the curriculum. *International New York Times*, 24 March. Retrieved from www.nytimes.com/2014/03/24/world/ europe/adding-coding-to-the-curriculum.html

Gardiner, E., & Musto, R. G. (2015). Introduction to the digital humanities. In E. Gardiner & R. G. Musto (Eds.), *The digital humanities: A primer for students and scholars* (pp. 1–13). Cambridge: Cambridge University Press.

Garza, A. (2014). A herstory of the #BlackLivesMatter movement. *The Feminist Wire*. Retrieved from http://www.thefeministwire.com/2014/10/ blacklivesmatter-2/

Gattenhof, S. J. (2004). *Young people and performance: The impact of deterritorialisation on contemporary theatre for young people*. PhD thesis. Retrieved from http://eprints.qut.edu.au/15934/

Gauntlett, D. (2011). *Making Is Connecting: The social meaning of creativity, from DIY and knitting to YouTube and Web 2.0*. Cambridge: Polity Press.

Gee, J. P. (2004). *Situated language and learning: A critique of traditional schooling*. New York, NY: Routledge.

Gee, J. P. (2013). *The anti-education era: Creating smarter students through digital learning*. New York, NY: Palgrave Macmillan.

Gilliland-Swetland, A. (2000). *Enduring paradigm, new opportunities. The value of the archival perspective in the digital environment.* Washington, DC: Council on Library and Information Resources. Retrieved from http://www.clir.org/pubs/reports/pub89/pub89.pdf

Glascock, T. (2015). Hipster Barbie is so much better at Instagram than you. *Wired.* Retrieved from http://www.wired.com/2015/09/hipster-barbie-much-better-instagram/

Goffman, E. (1956). *The presentation of self in everyday life.* Edinburgh: University of Edinburgh, Social Sciences Research Centre.

Goffman, E. (1974). *Frame analysis: An essay on the organization of experience.* New York, NY: Harper & Row.

Goggin, G. (2006). *Cell phone culture: Mobile technology in everyday life.* Abington: Routledge.

Goggin, G. (2017). Locating mobile media audiences: In plain view with Pokémon Go. In C. Hight & R. Harindranath (Eds.), *Studying digital media audiences: Perspectives from Australasia.* New York, NY: Routledge.

Gourlay, L. (2015). 'Student engagement' and the tyranny of participation. *Teaching in Higher Education,* 20(4), 402–411. doi:10.1080/13562517.2015.1020784

Grady, S. (1996). Toward the practice of theory in practice. In P. Taylor (Ed.), *Researching drama and arts education: Paradigms and possibilities.* London: Falmer Press.

Hamilton, W. A., Garretson, O., & Kerne, A. (2014). *Streaming on twitch: Fostering participatory communities of play with live mixed media.* CHI '14 proceedings of the SIGCHI conference on human factors in computing systems (pp. 1315–1324). Toronto, Canada.

Harris, A. M. (2014). *The creative turn: Toward a new aesthetic imaginary.* Rotterdam: Sense Publishers.

Hartley, J. (2012). *Digital futures for cultural and media studies.* Chichester, West Sussex; Malden, MA: Wiley-Blackwell.

Hartnoll, P., & Brater, E. (2012). *The theatre: A concise history.* New York: Thames & Hudson.

Haseman, B. (2006). A manifesto for performative research. *Media International Australia Incorporating Culture and Policy,* 118, 98–106.

Haseman, B. (2014). *Testing Times: Patiently waiting for the unforeseen.* Retrieved from http://www.tate.org.uk/research/research-centres/learning-research/working-papers/testing-times-waiting-patiently-for-unforeseen

Heathcote, D. (1984). *The collected writings.* London: Heinemann.

Heathcote, D. (2006). Foreword. In J. Carroll, M. Anderson, & D. Cameron (Eds.), *Real players? Drama, technology and education* (pp. ix–xiii). Stoke on Trent: Trentham.

Henry, M. (2000). Drama's ways of learning. *Research in Drama Education,* 5(1), 45–62.

Heppell, S., & Chapman, C. (2011). *Effective practice for schools moving to end locking and blocking in the classroom.* Retrieved from http://rubble.heppell .net/cloudlearn/media/Cloudlearn_Report.pdf

Hide & Seek. (2012). *99 tiny games.* Retrieved from http://hideandseek.net/ projects/99-tiny-games/

Hide & Seek. (2013). *The Hide & Seek Story.* Retrieved from http://hideandseek .net/story

Hirschberg, P., Gougherty, D. & Kadanoff, M. (2016). *Maker city: A practical guide for reinventing American cities.* Sebastopol, CA: Maker Media.

Hollands, R. G. (2008). Will the real smart city please stand up? *City,* 12(3), 303–320. doi:10.1080/13604810802479126

Hsu, H.-m. J. (2011). The potential of Kinect in education. *International Journal of Information and Education Technology,* 1(5), 365–370.

Hughes, J., MacNamara, C., & Kidd, J. (2011). The usefulness of mess: Artistry, improvisation and decomposition in the practice of research in applied theatre. In B. Kershaw & H. Nicholson (Eds.), *Research methods in theatre and performance.* Edinburgh: Edinburgh University Press.

Huizinga, J. (1938/1955). *Homo ludens: A study of the play-element in culture.* Boston, MA: Beacon Press.

Hunter, M. (2015). Rethinking industry partnerships: Arts education and uncertainty in liquid modern life. In M. Fleming, L. Bresler, & J. O'Toole (Eds.), *Routledge international handbook of the arts and education.* New York, NY: Routledge.

Igoe, T. (2016). Stop teaching programming, start teaching computational thinking. *Make.* Retrieved from http://makezine.com/2016/04/05/stop -teaching-programming-start-teaching-computational-thought/

InXile Entertainment. (2009). Line Rider. Newport Beach, CA.

Ito, M., Gutiérrez, K., Livingstone, S., Penuel, B., Rhodes, J., Salen, K., and Watkins, S. C. (2013). *Connected learning: An agenda for research and design.* Irvine, CA: Digital Media and Learning Research Hub.

Jackson, A. (2000). Inter-acting with the past – The use of participatory theatre at museums and heritage sites. *Research in Drama Education,* 5(2), 199–215.

Janesick, V. (1994). The dance of qualitative research design: Metaphor, methodolatry and meaning. In N. Denzin & Y. Lincoln (Eds.), *Handbook of qualitative research.* Thousand Oaks, CA: Sage.

Jefferson, M., & Anderson, M. (2017). *Transforming schools: Creativity, critical reflection, communication, collaboration.* London: Bloomsbury.

Jeffrey, B., & Craft, A. (2001). The universalization of creativity. In A. Craft, B. Jeffrey, & M. Leibling (Eds.), *Creativity in education* (pp. 17–34). London: Continuum.

Jenkins, H. (2006a). *Convergence culture: Where old and new media collide.* New York, NY: New York University Press.

Jenkins, H. (2006b). *Fans, bloggers and gamers: Exploring participatory culture.* New York, NY: New York University Press.

Jenkins, H. (2008). *Convergence culture: Where old and new media collide.* New York, NY: New York University Press.

Jenkins, H., & Bertozzi, V. (2008). Artistic expression in the age of participatory culture: How and why young people create. In S. J. Tepper & B. Ivey (Eds.), *Engaging art: The next great transformation of America's cultural life.* New York, NY: Routledge.

Jenkins, H., Ford, S., & Green, J. (2013). *Spreadable media: Creating value and meaning in a networked culture.* New York, NY; London: New York University Press.

Jenkins, H., Ito, M., & boyd, d. (2015). *Participatory culture in a networked era: A conversation on youth, learning, commerce, and politics.* Cambridge, UK; Malden, MA: Polity Press.

Jenkins, H., Purushotma, R., Weigel, M., Clinton, K., & Robison, A. J. (2009). *Confronting the challenges of participatory culture: Media education for the 21st century.* Cambridge, MA: MIT Press.

Jenkins, H., & Squire, K. (2002). The art of contested spaces. In L. King (Ed.), *Game on: The history and culture of video games.* London: Barbican.

Jensen, A. P. (2008). Multimodal literacy and theater education. *Arts Education Policy Review,* 109(5), 19–28.

Johnson, R. B., & Onwuegbuzie, A. J. (2004). Mixed methods research: A research paradigm whose time has come. *Educational Researcher,* 33(7), 14–26.

Kafai, Y. B., & Burke, Q. (2015). Constructionist gaming: Understanding the benefits of making games for learning. *Educational Psychologist,* 50(4), 313–334. doi:10.1080/00461520.2015.1124022

Kattenbelt, C. (2008). Intermediality in theatre and performance: Definitions, perceptions and medial relationships. *Culture, Language and Representation,* 6(7), 19–29.

Kelion, L. (2015). BBC Micro Bit computer's final design revealed. BBC News. Retrieved from http://www.bbc.com/news/technology-33409311

Kemmis, S., & McTaggart, R. (2005). *Participatory action research: Communicative action and the public sphere.* Thousand Oaks: Sage Publications Ltd.

Kennedy, G. E., Judd, T. S., Churchward, A., Gray, K., & Krause, K.-L. (2008). First year students' experiences with technology: Are they really digital natives? *Australasian Journal of Educational Technology,* 24(1), 108–122.

Kickstarter. (2012). *The best of 2012.* Retrieved from https://www.kickstarter.com/year/2012

Kirkman, R., Adlard, C., Rathburn, C., Gaudiano, S., & Stewart, D. (2010). *The walking dead*. Orange, CA: Image Comics.

Kirshenblatt-Gimblett, B. (2004). Performance studies. In H. Bial (Ed.), *The performance studies reader* (pp. 43–55). New York, NY: Routledge.

Krotoski, A. (2008). Hide & Seek: Alex Fleetwood wants to play with you. *The Guardian*. Retrieved from https://www.theguardian.com/technology/gamesblog/2008/jun/13/hideseekalexfleetwoodwants

Kuhn, T. S. (2012). *The structure of scientific revolutions*. Chicago, IL: University of Chicago Press.

Kuznekoff, J. H., Munz, S., & Titsworth, S. (2015). Mobile phones in the classroom: Examining the effects of texting, Twitter, and message content on student learning. *Communication Education*, 64(3), 344–365.

La Monica, P. R. (2016). Why Facebook could one day be worth $1 trillion. *CNN*. Retrieved from http://money.cnn.com/2016/04/28/investing/facebook-trillion-dollar-market-value/

Lammers, J. C., Curwood, J. S., & Magnifico, A. M. (2012). Toward an affinity space methodology: Considerations for literacy research. *English teaching: Practice and critique*, 11(2), 44–58.

Laurel, B. (1991). *Computers as theatre*. Reading, MA: Addison-Wesley Pub.

Lave, J., & Wenger, E. (1991). *Situated learning: Legitimate peripheral participation*. Cambridge: Cambridge University Press.

Ledgard, A (2007). *Visiting time and boychild: Site-specific pedagogical experiments on the boundaries of theatre and science*. Retrieved from http://www.wellcome.ac.uk/stellent/groups/corporatesite/@msh_peda/documents/web_document/wtx050363.pdf

Lemon, J. (2016). Pokémon Go: Residents call police as Rhodes swamped. *Sydney Morning Herald*. Retrieved from http://www.smh.com.au/business/consumer-affairs/pokemon-go-residents-call-police-as-rhodes-swamped-20160712-gq4hb3.html

Lenhart, A. (2015). A majority of American teens report access to a computer, game console, smartphone and a tablet. *Pew Research Centre*. Retrieved from http://www.pewinternet.org/2015/04/09/a-majority-of-american-teens-report-access-to-a-computer-game-console-smartphone-and-a-tablet/

Lenhart, A., Madden, M., Smith, A., Purcell, K., Zickuhr, K., & Rainie, L. (2011). Teens, kindness and cruelty on social network sites. *Pew Internet and American Life Project*, 28.

Lenhart, A., Smith, A., Anderson, M., Duggan, M., & Perrin, A. (2015). *Teens, technology and friendships*. Retrieved from http://www.pewinternet.org/2015/08/06/teens-technology-and-friendships/

Lévy, P. (2000). *Collective intelligence: Man's emerging world in cyberspace*. New York, NY: Perseus.

Little Big Planet. (2014). Little Big Planet (Facebook page). Retrieved from https://www.facebook.com/littlebigplanet/posts/10152307038246831

Lowood, H. (2006). High-performance play: The making of machinima. *Journal of Media Practice*, 7(1), 25–42.

Lowood, H. (2009). *Game capture: The machinima archive and the history of digital games. Mediscape Fall '09*. Retrieved from http://www.tft.ucla.edu/mediascape/Spring08_GameCapture.html

Lowood, H. (2011). Video capture: Machinima, documentation, and the history of virtual worlds. In H. Lowood & M. Nitsche (Eds.), *The machinima reader* (pp. 3–22). Cambridge, MA: MIT Press.

Ludlow, C. (2013). Alternative certification pathways filling a gap? *Education and Urban Society*, 45(4), 440–458.

Lupton, D. (2016). You are your data: Self-tracking practices and concepts of data. In S. Selke (Ed.), *Lifelogging: Digital self-tracking and lifelogging – Between disruptive technology and cultural transformation*. Wiesbaden, Germany: Springer VS.

MacNamara, C., & Rooke, A. (2007). The pedagogy and performance of Sci:Dentities. In *Creative encounters: New conversations in science, education and the arts*. London: Welcome Trust.

Mahn, H., & John-Steiner, V. (2002). The gift of confidence: A Vygotskian view of emotions. In G. Wells & G. Claxton (Eds.), *Learning for life in the 21st century* (pp. 46–58). Oxford: Blackwell.

Manjoo, F. (2011). *True enough: Learning to live in a post-fact society*. Hoboken, NJ: John Wiley & Sons.

Manovich, L. (2006). The poetics of augmented space. *Visual Communication*, 5(2), 219–240. doi:10.1177/1470357206065527

Manovich, L. (2013). Interaction as a designed experience. In U. Ekman (Ed.), *Throughout: Art and culture emerging with ubiquitous computing* (pp. 311–320). Cambridge, MA: MIT Press.

Marshall, B. K., & Picou, J. S. (2008). Post-normal science, precautionary principle and worst cases: The challenge of twenty-first century catastrophes. *Sociological Inquiry*, 78(2), 230–247.

Martin, A., Mansour, M., Anderson, M., Gibson, R., Liem, A., & Sudmalis, D. (2013). The role of arts participation in students' academic and nonacademic outcomes: A longitudinal study of school, home, and community factors. *Journal of Educational Psychology*, 105(3), 709–727.

Martin, C., & Ito, M. (2015). Teens without smartphones encounter a new digital divide. *The Conversation*. Retrieved from http://theconversation.com/teens-without-smartphones-encounter-a-new-digital-divide-40947

Marwick, A., & boyd, d. (2014). 'It's just drama': Teen perspectives on conflict and aggression in a networked era. *Journal of Youth Studies*, 17(9), 1187–1204.

McAuley, G. (1998). Performance analysis: Theory and practice. In *About performance* (No. 4, p. 1). Centre for Performance Studies.

McGeoch, K., & Hughes, J. (2009). Digital storytelling and drama: Language, image and empathy. In M. Anderson, J. Carroll, & D. Cameron (Eds.), *Drama education with digital technology* (pp. 113–128). London: Continuum.

McGonigal, J. (2003). *This is not a game: Immersive aesthetics & collective play.* Paper presented at the Digital Arts & Culture.

McGonigal, J. (2011). *Reality is broken.* New York, NY: Penguin Press.

McIntyre, A. (2007). *Audience knowledge digest: Why people visit museums and galleries, and what can be done to attract them.* Retrieved from http://webarchive.nationalarchives.gov.uk/20120215211132/research.mla.gov.uk/evidence/documents/audience%20knowledge%20digest.pdf

McIntyre, P. (2012). *Creativity and cultural production: Issues for media practice.* New York, NY: Palgrave Macmillan.

McWilliam, E. (2008). Unlearning how to teach. *Innovations in education and teaching international, 45*(3), 263–269.

Media Molecule. (2015). *Dreams.* Retrieved from http://dreams.mediamolecule.com

Mirani, L. (2015). Millions of Facebook users have no idea they're using the internet. *Quartz.* Retrieved from http://qz.com/333313/milliions-of-facebook-users-have-no-idea-theyre-using-the-internet/

Montola, M., Stenros, J., & Waern, A. (2009). *Pervasive games: Theory and design.* San Francisco, CA: Morgan Kaufmann.

Mori, M. (1970). The uncanny valley. *Energy, 7*(4), 33–35.

Morris, R. (2012). Imaginary museums: What mainstream museums can learn from them. In S. Macleod, L. Hourston Hanks, & J. Hale (Eds.), *Museum making: Narratives, architectures, exhibitions* (pp. 5–11). London: Routledge.

Murray, J. (1997). *Hamlet on the holodeck: The future of narrative in cyberspace.* New York, NY: The Free Press.

mySociety. (2016). *Better cities.* Retrieved from https://www.mysociety.org/better-cities/

Nakamura, L. (1995). Race in/for cyberspace: Identity tourism and racial passing on the Internet. *Works And Days 25/26, 13*(1–2), 181–193.

Neelands, J. (2011). Drama as creative learning. In Julian Sefton-Green, Pat Thomson, Ken Jones, & Liora Breslar (Eds.) *The Routledge international handbook of creative learning.* Abingdon, Oxon; New York, NY: Routledge.

Negroponte, N. (1995). *Being digital* (1st ed.). New York, NY: Knopf.

NESTA. (2010). *Beyond live: Digital innovation in the performing arts.* Retrieved from https://www.nesta.org.uk/sites/default/files/beyond_live.pdf

Neuman, W. L. (2006). *Social research methods: Qualitative and quantitative approaches* (6th ed.). New York: Allyn and Bacon.

Newman, J. (2008). *Playing with videogames.* London and New York: Routledge.

Niantic. (2012). *Ingress.* San Francisco, CA.

Niantic. (2016). *Pokémon Go.* San Francisco, CA.

Nicholls, J., & Philip, R. (2012). Telling tales in and out of school: Youth performativities with digital storytelling. In M. Anderson, D. Cameron, & P. Sutton (Eds.), *Innovation, technology and converging practices in drama education and applied theatre* (pp. 115–134). London: Routledge.

Nicholson, H. (2005). *Applied drama: The gift of theatre.* Basingstoke, UK: Palgrave Macmillan.

Nicholson, H. (2012). The performance of memory: Drama, reminiscence and autobiography. *NJ, 36*(1), 62–74.

Niemeyer, D. J., & Gerber, H. R. (2015). Maker culture and Minecraft: Implications for the future of learning. *Educational Media International, 52*(3), 216–226. doi:10.1080/09523987.2015.1075103

Noice, H., & Noice, T. (2001). Learning dialogue with and without movement. *Memory & Cognition, 29*(6), 820–827.

Norris, J. (2009). *Playbuilding as qualitative research: A participatory arts-based approach.* Walnut Creek, CA: Left Coast Press.

Obama, B. H. (2009). *President Barack Obama's inaugural address.* Retrieved from https://www.whitehouse.gov/blog/2009/01/21/president-barack-obamas-inaugural-address

Obama, B. (2016). *Weekly address: Giving every student an opportunity to learn through computer science for all.* Retrieved from https://www.whitehouse.gov/the-press-office/2016/01/30/weekly-address-giving-every-student-opportunity-learn-through-computer

Oblinger, D., & Oblinger, J. (2005). Educating the net generation. *EDUCAUSE.* Retrieved from http://www.educause.edu/educatingthenetgen/

O'Connor, P. (2013). Drama as critical pedagogy: Re-imagining terrorism. In M. Anderson & J. Dunn (Eds.), *How drama activates learning* (pp. 125–134). London: Bloomsbury.

O'Connor, P., & Anderson, M. (2015). *Applied theatre: Research: Radical departures.* London: Bloomsbury.

Organisation for Economic Co-operation and Development (OECD). (2016). *Automation and independent work in a digital economy: Policy brief on the future of work.*

O'Toole, J. (1992). *The process of drama: Negotiating art and meaning.* London; New York, NY: Routledge.

O'Toole, J. (2009). Drama for development and expression. In J. O'Toole, M. Stinson, & T. Moore (Eds.), *Drama and curriculum: A giant at the door.* The Netherlands: Springer.

Papert, S. (1980). *Mindstorms: Children, computers, and powerful ideas*. New York, NY: Basic Books.

Parkinson, H. J. (2014). Runner uses Nike+ app to draw penises. *The Guardian*. Retrieved from https://www.theguardian.com/technology/2014/aug/06/runner-nike-san-francisco-penis

Pesce, M. (2016). Mixed reality service. GHVR. Retrieved from https://medium.com/ghvr/mixed-reality-service-ce469783fd68#.stk8tzray

Phelan, P. (1993). *Unmarked: The politics of performance*. London; New York, NY: Routledge.

Pijbes, W. (2015). Netherlands: The battle for beauty in a virtual world: How museums can profit from the digital revolution. *Uncommon Culture*, 6(2), 138–145.

Poole, G. A. (1996). A new gulf in American education, the digital divide. *The New York Times*. Retrieved from http://www.nytimes.com/1996/01/29/business/a-new-gulf-in-american-education-the-digital-divide.html

Poole, S. (2014). The Truth about smart cities: 'in the end, they will destroy democracy'. *The Guardian*. Retrieved from https://www.theguardian.com/cities/2014/dec/17/truth-smart-city-destroy-democracy-urban-thinkers-buzzphrase

Potter, J. (2012). *Digital media and learner identity: The new curatorship* (1st ed.). New York, NY: Palgrave Macmillan.

Prendergast, M., & Saxton, J. (Eds.). (2009). *Applied theatre: International case studies and challenges for practice*. Bristol: Intellect.

Prensky, M. (2001). Digital natives, digital immigrants part 1. *On the horizon*, 9(5), 1–6.

Prentki, T., & Preston, S. (2009). Applied theatre: An introduction. In T. Prentki & S. Preston (Eds.), *The applied theatre reader*. Abingdon, Oxford: Routledge.

Punch, M. (1994). Politics and ethics in qualitative research. In N. Denzin & Y. Lincoln (Eds.), *Handbook of qualitative research*. California: Sage.

Read, C. (2014). 'Live, or almost live …': The politics of performance and documentation. *International Journal of Performance Arts and Digital Media*, 10(1), 67–76. doi: 10.1080/14794713.2014.912502

Reimann, P. (2011). Design-based research. In L. Markauskaite, P. Freebody, & J. Irwin (Eds.), *Methodological choice and design: Scholarship, policy and practice in social and educational research* (pp. 37–50). New York, NY: Springer.

Resnick, M., Maloney, J., Monroy-Hernández, A., Rusk, N., Eastmond, E., Brennan, K., and Kafai, Y. B. (2009). Scratch: Programming for all. *Communications of the ACM*, 52(11), 60–67. doi:10.1145/1592761.1592779

Rheingold, H. (2002). *Smart Mobs: The next social revolution*. Cambridge, MA: Perseus Publishing.

Rice, C. (2002). Interview with Condoleezza Rice; Pataki talks about 9–11; Shelby discuss war on terrorism. *CNN Late Edition*. Retrieved from http://edition.cnn.com/TRANSCRIPTS/0209/08/le.00.html

Richardson, L. (1994). Writing: A method of inquiry. In N. Denzin & Y. Lincoln (Eds.), *Handbook of qualitative research*. California: Sage.

Ringland, G. (2010). Frameworks for coping with post-normal times: A response to Ziauddin Sardar. *Futures*, 42(6), 633–639.

Robinson, K. (2001). *All our futures: Creativity, culture and education*. Sudbury: DfEE.

Robinson, K. (2001). *Out of our minds: Learning to be creative*. Westford, MA: Captsone Publishing Ltd.

Roet, L. (2015). *An artist put Tinder and LinkedIn profile pics side-by-side*. Retrieved from http://thecreatorsproject.vice.com/blog/an-artist-is-putting-tinder-and-linkedin-profile-pics-side-by-side

Salter, C. (2010). *Entangled: Technology and the transformation of performance*. Cambridge, MA: MIT Press.

Sardar. (2010). Welcome to postnormal times. *Futures*, 42(5), 435–444.

Sawyer, K. (2015). A call to action: The challenges of creative teaching and learning. *Teachers College Record*, 117(10), n10.

Schechner, R. (1992). A new paradigm for theatre in the academy. *TDR (1988-)*, 36(4), 7–10.

Schechner, R. (2002). *Performance studies: An introduction*. London; New York: Routledge.

Schofield, G. P., Bartindale, T., & Wright, P. C. (2015). *Bootlegger: Turning fans into film crew*. Proceedings of the 33rd annual ACM conference on human factors in computing systems (pp. 767–776), Association for Computing Machinery (ACM).

Schofield, T., Vines, J., Higham, T., Carter, E., Atken, M., & Golding, A. (2013). *Trigger shift: Participatory design of an augmented theatrical performance with young people*. Paper presented at the proceedings of the 9th ACM conference on creativity & cognition, Sydney, Australia.

Scott, R. (Writer). (1982). *Blade Runner* [motion picture].

Schwandt, T. (2001). *Dictionary of qualitative inquiry* (2nd ed.). London: Sage.

Selke, S. (Ed.). (2016). *Lifelogging: Digital self-tracking and lifelogging – Between disruptive technology and cultural transformation*. Wiesbaden, Germany: Springer VS.

Shaffer, D. W. (2004). Epistemic frames for epistemic games. *Computers & Education*, 46, 223–234.

Shaughnessy, N. (2005). Truths and lies: Exploring the ethics of performance applications. *Research in Drama Education*, 10(2), 201–212.

Shaughnessy, N. (2012). *Applying performance: Live art, socially engaged theatre and affective practice*. Houndmills: Palgrave Macmillan.

Shelley, M. W. (1818). *Frankenstein; or, The modern Prometheus*. London: Printed for Lackington, Hughes, Harding, Mavor, & Jones.

Shirky, C. (2008). *Here comes everybody: The power of organizing without organizations*. New York: Penguin.

Shulman, J. (1990). Now you see them, now you don't: Anonymity versus visibility in case studies of teachers. *Educational Researcher*, 19, 11–16.

Snow, C. P. (1961). *The two cultures and the scientific revolution*. London: Cambridge University Press.

Spaff. (2009). Look what we found in a cupboard today. *Media Molecule*, 8 September. Retrieved from http://www.mediamolecule.com/blog/article/look _what_we_found_in_a_cupboard_today/

Stake, R. E. (1995). *The art of case study research*. Thousand Oaks: Sage.

Standing, G. (2011). *The precariat: The new dangerous class*. London: Bloomsbury.

Stevenson, N. (2010). Cultural citizenship, education and democracy: Redefining the good society. *Citizenship Studies*, 14(3), 275–291.

Stewart, D. R., & Littau, J. (2016). Up, Periscope: Mobile streaming video technologies, privacy in public, and the right to record. *Journalism & Mass Communication Quarterly*, 93(2), 312–331.

Stringer, B. (2016). *Press release from O'Fallon police department*. Retrieved from https://regmedia.co.uk/2016/07/10/34798567498753.pdf

Stuart, K. (2013). Tiny Games and the idea of facilitation. *Guardian*, 10 April. Retrieved from https://www.theguardian.com/technology/gamesblog/2013/ apr/10/tiny-games-and-facilitation

Sutton, P. (2012). Shaping Networked Theatre: Experience architectures, behaviours and creative pedagogies. *Research in Drama Education: The Journal of Applied Theatre and Performance*, 17, pp. 603–616.

Sutton, P. (2016). Applied theatre, social media and glocalization. In K. Freebody & M. Finneran (Eds.), *Drama and social justice: Theory, research and practice in international contexts*. Abingdon: Routledge.

Sutton-Smith, B. (1997). *The ambiguity of play*. Cambridge, MA: Harvard University.

Tanz, J. (2011). Kinect hackers are changing the future of robotics. *Wired*. Retrieved from http://www.wired.com/2011/06/mf_kinect/

Taylor, P. (1996). Introduction: Rebellion, reflective turning and arts education research. In P. Taylor (Ed.), *Researching drama and arts education: Paradigms and possibilities* (pp. 1–21). London: Falmer Press.

Thompson, E. P. (1971). The moral economy of the English crowd in the 18th century. *Past and Present* (50), 76–136.

Thompson, J. (2006). *Applied theatre: Bewilderment and beyond*. Bern: Peter Lang.

Thomson, P., Lingard, B., & Wrigley, T. (2012). Reimagining school change. In T. Wrigley, P. Thomson, & B. Lingard (Eds.), *Changing schools: Alternative ways to make a world of difference* (pp. 1–14). London: Routledge.

Thornham, H., & Cruz, E. G. (2016). [Im]mobility in the age of [im]mobile phones: Young NEETS and digital practices. *New Media & Society*, 1–16. doi:10.1177/1461444816643430

Torok, R. (2015). ISIS and the institution of online terrorist recruitment. *Middle East Institute*. Retrieved from http://www.mideasti.org/content/map/isis-and-institution-online-terrorist-recruitment?page=29

Turkle, S. (1995). *Life on the screen: Identity in the age of the internet.* New York, NY: Simon Schuster.

United Nations. (2014). *World urbanisation prospects: The 2014 revision.* Retrieved from https://esa.un.org/unpd/wup/Publications/Files/WUP2014-Report.pdf

Vaterlaus, J. M., Barnett, K., Roche, C., & Young, J. A. (2016). 'Snapchat is more personal': An exploratory study on Snapchat behaviors and young adult interpersonal relationships. *Computers in Human Behavior*, 62, 594–601.

Vygotsky, L. S. (1933/1976). Play and its role in the mental development of the child. In J. S. Bruner, A. Jolly, & K. Sylva (Eds.), *Play: Its role in development and evolution.* New York, NY: Basic Books.

Vygotsky, L. S. (1980). *Mind in society: The development of higher psychological processes* Cambridge, MA: Harvard University Press.

Wales, P. (2012). Telling tales in and out of school: Youth performativities with digital storytelling. *Research in Drama Education: The Journal of Applied Theatre and Performance*, 17(4), 535–552.

Walker, R. (2012). Can Etsy go pro without losing its soul? *Wired.* Retrieved from http://www.wired.com/design/2012/09/etsy-goes-pro/

Wang, F., & Hannafin, M. J. (2005). Design-based research and technology-enhanced learning environments. *Educational technology research and development*, 53(4), 5–23.

Watershed. (2013). *What is a playable city?* Retrieved from http://www.watershed.co.uk/playablecity/overview/

Wenger, E. (1998). *Communities of practice: Learning meaning and identity.* Cambridge, UK: Cambridge University Press.

Westecott, E. (2011). Crafting play: Little big planet. *Loading… The Journal of the Canadian Game Studies Association*, 5(8), 90–100.

Whatley, S. (2013). Dance encounters online: Digital archives and performance. In G. Borggreen & R. Gade (Eds.), *Performing archives/Archives of performance.* Copenhagen: Museum Tusculanum Press.

White, D. S., & Le Cornu, A. (2011). Visitors and Residents: A new typology for online engagement. *First Monday*, 16(9). Retrieved from http://firstmonday.org/ojs/index.php/fm/article/viewArticle/3171

Wired. (2008). *The making of Little Big Planet* [Online video]. Retrieved from http://www.youtube.com/watch?v=WETeWdoz3cw

Wolf, G. (2009). Know thyself: Tracking every facet of life, from sleep to mood to pain, 24/7/365. *Wired*. Retrieved from http://www.wired.com/2009/06/lbnp-knowthyself/

Wotzko, R. (2012). Newspaper Twitter: Applied drama and microblogging. *Research in Drama Education: The Journal of Applied Theatre and Performance*, 17(4), 569–581.

Wyn, J., & White R. (1997). *Rethinking youth*. St. Leonards, NSW: Allen and Unwin.

Zemeckis, R. (Writer). (2004). *The Polar Express* [Motion picture].

Zemeckis, R. (Writer). (2007). *Beowulf* [Motion picture].

Zemeckis, R. (Writer). (2009). *A Christmas Carol* [Motion picture].

Zemeckis, R. (Writer). (2011). *Mars Needs Moms* [Motion picture].

Zimmerman, E. (2013). *Manifesto for a ludic century*. Retrieved from http://ericzimmerman.com/files/texts/Manifesto_for_a_Ludic_Century.pdf

INDEX